through the eyes of asperger's

through the eyes of asperger's

A Latter-day Saint Perspective

ROBERT CALLAWAY

atmosphere press

Note: This book contains information pertaining to people with disabilities and other issues, explaining the purpose of their lives here on earth, and how they can have successful, happy lives, while it focuses on those with Autism Spectrum Disorder. It contains inspiring information for anyone involved with any disability.

In the interest of protecting the privacy of certain people whose real identities are not essential to this true account, most names have been changed. All stories contained herein are based on actual life events. Ethan's account has been adapted. Any similarity of names in this account to actual people and families is purely coincidental.

TABLE OF CONTENTS

**My Own Life Experience Being a Member of the Church
with Asperger's Syndrome/Autism Spectrum Disorder**

My Sweet Wife's Wonderful Assistance

**Perspectives from Our Counselor
and another Close Friend**

Our Continuing Journey

FOREWORD
BY BRAD WILCOX

I first met Robert when he arrived in Chile as a new missionary. I was serving in the same zone where he was assigned. I noticed he was different from other missionaries and I worried. The transition to mission life is difficult and I wondered how he would weather it. I knew learning Spanish and adjusting to the culture would stretch him—especially because some Chileans have a way of being brutally honest when pointing out someone's weaknesses. I was afraid it all might prove too much for him. I was wrong. Robert rose above every challenge in remarkable ways. He had the love of his family and our wonderful mission president and his wife. He had the support of some faithful members of the Church who took him under their wings. Most important, he had the help of heaven. God and Christ were with him every step of the way.

Reading Robert's book has left me amazed at his courage, perseverance, and service. His life has not been easy, but he has never given up. He has learned, adapted, adjusted, and hung in there, and now he is reaching out and striving to help others do the same. He is strong in the Church. If he were one to look for excuses to be offended and leave, he could find plenty. Instead, he and his wife are serving in the temple. Robert's book—and his life—fill me with hope because I have an autistic grandson. I see the challenges ahead of my little guy and I worry, but I keep thinking, "If Robert can do it, so can my grandson." My grandson also has the love and support of family and Church members. Most important, he also has the grace and help from heaven that will get him through. It is the blessing that gets us all through.

Thanks for writing this book, Robert. Thanks for your courage and faith. Thanks for never giving up and for being a light to so many. Thanks for giving me hope. I am confident every reader will feel it as I have.

Con amor,
Brad Wilcox,
Author of *The Continuous Atonement*
and *Changed through His Grace*

PREFACE

This is a unique book in that Robert, the main author, has Asperger's Syndrome/Autism Spectrum Disorder himself. He writes about what it actually feels like to have Asperger's, about how it affects his emotions, and about the unique difficulties he had and is having as a member of The Church of Jesus Christ of Latter-day Saints, having Asperger's. He has stayed close to the Spirit of the Lord, which has helped him to better understand the role of Asperger's in his life, and which has also greatly helped him to know how to overcome many of the unique difficulties he encountered, being a member of the Church.

Robert wrote this book with the encouragement of various people in his life, and directed it to an increasing number of individuals in or out of the Church who have Asperger's Syndrome/Autism Spectrum Disorder, as well as to all those who are involved in their lives in any degree. He has done this to provide a great resource to all those involved with Asperger's/ASD who are at a great loss as to what to do to resolve extenuating situations, as he explains the processes of how to accomplish positive results. He details many helpful ideas as well as action steps to follow, based on our Savior's teachings, which bring great results in their lives. These are also illustrated in various, touching stories. He has proven how these steps work, and how this plan has worked in his own life.

In this book, Robert takes the person with Asperger's Syndrome on a journey, identifying with his emotions through similar experiences, and then he shows him how to work through and resolve problems, which the Asperger's person has an extreme desire to do every day of his life in order to feel more secure. The person with Asperger's actually does not know how to resolve many of his own problems, and he will need help from other good people. These problems arise from many of the more unique, odd situations encountered by having Asperger's, and especially by being a member of the Church, along with other issues he and other people would normally experience. During this process, Robert also gives much enlightening, helpful information to family members, friends, leaders, and teachers in the Church, as well as to any others who are involved with those who have Asperger's Syndrome, as he can relate "through his eyes" to what it personally "feels like" to have Asperger's Syndrome. Through this book, many of these people can also really help the person with Asperger's to resolve most of his problems. There are a great number of people who may not know about Asperger's with its associated characteristics, and may not even know that certain people have this disorder, as this Syndrome can be difficult to recognize. This contributes to some of the issues the Asperger's person experiences.

There are many books and much information available these days about Asperger's Syndrome and Autism Spectrum Disorder, which also give great help as to what to do about problems which arise specifically from having Asperger's. However, there is not information encompassing many more factors, which include being a member of a Church having Asperger's, whether active or not; unique situations encountered by being a member of the Church; how to resolve problems resulting from these situations; and how to incorporate Christ's teachings into the person's life to help him live a more normal life.

This book also contains information from close family members and friends to Robert, also written in their own words, explaining their own experiences relating to Robert and Asperger's Syndrome, and how they are instruments in helping him to resolve his difficulties and in helping him to live a better life, a Christlike life. They, as well as Robert, show how this is accomplished. This is all done for the purpose of helping those who are involved with Asperger's/Autism Spectrum Disorder realize each of their divine missions here on earth and how to fulfill them the way our Savior would have us do. This will bring more pure love and true joy to everyone. We hope this book will be a great treasure for you.

INTRODUCTION

This is a story about an individual named Robert who has Asperger's Syndrome, a disorder within the Autism Spectrum Disorder. It contains information involving him and those associated with him, including those who belong to the Church of Jesus Christ of Latter-day Saints. It contains the many issues he dealt with, being a member of the Church, before and after his diagnosis. It is written in a simplistic, straightforward manner.

Most of the book is written by Robert himself, who experienced these difficulties firsthand, where he describes his associated feelings. He writes of how he handled these difficulties in a positive way. Many of these issues are unique for someone who is a member of the Church with Asperger's/Autism Spectrum Disorder, being that many members of the Church live in a manner much different from the world's ways, with higher expectations. These issues arose from common Church life, such as when a child goes to Primary or a boy goes to Young Men's class; having a calling, and fulfilling assignments in helping others; or by even going to Sacrament Meeting. Members would see Robert's odd involuntary behaviors including involuntary movements and strange facial expressions, communicative difficulties in speaking with the proper words and in misunderstanding what people are saying, and reactions of sensory overload such as quickly putting his hands over his ears when a sudden, unexpected loud sound occurs, all characteristic of Asperger's Syndrome. These and other behaviors would make him appear very odd, rude, and not

Christlike, when in reality the opposite is true. Robert did not understand how he was being perceived, nor did he even know that he was behaving in an unusual manner. He thought he was acting normally. In fact, he had no idea how inappropriate his behaviors were, by how they were being interpreted. This made his family very uneasy, not only from his odd functioning, but also from the reactions of people around them. Some thought that Robert's family was not raising him properly. He was viewed by many as not having any disorder. Many people misunderstood him and some were harsh. Certainly, people could not be condemned for what they did not know. However, being Christlike is important.

There is no guide specifically for those who have Asperger's/ASD and belong to the Church, explaining the unique situations and issues involved and how to deal with and resolve them. This book is an attempt to meet this need, showing what Robert and other people did, while experiencing Asperger's, and how good people closely involved with them helped them to manage and resolve these unique issues. This book shows how Robert and these people stay close to our Savior, relying on His help with faith, and how this assistance, along with very important items which Robert accomplished during his life, resulted in a major improvement in his life, practically eliminating his Asperger's! Family members, Church leaders, teachers, and other members of the Church along with everyone else will also be able to greatly benefit from this powerful, inspiring information that deals with such a difficult and sensitive subject. They will understand what the Asperger's person diagnosed with Autism Spectrum Disorder is actually feeling and experiencing as he lives his life each day with this Disorder. Family members especially will know how to deal with and teach the family member with Asperger's, from this helpful guidance, which incorporates our Savior's teachings. They will also have improved lives themselves, and a better family relationship. This book should prove to be an extremely valuable resource in this area. Writing it has also blessed Robert's life so very, very much, as he truly desires to help other people have happier lives!

Let's begin on a wonderful journey, and discover some real solutions for living with Asperger's Syndrome and Autism Spectrum Disorder, which our Savior would like you to know.

my own life experience being a member of
the church with asperger's syndrome/
autism spectrum disorder

CHAPTER ONE
MY ASPERGER'S CHARACTERISTICS

"I can't take this!" Ethan shouted as he ran out of the room and very quickly shut his bedroom door. His father had just yelled at him as a result of another in a long series of his son's panic attacks. This young 8-year-old boy with Asperger's/Autism Spectrum Disorder had just yelled, "I'm not going!" after which his father shouted, "Yes you are!" when he was suddenly told by his father that he was going to be taken to the doctor to receive an immunization. His mother tried to calm her husband, who then told her with exasperation, "Sarah, I just don't know what to do anymore. Why does he have such meltdowns?"

His mother answered, "Try to relax a little. He has Asperger's, causing him to think and act differently, and I know it's very difficult to remember all the right things to say and to do around him that would make his life easier."

Her husband responded with agitation, "Isn't that the truth!"

This is very typical in the life of a person who has been diagnosed with Asperger's Syndrome/Autism Spectrum Disorder. A sudden announcement or change can be very frightening to him, when he has not received any advance information presented in a loving manner, to prepare him for the sudden change in his normal routine. Shouting at him would only intensify his negative reaction, causing his panic attack to be even worse, where he starts shaking and feels very upset and helpless. This happens because he is very sensitive and is easily frightened. Early intervention and especially being members of the Church of Jesus Christ of Latter-day Saints should greatly assist the person with Asperger's to lead a more normal life. However, being a member of the Church can present its own problems in this particular situation. You may be asking, "How is that possible?"

My name is Robert Callaway and I am in my late fifties. This book is a powerful story which I have written, consisting of my very unique personal life experiences with associated emotions. I will show you how I have positively progressed as an individual with Asperger's Syndrome, and how my characteristics have amazingly mostly disappeared. I will show you how my social interactions have become much more normal and how I socialize very well. I have done this to give you answers. Asperger's is very similar to a disorder known as "High-functioning Autism," both of which are within the Autism Spectrum Disorder. These are not learning disabilities, as people with these disorders are quite intelligent, nor are they any type of mental illness or disease; rather, these are neuro-developmental disorders, where the brain does not naturally develop in areas of social awareness and communication. As a result, those with this disorder naturally turn in toward themselves. Some areas of the brain are suppressed and other areas are more intensified, such as the sensory receptors.

This is an informative, inspirational, self-help book containing writings from my own perspective, through my eyes, experiencing Asperger's, rather than a book from a professional who has studied but does not have Asperger's Syndrome, thus not experiencing it with associated intense emotions himself. I am including what I have learned, how I have felt, how I have dealt with many issues, how others have helped me to cope in various unique interactive situations in a Church setting, and how Asperger's has become less of a factor in my life. I will show how Asperger's characteristics can effectively be greatly reduced in the child beyond what early intervention can achieve, and how family members play a key role in achieving these results by better understanding the Asperger's child and his thought processes, through my explanations. By fully applying the information in this book, the Asperger's individual will see very significant healing from his Asperger's/ASD.

I was born into a family belonging to the Church of Jesus Christ of Latter-day Saints, which was of great benefit to me, as my spirit really finds comfort in the gospel of Jesus Christ. I am much happier when I am closer to the Lord, Jesus Christ. My parents, Ralph and Mary, and my older sister, Susan, have also been active members in the Church. These family members have assisted me greatly, in the Lord's way, through some of the more unique, difficult situations I experienced in the Church and throughout my life. All this has greatly helped me to understand many vital pieces of information, which I will be presenting in this book. After a few introductory words, we will quickly start on a very fantastic journey.

It is noted that in today's world, there is much more information about developmental disorders within the Autism Spectrum Disorder, such as Asperger's Syndrome and High-functioning Autism, as to how they affect the brain as well as associated behavioral characteristics of those affected. As these characteristics can be reduced through manual training, it has been shown that young children diagnosed with these disorders can progress in a more positive manner if they are not specifically labeled with the exact disabilities they have, as this would give the brain a suggestion of hindrance. They can be taught that they can accomplish more than what was first thought they could. Therefore, this is one of the reasons this wide spectrum of disorders is now referred to as Autism Spectrum Disorder, or ASD. As those people with these disorders become older, more mature, and more accomplished, they can understand and are able to comprehend more about specific disorders which have been associated with their lives. This helps them to better understand their functioning within their life's experiences, so that they can progress even more effectively, reducing their characteristics even further. In this book, to make my references clearer and more understandable, I will be referring to higher functioning people with these disorders, who have been diagnosed with Autism Spectrum Disorder, as having Asperger's Syndrome.

It can also be noted that everyone in this mortal

world has some kind of physical, emotional, mental, social, or spiritual imperfections—or any combination of these—which result in personal reactions to difficulties in many forms of intensity. This is where assistance and appropriate intervention is very helpful. As a result, we could all be classified within a type of "Mortal Imperfection Spectrum Disorder." This is not to put us down, nor to make us think that we are not good enough to be able to progress, but to make us aware that we all need assistance and caring in a loving, Christlike manner to help us positively progress. Those with more pronounced disabilities or disorders will also need assistance and intervention specific for them so that they can progress and have happier lives. This book deals in a small degree with the educational intervention processes for those with Asperger's. However, it deals much more with the spiritual, showing how these approaches can provide help in a more efficient and effective manner. It shows how all individuals with disabilities, as well as their family members, are part of our Savior's plan, and how all this is connected.

In this book, I will be talking to a teenage boy named Ethan who has Asperger's/ASD, and also to his family: his mother, Sarah, Ethan's now single mother; and his younger sister, Alexis. They are all members of the Church. You will be able to easily relate your own personal experiences with Asperger's to theirs through similar situations and issues, with associated emotions, along with my own. I will be taking them on an amazing journey, in which all of you will be participating. I will be guiding them through life's experiences so that they will all achieve a much more positive outcome, having the needed tools to resolve their unique issues, with the Asperger's factor involved. Here we go.

"How are you today, Ethan? I am Robert. I hope you are feeling happy today."

"Yeah, I'm doing pretty well. I've had quite a hard life, though. My dad was the one in my family who didn't care about me as much, and didn't like it that I have Asperger's. He would get after me a lot for things he thought I was doing wrong, like the time when I was eight, he suddenly told me without any warning that he was taking me right then to get a shot. I couldn't deal with it, so he got upset with me." Ethan started showing a painful look. "I started crying and didn't feel understood at all. This was one of many times he treated me like that. Later, my dad divorced my mom, which was really hard on me. I wanted him to treat me better and stay with us."

Robert responds calmly, "Ethan, you have had some very difficult and unique challenges and trials in your life. I know what it feels like. I also have Asperger's, and I was just like you in many ways. We both have some extremely important information to share. We will both be able to explain what it actually feels like having Asperger's, so that family members and many other people will really be able to understand us and know how to help us better. There are even more ways now which will help us in a magnificent manner. Ethan, listen, I have some very important news for you. Your Asperger's characteristics and associated issues you have with members of the Church and other people can effectively be completely eliminated from your life! Does that sound exciting?"

"Yeah! That can really happen to me? It'll be terrific

to be able to fit in with people and be able to talk with them better. How's it done?"

"Your family and other people will be able to help you, and there is more you can simply do to improve yourself, after listening to the information I will be presenting to you. I will be taking you and your family on a very exciting journey which everyone will see. During this journey, I will show you and all the rest of those people like us who have Asperger's Syndrome what my family did to help me, all in a Christlike manner, even before I knew that I had Asperger's."

If any of you are not in this type of helpful family situation, there is still much that can be done to greatly help you, which I will be showing you.

"Throughout this journey, I will also be directing my helpful information to other people who are very much involved in your life, Ethan. I'll share ideas that could be new, surprising, eye-opening information to many of them concerning my thoughts and feelings about the many unique, difficult situations I experienced, and which you also experience, that would help them to better understand how to help you. My information will be a great benefit to them. This is also a very important purpose of the journey we will be taking. Even though I will be doing this, all the excellent information I will be presenting to you and others will be directed to helping you, Ethan, overcome many of the difficulties you experience having Asperger's, especially those you experience being a member of the Church."

Through this information, including what I will show to Ethan, family members will be able to overcome their own difficulties, those they have with the Asperger's child, and those they experience with other people in the community, while having a family member with Asperger's/ASD.

"This includes you, Sarah and Alexis."

I really care about all of you who have Asperger's Syndrome and related disorders, along with your family members and friends, and I would like to help all of you experience a much better life as I and my family have been able to, with Asperger's Syndrome involved. We are ready to start.

"Ethan, Sarah, and Alexis, let's begin this exciting journey together."

CHILDHOOD ASPERGER'S

There is much information now about the characteristics of Asperger's Syndrome/ASD.

"I am briefly explaining some of my characteristics of Asperger's to you, Ethan, as an identity reference. You will likely observe that my feelings toward my interests, and my behaviors and emotions, are just like yours."

This is also for all of you who have Asperger's Syndrome, as well as your family members. Later, I will show how these characteristics will connect with the unique experiences I had as a member of the Church, and how I dealt with them.

It is important to note that many characteristics of Asperger's which I will mention, such as higher sensitivities of the senses and great literalness; concreteness and detail in perception, thought, and communication; and increase in odd body movements, as well as greater dependency on parents, are also very common in young children, but children grow out of most of these characteristics. Those with Asperger's may not lose some or even many of their characteristics at all without personalized assistance, which I will be explaining in detail. Early intervention has been shown to positively assist with this. During this journey, I will show all of you how these characteristics can decrease very quickly, even more rapidly than ever thought possible.

A young child with Asperger's will show these above-mentioned characteristics, along with many others, in a more pronounced manner; yet, he may physically appear as other young children do, making this disorder more invisible.

"Ethan, you may be thinking by now, 'This is describing me quite well. People don't understand me.' You may relate more closely to these characteristics which I will be explaining, and you may easily identify and relate to these unusual patterns which were part of my normal behavior as a child."

Of course, my toys and play items were contemporary when I was a child. They are as follows:

My earliest recollections of my childhood are of when I was almost 5 years of age. I did not speak in a communicative manner until later in the year, when my parents put my name on the temple prayer roll, at which time I started speaking. I am very grateful that they did this. They were very excited and thrilled when I started talking. They said, "Oh, it's so wonderful that Robert is now talking. It's an answer to prayer!" I did not just start saying words, but I started speaking in complete sentences. After not talking during all this time, except for making grunting sounds, I would surprise my family and suddenly say, "What are we eating tonight?" My mind functions very logically, and I must have believed that I was not communicating unless I could say a complete thought very accurately. Other people with Asperger's/ASD may start speaking at an earlier age.

My speaking was still not very clear, but has improved over time, which is likely the case with many of you. I also exhibited many of the classic symptoms of Asperger's, which included suppressed motor skills, poor muscle coordination, odd walking and stance, strange movements with my arms, and other odd behaviors, such as playing with many round objects. Those on the Autism Spectrum usually have an intense interest in playing with all kinds of round objects, whether they are wheels, spools, little balls or marbles, rolls of paper or string, etc. As a child, I would throw a little wheel that came off a toy truck, like a bowling ball, and let it roll along the ground a great distance. I would like to put a pebble in a slingshot and shoot it straight up to see how high it would go. I would also do this with a toy called "Arrow-copter" and watch its shadow. I would use a water gun, shooting the water in the same pattern as a "Rain Bird" sprinkler, turning my arms forward and then back. Other young children without Asperger's may participate in some similar play activities, but I was drawn in more intently to these unique patterns, and I would stay involved with them for a much greater amount of time. I was very intrigued and fascinated with these types of activities. I later found out that other children along with some adults would see my unusual involvement in these activities and interests and wonder what was wrong with me. This led to some of the social difficulties I had in my growing years. Many people with ASD may also rock themselves and desire to be held more often. These unusual behaviors help to meet their increased needs for security.

I also had some other unusual kinds of interests. Having Asperger's, I have a very intense interest in very long items that are wound up, such as spools of string or rope, rolls of paper, skeins of yarn, and reels of recording tape or film (which were contemporary when I was young). I loved winding these by hand or by machine. I also loved using the playback equipment for tapes or film. When I wound these on the equipment by using the rewind or fast forward functions, I would intensely watch the tape or film unwind and get smaller on the one reel, while it got bigger on the other. As a child, I enjoyed unrolling a roll of paper, such as is used in a cash register, all through my bedroom, like a web, and then rolling it up again. Again, I would enjoy watching the roll get smaller and then bigger again. I was intently focused on the detail of winding, and I would wind as evenly as possible, trying to recreate the original wind. I would also do this with spools of sewing thread from my mother's sewing machine and with rolls of cord or rope. This is one of the Asperger's methods of learning brain, eye, and finger coordination. It was a productive play/learning opportunity for the Asperger's brain, which helped to develop my finger coordination.

My parents and sister thought this was quite unusual behavior and they were hoping I wouldn't be a messy person by how I decorated my bedroom with paper, but they saw how content I was with these activities and how much I enjoyed them, as these activities made me feel secure. They just knew I had different interests than most children. When my father came in, he exclaimed, "Wow, Robert, what have you done to your bedroom?" I answered with, "I'm just having some fun." He would then tell me, "Now remember to clean this up." I said, "I will." My parents knew I would be obedient to clean up afterward, and they let me continue with these types of behaviors, which I really enjoyed.

I especially liked making an afghan loom, which consisted of small nails in a long strip of wood, with a slot cut down the middle. I would enjoy spending hours using skeins of yarn, watching the yarn come out of the skein as it became smaller, and making an afghan or scarf. I still enjoy this activity. This is within the norm for an Autistic person. It made me feel happy, content, and secure.

I also enjoyed operating a radio station when I was a teenager. My father and I assembled my own little studio at home, and I enjoyed operating it, as well as assisting with our high school FM radio station as a disk jockey. This greatly helped me with pronunciation and with communication. In high school, I was taught how to be a professional announcer. My father was very helpful, and took an interest in my interests. He was guided by the Spirit to help me progress and feel needed and loved. I really appreciated his interest in me. My mother did the same.

"Sarah, this is something you can do to help your Asperger's child. He will thank you many years later for your interest and helpfulness. He will think back fondly on these times when he is older. This help and interest you give him will mean much to him throughout his life, will help him progress, and will help him feel much more secure."

There are certain quiet games I enjoy, such as chess and other "thinking" games. I enjoyed using a spirograph to draw and make complex, intricate patterns, due to my attention to detail. I was very creative and I loved using its round objects. I also enjoyed helping with the setup and the inflation, and then going on a ride in a hot air balloon. This was okay due to the fact that it is slow moving and I could hold on well. Fast rides such as roller coasters would scare me and overload my feeling senses, putting too much physical pressure on my body from the quick changes in direction, so I did not ride on them.

My muscle coordination is odd, awkward, and clumsy, due to a weakness in gross and fine motor skills as a result of my brain development. I have no interest in active sports, as I am very awkward with them. However, I have developed some coordination with calmer sports, such as bowling and golf. My handwriting is also poor, due to weak motor skills in my hands. I am able to type much easier. The Lord has compensated me in this way. My finger coordination was able to improve much more than my hand coordination. My parents knew that I had very poor handwriting. When I started high school, they were guided by the Spirit that I should take a typing/keyboarding class to be able to write well, which I learned very quickly as a result of my Asperger's brain.

I also have an extremely high, intense interest in one particular subject: weather. I've always had a great interest in weather. I would observe the sun's position by watching shadows move. As a young child, I remember sitting and watching a sun shadow move for an hour. I would note each season in detail, recording how much storminess would occur, especially snow depth. I had instruments to do this. I would study many weather facts in detail and learn information related to all areas of weather. I would enjoy wanting to explain what I learned to other people. Later, I received more weather measuring instruments as gifts from my father to measure temperature, wind, air pressure, etc. Again, he was quite helpful in my interests, for which I am very thankful. I would watch the wind instrument readout more intently, noting the varying wind speed and direction. It was an entertaining activity. I kept a weather log each day. I also reported some of this information to the media. I called in to some TV stations, where they showed my information along with other reports. My father also had arranged for me to do this.

Some time later, I could not put all my instrumentation out, which caused distress. Mental and emotional distress can occur when I am not able to be completely involved in my area of intense interest. I would feel very frustrated and depressed due to not being able to do things that I know make me happy. For instance, rental areas and condos I lived in later did not allow attachment of all my weather equipment. I felt uneasy around the people who made the rules, and there was nothing I could do to change the situation. I wanted people to understand my feelings and needs, but that didn't happen. I just tried to find something else to do, which wasn't as enjoyable. I knew when I could continue with all areas of weather measurement, I would have better mental and emotional support to help my wellbeing. This feeling would also be true for any person with Asperger's/ASD.

"You can relate to this, Ethan."

People with Asperger's and related disorders have a very intense interest focused usually on one or maybe two subjects, and can spend hours relating to another person every detail concerning this subject, as this brings them great joy. They completely miss the social cue that they are explaining too much detail for a much longer time than what the other person wanted to hear. They don't know that the person is bored and completely uninterested, but he doesn't want to be rude to people with Asperger's or Autism. These people also think extremely logically and concretely, and view general life in this manner. They don't understand that life isn't logical, and they cannot initially perceive it any other way.

Through my many experiences, I have been able to understand life in more ways now. Other family members and friends can cue me in, and let me know in social situations what other people are thinking. I can then know how to properly respond, such as saying, "Thank you for your compliment, and for your concern for me." This is something I would have otherwise completely missed. I have learned to ask, "How are you doing today?" I now understand that there are more people who have an interest in me than I first thought, when I talk positively with them and show a concern for them. Many of them are hesitant to talk to someone they don't know too well, especially if that person doesn't talk much to others. They show more interest when you are friendly with them, take an interest in them, and show that you care.

"This is a simple thing which you, Ethan, can learn about and do, which will help you feel much better. I will be guiding you through this."

Along with helping the Asperger's person to understand a little at a time about what other people are thinking, I am also able to help all of you who interact with the
Asperger's/ASD person to know what I, having Asperger's, am really thinking and feeling. This will help you
know and understand what the Asperger's child is not
able to tell you about his thoughts, feelings, and behavior.
I will be explaining this further.

Being very logical, the person with Asperger's needs a
very detailed explanation about the subject in any conversation, whereas other people would not need as much.
I don't need as much detail now as I did at first, but I especially need references to specific nouns, to prevent confusion. To make communication more clear and more
easily understood—and this equally applies to anyone in
any conversation—it is very important to refer to specific
names of people, places, and items, instead of using pro-
nouns such as "he," "she," "him," "her," "they," "them,"
"you," "it," "these," "those," "that," and "there." Doing
this would be extremely helpful. The word "thing" is also
too general and confusing. Adjectives are very helpful for
describing nouns, so the person would then know which
table in the house, for example. Once the reference to the
person, place, or item is definitely understood, then the
pronoun could be occasionally used to refer back to the
noun.

A person could say to the Asperger's person, "Could
you please put these plates and cups on the dinner table,
and make sure you have enough of them for six people.
Arrange them so that there is one plate in front of each
chair, and one cup is behind each plate." Giving instruction in this manner will help the Asperger's person to

easily understand and be able to help with confidence, feeling that he is worthwhile and is able to easily participate. This will prevent the occurrence of confusion issues for everyone. Once he has learned this instruction, he may not need as detailed an explanation each time, as Asperger's people are quite intelligent and can quickly manually learn concrete directions and explanations.

As is the case with many with Asperger's Syndrome, I was more content doing things by myself as a child, and I did not associate much with other children. I had one or two friends, but not close friends. I also did not have much of the basic communicative skills or social awareness which naturally develops with other children. I did not know of social cues or hidden social messages, such as a certain look on a person's face to tell me to change the subject I was discussing, which I completely missed. Later, that person said to me, in reference to one of his friends there after a cutting remark was made, "I'm going to make sure to save his face." As a teenager, I didn't know what he meant, as I thought literally. I was really confused in the social world. I also didn't know there was such a thing as body language. Deep inside, I wanted to be more social and wanted very deeply to connect with the other children, like the others were effortlessly doing, but I didn't have the ability. Their personalities were too different from mine, as they were generally more physically active and outgoing, so I preferred to do my school studies by myself and enjoy my family experience.

Some shy children may also be more comfortable by themselves for different reasons, feeling awkward around people they don't know very well, even though they have better social awareness than those on the Autism Spectrum. I didn't have this awareness, so I felt even more awkward around those I didn't know well. I looked at the ground to feel secure. As I wanted to be social, I enjoyed being with members of my family. We took vacation trips together, went to movies, and did other activities as a family. This especially helped me emotionally and spiritually as I was growing up, which I really appreciated. As an adult, I have learned how to very easily connect with other people.

"Ethan, I will be showing you how this was rather simply and easily accomplished. I can see that you are already really enjoying this journey we have started, as I see a happy smile on your face."

"This is really great! I just can't wait to learn how to be more normal, like you. There are many times I feel so embarrassed around people who are seeing all my differences."

"Yes, Ethan, I know how it feels. During all this time growing up, I kept wondering what was different about me, and why I was having such a different life experience than what other people were having. I am sure this is closely describing your own life experience, Ethan, along with your associated feelings, even though you have already been diagnosed with Asperger's/ASD."

I have since learned that Asperger's is more of an invisible disability. At first impression, I would look like I did not have any disability or disorder at all. I would physically appear normal, but then I would also exhibit many of the characteristics of Asperger's, including unusual expressions. This fact can easily cause great confusion when interacting with other people.

"I know this has also happened to you, Ethan. People

would think that you're intentionally acting odd to annoy people or to call attention to yourself. I know you've had some extremely upsetting experiences with this, which can be very traumatic. I'll help you learn how to communicate normally with people, and how to understand them, so that you'll respond to them the way that they are expecting. Your unusual movements and expressions can be easily eliminated! I'll also show you how your hearing sensitivities can be eliminated. You will no longer feel overloaded. You'll be able to adjust to changes in your routine very easily. You won't feel anxious or depressed nearly as much anymore. How does that sound?"

"That will be terrific!"

"This is all very possible. Ethan, you know that our Savior has His special plan for you in this life. Our Savior knows what is best for you. I have learned that Asperger's has been more of a blessing for me than a difficulty, because it has been a protection for my sensitive nature from the evils of the world. As I don't have as much social awareness, I don't naturally understand the social ways of how evil operates. I stay close to the Spirit, and I have felt through the Spirit of the Lord that this Asperger's path through mortal life is the best way for me, to help me in my progression. Our Lord has His plan for me and knows what is best for me, and I have accepted it wholeheartedly. All of this is true for you, too.

"I will show you, Ethan, how I stay close to the Spirit and how it helps me as I journey through life with Asperger's Syndrome. This will also help you realize these changes in your life. I will show you how the Lord will help you. I will also show you the Lord's plan for you, including the reason you have Asperger's. You'll see that you're not here on this earth with this disorder by chance. Our Savior definitely has a very important plan for you. You will enjoy having these answers to your life's questions."

INTENSE SENSORY SENSITIVITIES

As many of you may know, a common characteristic of Asperger's Syndrome is heightened sensitivity, which easily leads to sensory overload. The Asperger's brain receives sensory stimuli in a very intense manner, causing overload to occur easily. All of my senses are affected, some more than others. Hearing is especially affected. This is due to the fact that all little children have an inborn, innate fear of loud sounds and especially sudden, loud noises. The Asperger's characteristic reaction to loud sounds stays with him much longer through his life, and is more intense, generating an innate fear even as an adult, when a louder or disturbing sound occurs.

"I know you have the same issues, Ethan. I know how loud sounds can be really upsetting and frightening."

As an example, when a very loud motorcycle is passing by, I have to suddenly hold my hands over my ears. A surge of adrenaline has just occurred, and I have the extremely strong need to stomp or hit some object or hit my hands together, as this reflexive reaction is initially the most effective form of release. Other people may have to yell or scream. This is the response of the Asperger's brain to a loud, very irritating sound. It is like the volume is turned way up, and I cannot turn it down. Not only do I hear all sounds louder, but many sounds and certain frequencies—such as loud thumping bass in a vehicle, or very loud engines, or loud barking dogs—are very irritating and disturbing to me. This can be compared to how most people cringe at hearing fingernails screeching on a chalkboard. Loud, breaking glass sounds could even cause a reflexive panic attack, where I would jump, scream, and start shaking all over. These sounds affect me even now to some degree, but not nearly as before. My reactions now are much more normal.

Along with increased sensitivity to sound, it is difficult to understand people when they speak too quickly, as it easily causes overload in my brain. Comprehending and processing the information is very difficult when it comes too fast, plus it's harder to make out all the words. Speaking slower with a calm voice is the best way to communicate with an Autistic person. If someone is speaking too loudly or assertively, using aggressive language, or if there are other irritating and disturbing music or sounds in the area, I quite often have to hold my hands over my ears or leave the area, at times even now, though not nearly so much anymore. Any irritating sound or noise is like someone is shouting at me. Tuning them out does not really work for a person with Asperger's. He cannot effectively do this. Playing some pleasant music helps to cover unpleasant, disturbing sounds. Using some types of devices or covering the ears may also assist in reducing the volume level of undesirable noise. Wearing headphones or ear buds would appear quite normal in public. Various types of auditory treatments are also available to help permanently reduce the effects of undesirable sounds. I have found a simple technique that I will explain later, which also effectively reduces the effects of disturbing sounds and prevents anxiety attacks.

When I was young, I was coming home with my parents in the car once, when we passed an accident scene. It was nighttime, and the flashing lights from the police cars and ambulance were so powerful on my eyes that I had to close them and cover them with my hands. It was extremely disturbing to me, in addition to knowing that someone could be seriously injured. My parents had to calm me down using soothing voices as I was saying with an anxious voice, "This is too much for me." Soon my intense anxiety subsided. My parents were guided by the Spirit to know exactly what to do to help me calm down during these frequent episodes. I'm very grateful for all they did to assist me to feel better. They talked to me in loving tones, saying, "Robert, you are okay." They didn't want me to experience more discomfort than other people.

"I will show you, Sarah, and all you parents how you can utilize the Spirit of the Lord much more to help your Asperger's child more effectively. Many of his sensitivities will improve and he will thank you later."

Many quick bright flashes and quick movements are irritating to my vision. These stimuli easily cause sensory overload, resulting in an urgent need to remove myself from the situation. I would not look at them and I would leave as soon as possible. Modern LED lights, which have a definite rapid strobe-like appearance, are very irritating to view. This is also the case with very bright bluish-white lights. This color is more artificial, and the brain does not recognize this as natural light. This is why many people with Asperger's and Autism have a very difficult time with fluorescent lights in a classroom. It is irritating to their eyes, they feel more agitated, and they have a very difficult experience concentrating. These lights even pulsate to a small degree. I have experienced all this. Also, suddenly turning on a very bright light in a darker room, especially without notice, causes an intense, overloading, irritating reaction to my eyes and brain. It would cause a reflexive emotional reaction similar to a panic attack, where I would shout and start shaking, and I would have to close my eyes and cover my eyes with my hand.

Sudden or fast movements on a TV or while watching a movie are also extremely irritating, causing anxiety, and I have to look away from the screen or close my eyes. When these fast movements are occurring, it feels like someone is shaking my head all around, just as it does when there are quick, bright flashes or movements in the environment. This has not improved much for me. I have to live with it, doing what I can do to not observe these stimuli, including closing my eyes, covering them, or even having to leave the area, in order to prevent these effects. Looking at some pleasant nature scenery helps me feel better.

Another time I was riding in a vehicle going normal speed when suddenly a very loud car came up quickly behind us, then passed us way too fast with an extremely loud engine. That driver had a need for power and speed, but he was making it very unsafe for other drivers. All this set me into an intense anxiety attack. Again, people around me had to help calm me by using soothing voices, telling me things were okay, and I had to wait until my reactions subsided to function more normally. This can still happen to some degree.

Any type of anger or aggression overloads me emotionally, physically, and spiritually, causing emotional upset and a need to have it immediately stop, or I need to quickly leave the area. Any type of aggression, such as being forceful and powerful with words and aggressive language, angrily shouting, as well as someone driving a vehicle extra fast and recklessly, are examples of what I need to avoid in order to prevent emotional upset. Intense anxiety attacks can result from emotional overload, where the person feels very anxious and starts shaking and breathing hard, and may yell out and hit some object. Even driving or being a passenger in a vehicle in traffic with some aggressive drivers or loud vehicles nearby causes overload, and I function much better when I avoid that environment. I am reminded to pray at the time, which does help. I am not in a vehicle as often as most people, and I am mostly in areas where less of this occurs. I do very well in a calm, peaceful, tranquil setting. I notice that I can function much more normally in this type of environment. If there has been an aggressive or emotionally disturbing occurrence which has not been resolved, I will continue to feel greater emotional overload and great anxiety, and I will not be able to function comfortably or feel at peace until the situation has been resolved in some manner. Parents can be of great help to their child with Asperger's/ASD by lovingly talking to him, reassuring him, and also by enlightening appropriate neighbors and members of the Church and enlisting their help to reduce or maybe eliminate some of the more aggressive situations where appropriate. When the Asperger's child sees this progress, he feels much more comfortable and more at peace, even though he knows that there will always be problems in his life. He will remember and appreciate his family's assistance and concern for him all through his life, which he will look at with loving memories.

I had an experience where an aggressive dog was loose at times. This was when I was going to school, and I was walking to the bus stop in the morning. I was going down the street when the dog came out in front of me, growling, and not letting me pass. I was told later that he was protecting his property which was close by, but the dog didn't know how far from the property he should still protect. He was acting on instinct. I had to return home and have my mother let the neighbor know what was happening. I said, "Mom, the neighbor's dog won't let me go down the street, and I'm scared he's going to bite me. Can you take care of this so I can go to school?" I was upset and shaking. My mother said, "I'll call and let them know."

She wasn't able to get an answer, so she said, "It looks like the dog isn't out now, so try again, and I'll watch. If the dog comes out, I'll drive you to the bus or to school if the bus has already come. I will also watch for you when you come home."

This made me feel much better, so I went back out and the dog was not there anymore. I got to the bus stop when the bus was just coming, so I was able to go to school okay. I still had great anxiety about coming home, but it went fine that afternoon. I had told my parents, "They are breaking the law, and this needs to stop or they should be reported." Later, my father was able to talk to the neighbor about the situation, who then said, "The dog does get out at times, so I will make sure that he doesn't get out loose anymore." This made me feel much more relaxed. My parents gave me great reassurance, along with assistance to resolve the problem, which I really appreciated. Does this sound like an appropriate solution to all of you? Support like this will help your Asperger's child to progress, as he will feel more secure. He will know that more situations will occur, but this will let him know that he can trust his parents to help him feel calm when they do occur. This type of early intervention will greatly supplement other early interventions. If his parents are not in a position to help the Asperger's child, then his siblings, other Church members, or other friends can effectively accomplish the same results.

"Ethan, you know that your mother has helped you, even more than you realize. I know that you really appreciate all she does. Your sister loves you and has also helped you."

All I have explained so far shows how the family copes with the increased sensitivities of the Asperger's child. They know his differences and what he needs in order to cope with living in society. While they may know how to help him, the family might have a more difficult time coping with other people's reactions. As members of the family live to be guided more by the Lord's Spirit by living the gospel, they will be able to help other people understand these issues related to Asperger's Syndrome in a loving way, so that these reaction issues will decrease. Difficult situations will become better. I will be explaining this further. Let's continue.

I have more sensory sensitivities, such as my sense of smell, which is also increased. I have pleasant memories of many situations where a good scent was involved. Often, when I notice the same scent, a vivid picture of my past experience is brought back to me, with all the sights, sounds, and good emotional feelings of that time. This is one of God's gifts to me. When there is an undesirable, more pungent odor or smoke smell in the area, as my sensitivity to it is also greatly intensified, I have to leave by going indoors or in a vehicle, somewhere away from the odor.

When I was a child, my mother would give me various fruits to eat, such as an orange in my Christmas stocking, or fruit salads and strawberry or peach desserts. She really wanted me to eat them, but I just could not eat very much. It was like eating lemons straight. They were very bitter and way too strong. We found out that my sense of taste is increased as well. Many stronger-tasting foods, such as citrus fruits and some vegetables, overload my taste senses and even sting my mouth or can cause a very unpleasant flavor. To me, they are extra bitter or sour, like they would be to a very young child. In order to eat these foods, they need to be diluted by being mixed or blended with enough other milder foods, such as milk, yogurt, bananas, and good flavorings which are very tolerable. Even now, certain flavors are still extremely unpleasant to me.

"This has probably happened to you, too, Ethan."

My sense of touch is not so prominently affected as with other Autistic people. However, many do not like to be touched at all and do not like the feel of certain types of clothing, such as corduroy. Many Autistics also resist the wearing of a dust mask. Along with the feeling of intense physical discomfort, it can feel extremely intrusive and intimidating, causing sensory overload. It can also cause extreme anxiety attacks, producing the sensation of not getting enough air. It is compared to when a person comes up behind another person and puts both his hands tightly over the other person's face, then keeps them there. This sensation affects me now, and it especially bothered me when I was younger, when I had more touch sensitivities. When relatives would come to visit and hug me as a child, it was very uncomfortable. They would come and squeeze me in their arms, and kiss me on the face, as they were showing their love. They did not know that they were putting me in an extremely uncomfortable position. I know that many children feel this same way, especially boys, but with Asperger's, it is way more uncomfortable. These sensitivities decreased when I became an adult and my brain was more developed. I like to hug more now. I still have a great sensitivity to any kind of poking and pain.

I also have an increased sensitivity to motion. When I am in a vehicle, I do much better if the starts, stops, and turns are gentle. When the driver is aware of this, he can drive more smoothly and gently. If there is a need for a quick stop, such as the traffic light turning red, the driver could say, "We need to stop fast. Hold on!" Preparing me even one second before, if possible, greatly reduces the effects of a quick stop for me.

There are positive sensations of touch which are very calming and soothing for the Asperger's/ASD individual. Smaller, very smooth items such as dry beans, and very soft items such as the soft fur of a rabbit or kitten create a more welcoming and desirable sensation with his hands. This is a calming intervention technique which is very helpful. Effective, gentle massages may also help soothe many people with ASD.

"Many of these reactions and sensations which I have been describing may be very familiar to you, Ethan."

Another characteristic that I have is that I am quite witty. I love good humor. People's conversations quite often remind me of good jokes to tell. For example, I would ask, "Why did the chicken <u>not</u> cross the road?" Then I would tell them, "Because he was too chicken." I like to tell good jokes and watch good humorous shows. I understand funny, simple, family shows better than other types of movies with a great amount of action or drama, which can be very overloading, emotionally. This is due to the fact that my mind understands family programs of a calm and concrete nature, as a young child would, much more than those which are more abstract or aggressive, or with a great amount of drama.

Another symptom of Asperger's Syndrome is not having the desire to make eye contact. There were many times when people would say, "Look me in the eyes when I'm talking to you." I would not be able to do it. It makes me very uncomfortable. It is a very unpleasant, disturbing feeling to look at someone's face and eyes and see all the movements, which are very strange to me. It causes sensory overload, even now. When I would not look at someone's face when asked to, he would think that I was trying to be disrespectful. He did not understand that it was overloading to me. I couldn't tell him that I wasn't able to look at his face, so he would say, "So you don't think that much of me?" Some people may actually say this when the Asperger's person doesn't look at faces. When I was younger, I didn't know that looking at someone's face made him feel more important. Now that I have learned this fact, I am looking at people's faces more, so that they feel that I care more about them.

"This is important for you, Ethan, and also for your family to know about you, so that you will have better interaction and communication with other people."

It is even more visually overloading when I see a woman's face overdone with makeup, especially her eyes. It becomes way too noticeable, standing out, drawing excessive attention to certain areas and away from her face in general. For me, a lesser, appropriate amount would be more pleasant to view, making her appear more natural. For women, wardrobe and makeup are nonverbal communication. Earlier, I didn't understand body language, of which I had no knowledge during much of my life, except for simple smiles, etc. This makes eye contact even stranger. I found that I can verbally communicate better by looking at some stationary object, or toward the person in general, but not at the face. This way, my mind is not distracted and my communication is clearer. Through the years, I have been working on this by asking the Lord for help to be more comfortable looking at people's faces, and there has been improvement. I am now able to look more at people and their faces.

When I was in school, it was hard to look at the teacher as much as the other children did. Some teachers thought that I was extremely shy, when that was not really the case. When I became an adult, I was able to look at the ward members of the Church more. I later learned that by my looking at them, they felt that I was more interested and more caring about them. This is a good social skill to learn. However, I still have some difficulties remembering this, and I often need to remind myself to look at people while I am having conversations with them.

When I was not looking at people's faces very often, it took me much longer to recognize a new person, like someone I had met more recently or had seen very few times. If I saw that same person later, I quite often didn't recognize him or I confused him with someone else. This especially happened when I saw the person in another setting or in another location. If I were with someone at the time, I quite often would have to ask about that person, to verify his identity. I would ask, "Who is he?" or "What is his name?" I would do this discreetly, which I have done much of my life. Along with doing this, I need to see that person several times frequently in order to start recognizing him myself, wherever he may be. For someone I haven't seen often, or if it has been quite a long time since I last saw him, after greeting him I would look at him and ask, "Remind me of your name?" That person would know that I am showing interest in him, and would positively respond to me.

"This is something I know will help you, Ethan."

COMMUNICATION DIFFICULTY

A very common, well-known characteristic of Autism Spectrum Disorder and Asperger's Syndrome is difficulty in communication. My communication difficulties have slowly improved through my life, through the teachings from my family and friends, and from good interactions with other people. One communication difficulty which I had and which others with these disorders have, is strug-

gling with enunciation and pronunciation as young children do. They tend to quietly mumble their words, which
makes it difficult for them to be understood. Intervention
with speech therapy and loving help can assist with this
issue. However, they will still have a harder time with
expressing their thoughts, which I will explain. They
have a tendency to be blunt, which can make them appear rude. This tendency can improve over time. Even
though I can think well and speak better now, I have had
a great struggle to think of how to express my thoughts
using the right words, or to know if I am really understanding the main thought in a conversation or identifying the proper information. This especially happens
when the information is given nonverbally or is given
with less detail. This is not uncommon. You can all relate
to this. Everyone experiences communication difficulty to
some degree, but with Asperger's this problem is greatly
increased. Here is how the Asperger's mind interprets
communication:

Many times when I express what I am thinking, I am
not sure if the person understands all my actual
thoughts. Due to this and the lack of social awareness,
including unawareness of nonverbal communication, facial expressions, and body language, I have an increased
need for detailed verbal feedback from the person, indicating that he actually understood my thoughts and
communication. Much of the time, this feedback does not
occur, or it tells me something completely different.
When this happens, it is my nature to explain or ask the
question in a different manner, not to provoke, but to try
to clarify what I am thinking that the person did not understand. This may occur several times before I get the

right feedback, if the feedback happens at all. I would ask, "What do you mean by that?" The person would then appear exasperated at me from my questioning, due to my unique social unawareness. Many times, I would not know that the person actually did understand me, because I didn't understand his body language telling me. He would then not understand why I was explaining or asking again, and would think that I was trying to provoke or irritate. Many would especially wonder why I was trying to irritate, knowing that I am an active member of the Church, and would think that I should know better.

"So you are saying that your sister and her husband are traveling out of state tomorrow to get your nephew and his wife?" I asked this, when my neighbor told me that he was going to have some family come and stay with him for a few days. I had brought up a fun subject, trying to show some interest in my neighbor, a good acquaintance of mine and an active member of my Church ward. He said that his sister is bringing his nephew, along with their spouses. "I'm not sure what you mean. Do you mean that your sister's son and his wife are coming? Did you say that your sister is coming to stay also?"

My neighbor said in exasperation, "How many ways can you ask the same question? Don't you understand? I said that my sister and her husband are going to get my nephew and his wife. They don't have transportation at the moment. They will all come here to spend a few fun days together. I know you mean well, but I don't know why you don't understand me the first time. I guess that I need to explain everything to you in extreme detail. Someone needs to teach you how to properly socialize with people."

I left feeling quite hurt. I had thought that I was communicating well, but that my neighbor was too vague. I wasn't completely sure exactly who was actually coming to visit him or the number of people. I didn't know why he was telling me about how I was talking with him. I was just trying to have a normal conversation with him, trying to understand all that he said. After our conversation, he told his wife about his experience with me. He related, "I don't know about him. He didn't understand me when I was speaking like I do with everyone else. He kept looking at the ground during much of the conversation. He behaves like he's still a little kid. What do you think is his problem? Haven't his parents taught him how to interact with people?"

"What do you, Sarah and Alexis (or a family member of the Asperger's person), think about this conversation I had a long time ago? What do you think you could have done to help me communicate better at that time? Would it have helped if the neighbor had been informed about my disability?"

Asperger's people have a much greater struggle with communication, and other people do not understand how deeply I am trying to learn to communicate. I have noticed that some individuals, especially those who have the Spirit of the Lord with them more often, do understand me better and do not perceive I have much difficulty with communication; thus, I have better interactions with them. The Spirit helps them be more aware of various types of communication and difficulties other people have.

"Ethan, you have probably experienced very similar

patterns in your life, more so than what other people experience with communication difficulties. Does this experience I related sound very familiar?"

"Yeah, I've had this happen to me many times. I'm so happy to know that you've had the same experiences, and know how to resolve them. Show me more."

"Okay. Through more experience and practice with communication, your skills will improve and your life will become better, as my life has. During our journey, I will be showing you, as everyone will see in this book, how this is to be accomplished."

Communication is a key factor in a person's life, and has a great influence on everything he does. Every person needs to feel that he or she is understood. Every person also needs to feel that the other person is showing interest, making him or her feel worthwhile.

I have also noticed that when someone interrupts me when I am attempting to express a thought, or if other loud sounds or other sensory stimuli such as flashing lights or rapid movement start to occur, thus overloading my senses, that I completely stop talking that very instant. Many times I cannot think of exactly what I was saying in order to finish my thought. I may have to start over completely. Again, this happens more intensely to me than with other people who don't have ASD, although not so much now.

If I am responding to a statement or question, I may not know if I have responded sufficiently, over-responded, or if I am responding to the core of the question. As mentioned, when I ask someone a question, many times it is more difficult to think of how to properly phrase the question. I might ask, "What is happening here?" A better way to ask would have been, "I noticed that the two workers have left. Are they outside doing something?" When the person is thinking in a much different way than I am, he may answer my question in a very vague manner, leading to my asking for more detail. He could say, "Those people have gone over there to take care of that problem." I would then say, "Who went where to do what?" When this occurs, it appears that I am prying for information, when I am actually only asking a simple question to receive a simple, clear answer. Instead, he could say, "My two workers have gone outside to clear the snow." Other people would already know what he meant, quite often through body language. As he does not understand this about me, not knowing my differences, he may easily become quite irritated.

"This may be very familiar to you, Ethan, and you can still remain confused after the conversation. You want to understand other people better, and you really want them to understand you. I know that you become quite frustrated when they don't. You say to yourself, 'What can I say to make him understand me?' You see that this can very easily be compared to experiencing a language barrier."

I understand verbal communication very literally. When I trust someone, I take what the person says as true. If the person is using sarcasm or some innuendo, I usually need an explanation so that I can understand the true meaning. I don't know how to read between the lines. As my social skills and social awareness are drastically suppressed, I have problems with reciprocal communication. Even with feedback, I have difficulty taking the perspective of another person, even though I am a very empathetic person. I used to be completely unaware of nonverbal communication (body language), and I would unknowingly display unusual, involuntary non-verbal communication, such as involuntary facial expressions. For example, I was not aware that I was smiling when someone was being angry toward me for a reason of which I was unaware. The person would then increase his anger, causing me great hurt, distress, and anxiety. This could make me smile even more, as I was completely unaware. This is very common among those with Asperger's. I would also involuntarily make other odd facial expressions, turn my head very quickly, and unknowingly move my hands and arms in an odd, unusual manner, especially when I was in an uncomfortable social situation. People would think that I was trying to irritate them. Many times, even now, others would tell me that I am making odd facial expressions, such as when I am reading something in the distance.

Many people with this Syndrome and related disorders also have an increase in tic behaviors, other forms of nonverbal communication, such as tapping, twiddling, fiddling with hair, picking or scratching, touching their head, clapping motions, waving arms, etc., and not being able to sit still or stand still (similar to ADHD), especially when they are experiencing uncomfortable or distressing situations. As these are also involuntary behaviors, other people don't understand the reasons for the increase in these behaviors either. Many people may become very annoyed at this, and they prefer to not be around the Asperger's or Autistic person. He then becomes completely confused, and doesn't understand why they respond in this manner, appearing unfriendly.

"Again, does this sound familiar, Ethan? Many of these characteristics can diminish over time, especially when consciously trying to make improvements, as I will be showing you during our journey."

Another communication difficulty I have is with telephone answering systems and voice mail. My mind does not function well to think of what to say in a message, when there is no one to whom I am actually speaking. I just hang up. Recently, with practice, I have been able to leave brief messages. Typing messages in a two-way live conversation, such as texting, creates the same difficulty. I communicate best in a two-way live verbal conversation, where there is a greater chance for faster concrete feedback to assist me with communication during that very moment. Also, seeing the people, whether in person or by utilizing any of various online video apps, helps me to communicate better, so I know that the person is actually listening to me. This is how my Asperger's mind initially functions. With practice, these communication difficulties will improve for anyone.

Some of you may not have all these same difficulties. Younger people with Asperger's may really enjoy using smart phones in various ways to communicate, and may find that method easier because they are not actually seeing the person, thereby reducing associated anxiety. Their brains may develop in slightly different ways. They may also spend as much time playing video games and surfing the web as other people do, as they feel comfortable and secure with this activity.

"Ethan, you may be very good at this."

For any of you with Asperger's/ASD, it is better to not do this excessively, as it has been mentioned that extreme use and constantly looking at the screen could very easily cause some harmful effects on your brain, and with your eyes when you become older. It can cause various vision difficulties along with ADHD. Sitting too long can cause some other health problems to develop as well. All this will also slow your normal development and keep you from learning social skills and developing more social awareness, when you are not around other good people who can help you learn them. Interacting in person or through a video call with other people who know you or are acquainted with you is the fastest, most effective way to develop more social awareness and to learn important social skills, rather than by texting or using email.

All these characteristics and difficulties I have discussed so far have a common, underlying connection in the Autism Spectrum Disorder; however, there are also many variances among those with Asperger's Syndrome, thus indicating somewhat of an "Asperger's Spectrum Disorder," within the Autism Spectrum Disorder.

UNAWARENESS OF INVOLUNTARY MOVEMENTS

I have had some unique experiences throughout my life as a result of Asperger's Syndrome. Many people would not understand my behaviors, the way I would move and look at things, and the way I would understand what people are saying. I will explain my experiences with involuntary movements in more detail. As mentioned, I would excessively move my arms and hands all around, scratch my head, etc., especially when I am put in an uncomfortable situation around other people. At the time, I did not even know I had any problem with this. (Later, I became more aware of this through the help of other people.) As a result, people would think I was intentionally trying to act strange with them to get attention in an immature way, or wanting to treat them in a poor or rude, disrespectful manner. Of course, I didn't know what was happening. They would then respond to me accordingly by getting angry, acting rude, punishing me by not being respectful or allowing me equal opportunities like being able to associate with the group or to do activities with them, and blaming me for doing something wrong when I was not aware of it nor was I intending to do anything wrong or hurtful. To my surprise, they would treat me as a troublemaker, causing much sorrow and depression for me and my family.

One time I was asked to clean the men's room in our Church meetinghouse. I was doing my best when the person who assigned me came and asked, "How is the restroom coming along?" I told him I had done the best I could and the work was completed. We went in and he said, "This area here needs to look better." I thought it was okay, and then unknowingly I started moving my arms and scratching the back of my head excessively, as I was feeling uncomfortable with him. He asked, "Robert, what are you doing?" Just then, two more guys came in and also saw what I was doing. They thought I was acting strangely, and the first one exclaimed, "Look at him! Isn't he the sight? Let's take our break while he finishes cleaning what he didn't do." Apparently I had been rubbing the back of my head even more, feeling very uneasy and awkward, when I responded, "I have cleaned everything that needs attention here." They saw how naïve I was and tried to take advantage of me, as they knew I had finished my cleaning. They were irritated at my actions and were becoming more upset, as they thought I was intentionally acting that way to annoy them. "Robert, why are you causing us so much trouble?" they asked.

I then said, with much sadness, "I didn't know I was. What do you mean?" They thought that I was just trying to be funny with them to irritate them even more. They were then more upset with me and walked away. They started telling some of their friends about this experience, which made them really laugh. I felt very sad, like I could not be accepted by any group of people. People in other minority groups also experience this, which makes it more difficult to interact with others.

"After reading this, what do you think about this particular experience? Many more of you with Asperger's, along with you, Ethan, may have had frequent similar experiences, where you've tried to be more sociable and helpful, and have experienced very similar emotions."

Being active in the Church, I was also viewed as not being Christlike, which was a total misunderstanding. They would think I was normal, that I was just making excuses whenever I exhibited any characteristics of Asperger's. This has happened all my life. I did not know why they were truly upset. This was only intensified and traumatic to me, as my emotions were more like those of a younger child. I have greater sensitivity, emotionally and spiritually. It was better for me to stay away from those people who would not understand that I was not that type of person, even after I had made the attempt to explain. They would think that I was only attaching the Asperger's Disorder to myself as an excuse, believing that I never had it. They did not understand about Autism Spectrum Disorder. I have not been able to trust many people in my life as a result.

"This is probably describing you completely, Ethan."

It is also surprising to me to know that many of these people are members of the Church. I do not hold judgment on them, however. I know that no one is perfect, including me. They are still progressing, as I am.

It should be noted here that there are people who have certain other types of disabilities or disorders, which could cause them to exhibit many types of undesired involuntary movements as well. One of these disorders is Tardive Dyskinesia, where frequent involuntary movements and expressions occur, such as sticking out the tongue, usually as a side result of certain medications. As more information is discovered these days about physical disorders, more and more people are becoming aware of certain unusual behaviors that some individuals exhibit, learning that these behaviors are not intentional and that these people are not trying to be rude.

With Autism Spectrum Disorder, however, these involuntary movements and expressions, a natural result of ASD, are also accompanied by an obvious lack of social awareness and social skills, along with some shyness and anxiety. This compounds the problem, where people are generally more confused, not knowing what is causing several undesirable characteristics to occur together. This contributes to more misunderstandings of the person with Asperger's/ASD, and a greater likelihood for him to experience a more traumatic moment, such as what was just described. Traumatic moments more easily occur for the Asperger's person, due to his increased sensitivity.

When I experienced these situations in my life, I felt upset and sad, and wanted the issues to be quickly resolved. I needed help to clear up misunderstandings. This is very true for young people with ASD—they need good people to advocate for them, which will help them feel more important and worthwhile. As association with those who are more understanding of the Asperger's person will greatly help; it is very important for us to be more Christlike and accepting of those who live with a disorder. This is also true for anyone with any disability, and those who are experiencing other major issues.

I did not actually learn about Asperger's Syndrome and realize that I had it until I was 36. There was no information about it when I was a child. Now that I am aware of my disability, I and my family can explain it to others. Many can understand it and not use it against me as other people have. They appreciate the enlightenment and know what to do to help me with my difficulties. They now treat me better. I can trust and depend on good people by what they say—and especially by what they do. There are a few who thought I never had anything wrong with me and would treat me with respect. Over the years, I have noticed that these are generally more spiritual people who can accept differences, and are guided to understand me better. I can relate to them very well and they help me in my progression in and out of Church settings. As I am more comfortable around them, my involuntary movements are greatly reduced.

I have also noticed that associating more with other

good people who don't have Asperger's Syndrome or Autism helps me to understand life better and I can progress more easily. Even though those with Asperger's or Autism are great people, I learn more about social awareness, communication, and various social skills—which help me prevent the unintentional appearance of rudeness—by being around good people who are functional in these areas, as I have to learn these skills manually. These social skills do not come naturally, as they do to those who don't have this disability. This helps me to help those with Asperger's and similar disorders, as I enjoy socializing with them and helping them.

"With help, Ethan, you can find some good, spiritual people to help you in your life experiences, and then be able to help others by sharing what you learned."

In general, it takes me longer to be able to trust someone. As my emotions are more like those of a child, I have a greater need for love and security. Associating with those who are more spiritual and understanding, whom I can trust, helps to fulfill my emotional needs. Also, those assigned to me for ministering within the Church can truly help me by checking in and seeing how I'm doing. I know that explaining these feelings will help more people who interact with those with Asperger's be aware of this Spectrum Disorder, and then more people will have a better understanding of what those who are similar to me are really experiencing and feeling.

It is very important to make sure that the person with Asperger's is not told or treated in any way to indicate that he is a troublemaker or that he is doing something wrong, when he is really not intentionally doing this. Otherwise, he will keep thinking that he is usually doing something wrong, or that he is not completely capable of doing something right, no matter how much he is trying to do right. He will feel that he is not good enough and may quit trying, and he will feel that he does not belong to, nor is able to fit in with any group of good people. He will feel not wanted or not needed. He will feel very upset, depressed, and insecure. He may become inactive or worse. Understanding what they are really thinking and feeling, and showing true compassion and empathy are the best ways to help people with Asperger's and similar disorders to progress. People in other minority groups, such as certain races or other disabled people, are also quite often left out and even belittled. They don't have friends or people they can trust, so they stop communicating and are very lonely. Showing Christlike love and including them in good activities in a loving way, where they can easily participate, is extremely important. I have been left out many times and I have felt very upset and quite depressed, lonely, and not needed. We should develop an outreaching attitude, combined with showing our Savior's love. This is described well in Edwin Markham's poem:

> He drew a circle that shut me out—
> Heretic, rebel, a thing to flout.
> But Love and I had the wit to win:
> We drew a circle that took him in!

Wow! What inspiring words these are! During our journey, this book will show you how to interact with Asperger's individuals and those with similar or other disorders, how to include them even more, as well as how to help them feel calmer and more settled.

I have to handle life's situations in a different, many times more difficult way. Staying close to the Spirit and good people helps to make this more difficult way much easier. Staying close to the Lord is a better "workaround" for those with Asperger's.

"I will be showing you, Ethan, some excellent information about how this is accomplished and how you can have a happy, fulfilling life experience. Let's continue on our journey."

SCHEDULES AND ROUTINES

Staying in a routine is very important to me and to others diagnosed with Autism Spectrum Disorder, and it is very difficult for them to make any change from their comfortable routines. This is due to the fact that people with Asperger's Syndrome have an amazing ability to recognize patterns, and they are very comfortable and secure with them. I become really anxious and distressed when schedules change. For example, changing to Daylight Savings Time is very difficult. It is easier for my mind to not change the time, but to just do something which is scheduled, like going to Church, an hour earlier. I can then gradually adjust to changing the time.

A change in schedule affects me and others with Asperger's even more when it is not announced. I can cope with life's changes easier when good people who stay close to the Spirit assist me to prepare me for the change.

"Sarah and Alexis, this information is for you."

It is very important for me to be told of changes with

as much advance notice as possible. If this is not possible, then showing increased love and comfort during the change will be of great assistance. Explaining all the good reasons for the change helps with the way the Asperger's mind processes information. Doing this in a gradual, calm manner really helps to prevent emotional overload and meltdowns, especially with children.

There is an intense effect on people with Asperger's when the change is of a greater magnitude, such as a major event being cancelled at the last minute or a sudden change of address. Many changes even frighten them and can easily cause emotional overload. It also causes loss of trust and the ability to depend on something. Help them to feel more secure by showing love and by showing how changes can be for the good. Show them that we cannot always control bad changes, but that we can do positive things to help ourselves feel better, like doing good things to help others. Suggest to them the good ways they can easily help other people. Doing this will generate a positive attitude in them. All this has been a great help for me, and it is still needed. I need to count on some things that don't change, things in which I can trust. Finding these items, such as music, is very important in the lives of Asperger's people. I also have the intense need to count on certain people whom I can trust and with whom I feel safe. I especially need these people to assist me with changes.

I know all that I have been explaining is extremely important in the lives of people with Asperger's, as I know what it feels like and how I think in these changing situations, having Asperger's myself. I know that there are many changes in life, and I am sharing with you what has helped me. Staying with what doesn't change really helps. There are some school subjects that are like this, which I feel very comfortable learning, such as mathematics, grammar, and music. This is true for many with Asperger's. This also matches with my spirit, which needs to trust. I can especially count on our Savior, Jesus Christ, and the gospel He taught, as He does not change and is perfect. I also receive added comfort through the gift of the Holy Ghost, which helps me with changes as well. This is another way to help people with Asperger's deal with changes. Pray that this Spirit can be with them to help them. Keep this Spirit with you to help you with your positive interactions. To illustrate this issue of sudden changes, here is a true story about people I know.

A boy named David had been diagnosed with Autism Spectrum Disorder. He has just turned nine and has started fourth grade. He has been in early intervention programs, but he is still having many difficulties at school. At first impression, he looks normal and he is quite intelligent, but he has a hard time doing his reading assignments. He sometimes cannot quite understand what his teacher is saying and at times he appears anxious and irritated. He has been given an adult tutor who takes him outside during part of his class time to help teach him. David and his tutor, Jenny, sit on the swings as she teaches him what the other students in his class are learning inside. He feels much less irritated and less anxious while outside. He is learning very well and feels very secure with her.

A few weeks have gone by when suddenly, one Monday, Jenny is not there. David quickly finds out that Jenny won't be there anymore. His teacher informs him that she had to make a sudden change in her life and move out of state, closer to her family. A rather serious family emergency had just occurred, and Jenny had to move in with her sister. On hearing this, David quickly has a reflexive panic attack, where he starts to yell, hit his hands together, stomp his feet, and he starts breathing very heavily and rapidly along with much trembling, and shouts, "This isn't fair! Why are you doing this to me? I don't like this. I can't stand it! I'm not coming to school anymore!"

David's teacher works on settling him down, saying in a kind, loving voice, "It's okay, David. I will help you. I didn't know that Jenny was going to leave until last night. There was nothing I could do about it."

"So what am I going to do now?" David sobbingly asks, still trembling a lot.

His teacher gently responds, "I will work with you so that you will feel more comfortable, and I will go out with you during recess and explain more to you about anything you don't understand." This really helped David feel more secure and settled again. His teacher continued, "We are working on getting another tutor to help you. We are looking to find someone who understands you really well."

David responded, "I will like that." This shows that being Christlike to a person with Asperger's/ASD, even outside of a Church setting, will always be very beneficial when sudden changes happen. This is what my parents did for me when changes occurred, for which I am very grateful. Again, the Asperger's person will remember this positive assistance throughout his life.

"Ethan, you have experienced changes like this in

your life, so this information will be comforting to you. I can see that you are even more excited going on this journey. Let's continue."

I also have more of the need for order in my life. My mind is less stressed if everything is more organized. My father would say, "A place for everything and everything in its place." Assembling a jigsaw puzzle exercises my brain as I recognize patterns and order, and "put everything in its place." I, along with many people with Asperger's, can also pick up on small details in common items everyone sees or uses. For example, we would immediately know how many bends there are in a standard paperclip, when asked. Other people may not know this right away, even though they may frequently use paperclips, but we know it's three, from our ability to recognize and remember patterns and detail.

Also, along with recognizing patterns, I am able to remember sequences of numbers extremely well. I am able to associate them in a mathematical pattern, which helps me to remember the sequence. For telephone numbers, I can also recognize the pattern they make on the telephone keypad. I do this when I make it a point in my mind to remember the number. The same is true of memorizing the spelling of a word. I easily see and recognize the arrangement sequence of the letters in a pattern. Once I see it and I tell my mind that I need to remember this new word, it is always there. Doing these or similar exercises can help people with Asperger's to feel more organized, have more trust, and feel more settled in their minds. This gift of recognizing patterns is a great compensation for their life's struggles. As they, along with the rest of us, are recognized for their talents and skills, they will feel more important, more worthwhile, and will feel more a part of society.

"What I have explained is all very good information for those who interact with Asperger's people, including you, Sarah and Alexis. I can see that what I have told you up to this point is allowing both of you to feel some emotional relief, as you understand more about Ethan's feelings and how he thinks. Let's continue with some more important information."

SIDE DISORDERS

I have noticed that there are three main side disorders which can accompany Asperger's Syndrome. They are: Non-combative Post Traumatic Stress Disorder, Generalized Anxiety Disorder, and Situational Depression. Other people with Asperger's and many others without Autism Spectrum Disorder may experience varying degrees of these disorders, and may experience related disorders as well. Because my emotional state is more like that of a child's due to Asperger's, I am more sensitive to negative emotions and aggression. When people treated me in a negative or angry manner, due to misunderstandings which occurred through much of my life, it was very traumatic to me, thus causing PTSD. I then had a greater need for peace and calmness, so that I would not be upset. This is one of the major points to remember when interacting with someone with Asperger's: Never be aggressive, or even use a raised voice, but rather be calm, loving, and kind, and establish appropriate boundaries to create a sense of security. Make this a priority item to remember.

Non-combative PTSD is a disorder where intense experiences with negative emotions, loud and not so loud frightening sounds, and aggressive situations which were traumatic cause stress later in life. A similar emotion or act later in life could trigger the traumatic experience again, causing the same trauma, anger, and anguish as though it were occurring for the first time, which also happens with Combative PTSD. Sensory and emotional overload occur, which could cause a panic attack or meltdown, associated with PTSD and Asperger's Syndrome. This can repeat itself many years later.

Confrontations and aggression, or anything which causes sensory or emotional overload can also easily trigger anxiety and panic attacks, part of Anxiety Disorder, which is very common among those with Asperger's or similar disabilities. With Anxiety Disorder, the person may have prolonged periods of heightened anxiety in some uncontrollable situations, where he would feel very unsafe or insecure, often shaking and yelling out. This easily happens when he doesn't feel safe where he is or if there's no one to help him. He doesn't know how to resolve this. He may feel very lonely and may also feel very frustrated within himself, like he is not good enough. I have felt all this. When an anxiety or panic attack occurs, the Asperger's person may commonly have a prolonged period of shaking or jitters, which may be more intense than with other people. For some, it could be compared to having a mild seizure attack. Many of you may have experienced this.

With Anxiety Disorder, I have a continuing battle to feel comfortable being outside or in places where there is the possibility of loud sounds occurring. It is also challenging to be seen by someone who has been aggressive or angry toward me, or with whom I have had difficulty with communication. I feel very awkward in these situations, and it could easily come to the point to where I feel quite scared. It is a distressing situation for me, easily causing an anxiety attack. Even riding in a vehicle in heavy traffic or with sudden stops can also cause anxiety attacks. Loving intervention from other good people will go a long way to greatly subdue these disorders, reduce the overload, and help the person with Asperger's feel secure and more at peace.

Situational Depression is common among those with Asperger's Syndrome and other disorders. During my life, I have not had the normal life experiences that others usually have. I have not been able to be in a normal working situation during my life, except for about 14 years. I have not had the close friends I needed. I didn't get married until age 45, nor have I had my own family with my wife. Many with Asperger's may not even have had these experiences. I am not completely capable of viewing the regular working world the way that other men do. I receive a disability insurance benefit, which isn't all that much.

When people don't positively respond to me the way they do with others, or even respond at all, some unpleasant situations are created. I tend to easily feel sadness and feel left out. When depression increases, I have a loss of interest in activities I normally enjoy, along with experiencing the other more common characteristics of depression, such as confusion and loss of energy. I feel more depressed with greater insecurity and anxiety due to negative situations, even though I try to do what I am capable of doing to improve the situation and be happier. Praying does give me some comfort.

At times, Situational Depression is more pronounced than other times, depending on the external environment and situations occurring, such as when the person is ignored due to his differences. It can also become more cyclic. Frequently, when an event causing PTSD occurs, with its associated reflexive anxiety or panic attack, and the initial shock subsides, I have had increased depression and anxiety the following day. This could also be referred to as Depressive Anxiety Disorder. This disorder could be longer-lasting, depending on the current undesirable situations. It frequently occurs with imbedded Depressive Anxiety Attacks, where the person easily reacts to aggressive or unpleasant stimuli and feels very depressed. Depressive Anxiety Disorder can also occur when an enjoyable activity has finished and the person experiences a letdown. This can especially happen when there are no other immediate fun plans. He can feel very depressed along with great anxiety.

"This is exactly what has happened to me. I just didn't know what it was."

"Thank you for your thoughts, Ethan. When any of the above-mentioned unpleasant stimuli have just occurred, then smaller unpleasant situations, external negative emotions or aggression, or feelings of loneliness can more easily cause stress and trigger these side disorders, panic attacks, anxiety attacks, or meltdowns. This is very familiar to you, Ethan, as you know."

This is also very familiar to others with Asperger's, and to those of you who are more sensitive and have tender emotions. All of you would desire that any unpleasant situations would not occur, or would be very small ones, so that you would not have to experience these above-mentioned disorders as much in your life. Remember that our Savior is in charge, and He will allow us whatever situations He feels is necessary for us to experience, and sometimes we put ourselves in less pleasant situations from poor choices we make at times. If you are having a bad day and say something rude to a family member, such as, "Don't talk to me that way," that person may respond negatively to you, saying, "I don't want you around me anymore," causing you to feel very depressed. What we learn from this is to remember to be more Christlike, thus preventing this situation. Instead, you could say, "I really appreciate what you did to help me today with my schoolwork." Being kind to others will help us to feel much better. When the Lord allows us to be in unpleasant situations, we should know that He is helping us to progress in positive ways. As we become more humble, willing to submit ourselves to Him and put our trust in Him, He will help us through these unpleasant situations and make them easier to bear.

As an example, one very unpleasant situation occurred when my young nephew passed away. Cell phones were not much in use at that time yet. I was at work that day. We were previously told in a meeting that when someone called our work office with an emergency, the secretary or office worker would go find the worker immediately and let him know of the emergency. We would always let the secretary know at which building we were working. At this time, my mother called the work office to let me know that my nephew was about to pass away that morning. She said, "I need to talk to Robert right away. There's about to be a death in our family!" My parents were on their way to the hospital and wanted to get me to take me there, also. I happened to be working in the building closest to where they could easily pick me up on their way. I was a half mile from them. However, the secretary told her that it was not known where I was at the time. I had already called the office and explained where I was. The office worker had been treating me poorly during this time, when he already knew that I had Asperger's and the characteristics associated with it. My mother kept trying to locate me, but it did not happen. The office workers were not cooperative. My parents had to go on without me to the hospital, where all the family had gathered, everyone except me. I had no idea that any of this was occurring. Later that afternoon when I was at home, my mother called me to let me know what had happened, along with my parents' attempts to get me. Missing out on a grievous event as this, along with the closeness I needed with my family at the time, due to the workers' attitudes toward me, made this experience and the intense emotions associated with it much worse.

If this had happened to you, and you didn't have a phone with you, how would this have made you feel—if there had been a way to contact you, but it didn't happen? What would you have done? You certainly would have felt a mix of great emotions which would have made you feel helpless, depressed, and upset, along with feeling anxiety and even anger, along with normal grieving. What can you do to help yourself through all this? What would be the best thing to do at this moment?

This traumatic experience caused great depression,

along with adding to the PTSD which I already experienced. Prayer was the best way I was able to deal with this experience. Members of my family also greatly comforted me during this time. I still had to let my emotions out, and I cried a lot for the first few days afterward. I prayed that I would not have resentment toward these people. I realized that the Lord wanted me to experience this in order to help build my character, and to help me to learn to not be angry with other people. I will show you later how situations like this do not affect me now like they did, and how they do not cause these side disorders to occur much at all.

This is a sample of many other traumatic experiences which occurred in my life. Some of these will be described in greater detail later, as examples of what you, having Asperger's/ ASD, may similarly experience, and I will show you how I dealt with them. Again, they are more traumatic to me because my sensitivity due to Asperger's Syndrome is increased, and they easily affect my very tender spirit. Many times, I experienced tremendous grief and mental anguish, and I cried a lot as a result of certain, intense situations I experienced throughout my life. I have had prescriptions of medications to help control these disorders, but they did not help. Even at low doses, they made me feel worse, and I had bad reactions to them, so they were discontinued. However, some people's disorders and anxiety can be helped with certain medications with careful monitoring. (I have a specialized medication now which does help with anxiety.) They can also be helped by meeting with a counselor who is proficient in understanding Autism Spectrum Disorders.

I am working on controlling the PTSD and Situational Depression, along with associated anxiety, the best I am able, with the Lord's help. There are simple methods to use which can greatly reduce these side disorders. They can be managed to where they are hardly noticeable. Later I will be explaining how I do this. I do my best to be positive while I do what good I can. Priesthood blessings have also been a great help.

Here is one way Situational Depression can be easily reversed. Those of you who interact with the Asperger's person, can help create positive, exciting situations to help alleviate the negative situation causing the depression. You could all go out for dinner or see a good show, you could go to visit some good friends in the area or have them come over for a good meal and socializing. Help him be involved in positive activities so that he is not idle very much. Depression increases when a person is more idle. Idleness increases when there is more depression. They feed into each other. In this case, he may then turn to spending excessive time playing video games, watching movies, or chatting online. Help him keep his life more balanced. Another way to help the depressed person is to listen more empathetically to him, and respond with positive communication. Remind him of his many blessings, and how much you love him and need him around. Let him know how important he is. Spending quality one-on-one time with him is one of the most important Christlike behaviors you can do for the Asperger's person. This will have a great influence on him and he will remember it throughout all his life.

I know that the adversary wants us to feel depressed. This is one of his tools. He wants us to feel this way so that we will have negative thoughts, think that there is no hope, and not think about our Savior. Some people have these side disorders, some more than others, which are linked to a disability on the Autism Spectrum or related brain disabilities, or any physical disability which reduces our performance as compared to most people. This performance reduction can easily intensify anxiety and depression. I know that the Lord will help us to suppress these disorders, as we desire this, and as we put forth our best effort to stay close to the Lord, earnestly pray, and live His gospel. Then as we do all we can to help ourselves improve, He will assist us. Helping others in positive ways and doing good, worthwhile projects are some very excellent ways to help suppress Situational Depression.

Some thoughts from Elder Boyd K. Packer have been a tremendous help for me as I've experienced these side disorders. They have diminished as I have incorporated these ideas in my own life. He said, "I work on keeping my thoughts positive. As the years passed I found that, while not easy, I could control my thoughts if I made a place for them to go." I can replace thoughts of grief, anger, disappointment, anxiety, insecurity, or fear, as well as depression, with better thoughts and with good, peaceful music. "I also love the sacred music of the Church. The hymns of the Restoration carry an inspiration and a protection for me." Many times I turn on calm, relaxing music or think of an uplifting Church hymn.

Deep breathing also works very well when I experience a PTSD episode or panic attack. I exhale completely. I then slowly take a deep breath. I repeat this until these episodes are greatly reduced. I also do positive self-talk. "Thoughts are talks we hold with ourselves." I think, "It's okay now, it's safe now." Some other positive self-talk would be saying to yourself, "I am a very important and worthwhile person, a literal child of our Heavenly Father." "I have great potential and I am capable of doing much good." Doing what the Lord would have me do allows prayer and spiritual guidance to help me.

"Later, I will explain some fantastic methods which will further suppress these disorders and Asperger's characteristics which can be very annoying to yourself and others. I will also offer you great information to help your family to be able to handle your Asperger's situation."

This information will also help each of you deal with issues you experience in and out of the Church, having Asperger's/ASD. Each of you, along with your families, will then experience some very marvelous results. There will be a renewed hope and everyone involved will progress and have a better life. I will show you how it happened for me and my family and I will show how it will happen for all of you, too.

"Ethan, it has been very enjoyable taking you this far on this journey with me. I know that you have already progressed. I have seen your excitement and great joy, having come this far on our journey!"

"You're right! I'm very happy and excited about everything you've taught me. This is great! Mom and Lexi, are you excited too?"

"Yes, Ethan, we're very happy that we're going on this journey together. Lexi and I are learning more about you, and we're truly joyful especially for you and what you are learning."

"Ethan, I see that your family is happy for you and also very excited with what they have learned in order to help you. They are seeing how they can have a more loving family relationship with you. I am looking forward to helping you feel much happier in your life, be able to communicate better with others, and understand more about yourself, as we continue on this awesome journey."

CHAPTER TWO
EXPERIENCES AS A MEMBER OF THE CHURCH WITH ASPERGER'S SYNDROME/ASD

"Why is he being such a brat?" "Why is he acting so childish?" "He is acting so immature, just trying to get attention by being disrespectful!" "Don't his parents know how to teach him how to behave, especially after going to Church every week?" These are just a few of many "judgmental" accusations presented directly or indirectly to the family of a person with Asperger's Syndrome. These people are unaware of this disability, it being harder to perceive. They think that the person is normal, and just "acting out" but knowing better. Many years ago it was thought that this disorder was caused by the parents, by how they were raising their child, that they were mistreating the child or not teaching him properly, causing him to "act out." Now we know that Asperger's/ASD is a physical developmental disorder in the brain, resulting in these unusual characteristic behaviors previously mentioned, such as involuntary movements and facial expressions.

When other people are told about the child's real disability and what he is experiencing, and they choose to not believe this information, then this tells us something about how these people are, by how they still treat him. We need to pray for them. This also shows what the child has to deal with, being in the Church with higher expectations of living. His trials and social demands are thereby increased, especially when he has been active and faithful in the Church.

Here, I will explain more about some of my experiences in the Church, some positive and others not so much, and some quite intense, as Ethan knows. Before I knew I had Asperger's, my family and I didn't know why I was having these experiences, and why I was behaving the way I did. When I was diagnosed with it, I found that I was in a very small minority group of people at that time who were diagnosed with ASD. I didn't know that I had Asperger's Syndrome until I was 36, being that it is an invisible disability and was quite rare at the time. It was just then being discovered. Now it can be diagnosed in a person much earlier in life, as there is much more information available today. I have learned that Asperger's and Autism were not nearly so prevalent before I was diagnosed. Only one in about 4,000 were diagnosed with Asperger's when the Autism Spectrum Disorders were discovered. The Autism rate has dramatically increased since then, partly because it is much easier to diagnose. There are over 3 million children in the United States with this disorder, plus a great number of adults. This being the case, there are many more of you who have this disability, have a family member or members with it, or know of an extended family member or friend diagnosed with Asperger's/Autism Spectrum Disorder. Some unique experiences occur in the life of the person with Asperger's, as well as for the family. Many of these experiences are even more unique in the Church setting, as I have experienced them myself. I will explain further what it felt like to me.

"You will find that this part of our journey will become more interesting, Ethan, as we continue along."

CHILDHOOD EXPERIENCES WITH ASPERGER'S

When I was a young child, I knew that most kids were different from the way I was. Their personalities were different, and the boys were generally more active and outgoing. At the time, I thought that I was normal, just a different personality. I didn't understand why I had very few friends. I liked being by myself at home, and with my family more. However, I felt very sad that I didn't have the friends and relationships that many of the other children had. I have learned that people with Autism and Asperger's have an even greater strong need to have a "safe" person to be around and a "safe" place to be or to go. They have a great need for love and security. They have a very strong desire to connect to and interact with many other good people whom they can trust, and who can understand their sensitive feelings, as they do think differently and understand life in a very different manner. They have a great need to feel validated.

"Ethan, you know what I mean. I will be discussing this in more detail during our journey."

I didn't like much of the outside world when I was young. It was quite overwhelming to me. I was scared of large animals. I needed to stay away from big dogs and other larger animals. The earliest I remember was being on a horse with my sister Susan, when I was about four years old. I was not happy. I was scared and wanted to be off. It was a very large animal compared to me. I have never had the desire to be on a horse again. I am not really an animal person. I didn't especially like holding cats or other small animals. I was scared of their sudden, unexpected movements and behaviors. There are variations of this within the Spectrum, where some of us need calm animals to help meet those needs of love and security. Others find that animals can help them feel calm and comfortable, especially when there are not enough people around who understand them.

As mentioned, I did not start talking until I was five years old, when I started talking in sentences. Others with Asperger's may talk sooner than this. Again, my mind has always thought very logically, and I must have thought it was illogical to say just single words, thereby not communicating much at all. Also at that time I started kindergarten, where my parents had me in speech therapy. My pronunciation, and especially my enunciation, was poor, and it was difficult for me to speak and communicate. Since the speech therapists didn't know I had a disorder, they helped me the best they could. I still have difficulty pronouncing some English words, especially those where an "L" or an "R" follow a consonant. Extra practice with pronunciation can be a great help.

Speech therapists can also help with the enunciation of these words.

All the events which happened at that time are my earliest memories. Some of my experiences in kindergarten were pleasant, such as hearing an enjoyable song, and others were not, like being blamed for doing things I had no idea were bad, such as playing with an item which I was never told not to touch. I was asked, "Why are you taking this apart?" I answered, "I saw the other kids doing it." What I had done was shown to several other teachers, who then told me that it was wrong to do, indicating that I did something bad. I didn't know it was wrong and I actually wasn't intending to do anything wrong. This made me feel less secure. I remember feeling very uneasy, afraid while being away from home when I first started kindergarten, as I was away from my "safe" person. The adults at school didn't understand my unique behaviors, also causing my uneasiness being there.

"Ethan, you probably had similar feelings and experiences at that age, along with others."

During this time, I had not developed proper balance. It was discovered that my eyes were not focusing together, which was later corrected by surgery. I was scared of falling into a swimming pool or off a ladder. This was compounded by the innate fear that little children have of falling. I had to teach myself balance all through my life, mainly by practicing on a bicycle. I also practiced in a swimming pool with the help of float devices. At times I still have some difficulties with balance, and I have to hold the handrail when using stairs.

Since all of my physical senses are intensified with

Asperger's, a particular view was very appealing to me. I remember seeing a display in a California shopping mall plaza, where water drops would come down on vertical wire-type strings arranged in a circle. There were various sizes of circles, each with strings hanging down about 30 or 40 feet into a very beautifully landscaped arena with little ponds and lush growth. When I lived there, I would remember the pleasant aroma of evening barbecues from neighbors, as well as our own, when I would go into our backyard. This made me feel very happy.

At this time, I remember going to Church each week with my family. I remembered the uniqueness of the building, its beauty, its unique fragrance inside, and the special feeling I experienced there. People there would treat us very well, including myself, as my behaviors were similar to those of most five-year-olds. I also re-member feeling the loving closeness with my family when we had our weekly family home evenings. This made me feel very safe and comfortable. For example, one summer evening we had a barbecue dinner. We sang a hymn and had a lesson, which included tossing a bean-bag onto a target to illustrate how to achieve goals. We played a board game for an activity and then had ice cream. I looked forward to each of these evenings of fam-ily togetherness. Even though I didn't fully understand it at the time, I was feeling the Spirit of the Lord and family love in the home and during our gatherings. This is very important.

"I know that you can really relate to these loving ex-periences, Ethan, which make you feel very happy and secure."

When I was six years old, we moved to Utah and I got

to see snow for the first time in my life. I remember it being a very new and different experience for me. It was like a magic white blanket had been put down overnight. I had to be careful to balance on it.

I felt better spiritually when we moved to Utah. The neighborhood and ward were very friendly. The majority of the families in the neighborhood were active in the Church. An elementary school and Church meetinghouse were near us, and experiences there were much better for me than they were in California. People were more friendly and respectful. I felt more safe and secure. Around this time, I remember seeing and enjoying two classic movies: *Mary Poppins* and *The Sound of Music*. I liked *Mary Poppins* with all the magical events it portrayed, as well as the great music. I also enjoyed the great classic music in *The Sound of Music*. It was very calming and uplifting to me.

I remember going to an amusement park called Lagoon. Due to Asperger's and my balance, I was not interested in the fast thrill rides, but really enjoyed the slower rides, such as the carousel and the cars on a guided track. These were slow and on the ground, which made me feel safe. Around the time when I was eight years old, I was able to ride a bicycle with training wheels, which were more commonly used at the time. Soon after, with much work, I was able to learn to balance and ride it normally, but not fast. I was very excited about my accomplishment. (Other people within the Spectrum ride bicycles faster and are quite fearless as they do so. Due to the wide range of behaviors and varying types of Autism, this disorder is appropriately referred to as a Spectrum Disorder.) Later, I had my own bicycle and I was very interested in attaching a speedometer to it. This was not to see how fast I could go, but rather, to watch the speedometer dial indicator move and watch the mileage numbers change on its odometer. This was also a very fascinating activity for me.

When I turned eight years old, I joined the Cub Scout program. I enjoyed learning and accomplishing much during that time as a Cub Scout, such as building a crystal radio set, and of course, the pinewood derby cars. It was very fun, as many of you know, when the pinewood derby car race began. I was very excited, as I knew that having a heavier car would increase its chance of racing faster and finishing sooner.

"I know that you, Ethan, were also very excited when you raced your pinewood derby car. You were happy to see it go faster than most of the other cars, or even win, just like the other boys were hoping for their cars."

All the boys had the compelling desire and excitement to participate in this race. I was very thankful for the help my father gave me in getting my racecar ready. I received help mainly from my father to accomplish the other requirements to advance. I also received some help from some of the leaders, but had less interaction with the other boys. I was excited to achieve the advancements and earn awards. It was quite easy and fun to complete the requirements in Cub Scouts and Primary, which also gave me a feeling of great accomplishment.

"I know you had these same feelings, Ethan."

"Yeah, I sure did. It was so fun and exciting to earn awards in Scouts and advance in Primary. It was very easy to learn and memorize what I needed, so I could pass off each requirement. I also enjoyed how my mom encouraged me and how comfortable I felt at home when she taught me so much about the gospel. I just feel safe at home."

"Ethan, that's how I felt too when I was that age. It's wonderful you have a loving mom and sister in your life to help you progress and advance in this way."

Later, as a Boy Scout, I did not progress very far, as I was more limited with Asperger's as to what I could physically accomplish and enjoy. I was also limited in my good interactions with the other Scouts. They were not very interested in me and most leaders would ignore me instead of finding ways to involve me in the programs. This was mainly due to the fact that none of us were aware of these lesser-known disorders, nor did anyone have the knowledge of how to best interact with those who unknowingly had these disorders. Being older, my unusual, different characteristics—such as those with social awareness, communication difficulties, and involuntary movements—were becoming more obvious, and this was confusing to everyone. While I didn't know I had a disorder, I did the best I could. Others with Asperger's in the scouting program have varying interests and abilities, and some can accomplish more and advance farther, especially when not being told of any limitations.

"I understand that you achieved a little more than I did in Scouts, Ethan."

I mainly enjoyed doing fun activities with my family. When I was young, we would go on a trip each summer to visit family in California. Since I think in more of a mathematical manner, when we were traveling in the car I would be looking at a map and checking the number of miles between towns. I would also be intensely noticing the different climates as we traveled into new areas. I would be looking out the windows, seeing everything in great detail as we traveled along. I also enjoyed visiting our relatives. My grandma Irene lived by the ocean. She was very spiritual and I felt safe around her. When we arrived there, she said, "Oh, I'm so happy to see all of you. Thank you for coming! I always enjoy seeing each one of you. It's been awhile since you were here." She wasn't able to travel to our home, so she saw us only when we went to visit her. It was fun seeing her and going to the beach. The ocean scent was in the air. Due to my balance, I would go in the water only several inches deep. I did not learn to partially swim until much later in life. However, it was a very neat experience to walk on the sand and hear the ocean waves and birds. It was fun to stand at the edge of the water and look out across the sea to where it met the sky. This was such an amazing sight! I was really excited going to see the ocean at the very beginning of our vacation trip, and I could hardly wait until it was in view.

When we were there, I remember in particular going to a couple of fancy restaurants. Again, with my senses intensified, I really remembered the good sights and sounds, such as a beautifully decorated gas fireplace with lush decorative seaside-type vegetation, as well as the pleasant aromas and good food there. They were both at the beach, and one was actually off the shore, over the water, so I could see and hear the ocean as well. For me, this experience was one of the great highlights of our vacation trip.

When we went to visit my other grandparents, Richard and Verda, I could really feel the spirituality and love in their home. When we arrived, they would say, "Welcome to our home. Oh, it's so wonderful to see all of you!" They were very pleasant to be around and I felt safe with them. I really enjoyed visiting them. While there, we would have family gatherings with other relatives, have barbecues, and enjoy our friendship, which I especially needed to help my spirit heal and feel better. I have a favorite aunt and uncle, Frances and Bob; I always enjoyed visiting them or having them visit me. They were easygoing and casual, which is more my type. This makes me feel very relaxed and peaceful. This shows how spiritual members of the Church have a great influence on children and those with Asperger's. All children are affected this way, but children with Asperger's have an added security need, longing for "home" but not quite understanding it.

"I know that you, Ethan, really enjoy visiting your relatives also."

My father, Ralph, was a landscaper, and I enjoyed what he designed for various properties. I also enjoyed assisting him with developing our own landscapes in our yards each time we moved, which was every few years. These landscapes were very beautiful. He artistically designed everything in detail on a large page before creating it on the ground. He showed me the application of the common saying, "Plan your work and then work your plan."

When I was in elementary school, I had a higher ability in math, grammar, and spelling. As we didn't know about Asperger's Syndrome or Autism Disorders at the time, my family and I didn't know that Asperger's was the reason for these higher abilities. I wasn't thinking about having higher abilities, either. I was just content doing my schoolwork, and doing the best I could, putting forth my best effort.

"Ethan, have you had a similar experience in elementary school and middle school?"

In elementary school and all the way through high school, I would get colds and the flu much more than most of the students. Children's immune systems are still developing, and they aren't as strong as adults' immune systems. However, my immunity was even worse, mainly due to extra stress and anxiety. My mother would go and bring my schoolwork home for me to do, so I would remain current with my assignments. Again, I look back at her caring ways, which I really appreciate. One math teacher was presenting a new concept on the board for the class on the day when I wasn't able to be there, when I had the flu and pneumonia. He knew that I was a good student in the class, so he outlined the entire presentation on a paper, along with the assignment. I understood it and was able to do the new assignment at home as if I had been there. This shows how good teachers can work with students, no matter their situations. They can have a very positive influence on children with Asperger's Syndrome as well, and help them to efficiently learn.

The teachers would also help me when the other kids would tease me or make fun of me. At times, the kids called me names or would talk disrespectfully to me, and sometimes would be a bit more aggressive, but the teachers and school administrators would speak to them and help them to understand. Many of these students were having family issues, and would act out like this or in a bullying manner as a way of dealing with their emotional issues. These students' behaviors were not as aggressive then, as they are now. Teachers and administrators can now work more closely with these students and their families, and provide resources to assist them with their problems, so that more students will have a positive learning experience at school, including those with disabilities. I will be giving a powerful example of this shortly.

"I know that you, Ethan, and all others with Asperger's Syndrome/ASD have been teased, made fun of, and bullied at school and maybe even at other social settings, like during youth activities. This is more common among those with disabilities, as it has been for me. However, we should always be proud of who we are, and still choose what's right."

When I was finishing high school, I wasn't getting sick as often. As I was becoming older, my health was starting to improve. A couple years later, I found some excellent nutritional products which helped me to stay well much more of the time. This helped me socially, as I was able to spend more time interacting with people, utilizing the information my parents had taught me. When I was a child, interacting less often due to illness was one of the reasons my social skills were slower to develop. Helping the Asperger's child stay healthy will be a great benefit to him, allowing more social assistance during his school years. He will be able to spend more time with his interests, also allowing faster brain development. This is another good intervention technique.

Again, when I was about eight years old, I had a very intense interest in genealogy. My mother worked on it often, and I desired to make my own large multigeneration pedigree chart. I would spend hours writing as much detailed information about my direct-line ancestors on this chart. This has proven to be a tremendous asset to me, as I still really enjoy family history, and I verify this detailed information online, from the family tree records.

"Ethan, you also have probably had intense interests in certain areas when you were growing up, such as music and mathematics, for example."

MY ASPERGER'S EXPERIENCES AS AN ADULT

I graduated high school with an A- average. I have an above average IQ, which is more common in people with Asperger's Syndrome. I understand this is due to the fact that because certain areas of the brain were suppressed in their development, such as the communicative and social function areas, then other cognitive areas of learning (along with sensory sensitivity) were accordingly heightened, all based on the neuron patterns in the brain. This results in the IQ being above average, along with some savant situations, where the person has great knowledge and talent in a particular area, like music. However, I don't view myself as above anyone.

As I am of a sensitive nature and my tender spirit cannot deal well with any type of aggression, I had no interest in the military service. I wouldn't physically qualify for it either. This was not to be any part of my life. However, I am very interested in our country's freedom, and I really appreciate and support the service which others have given to protect our freedoms and keep us safe. I do participate in the election processes each year.

I was able to go to college for a couple of years after graduating high school, taking a lighter load so I could more easily handle everything there, without feeling overwhelmed. I lived at home while doing this. At age 21 ½, I was able to go on a full-time mission for my Church. I went later due to the effects that Asperger's Syndrome had on me, emotionally and socially, although I did not know the reasons at the time. I went when I felt more ready. Going to college for a couple of years and having that social experience really assisted me in being ready for a mission. My Church leader didn't want me to go, thinking I had some major mental and emotional problems, which were not the case. Asperger's Syndrome was not known at that time, and without the information concerning it, people were more easily confused. I knew that I would be going, and my patriarchal blessing also mentioned it. My father had to insist that the stake leaders send in my paperwork. The Spirit had told us both that I was to go. I had a very successful mission in South America, which helped me progress as well.

"As I discuss these achievements in my life, and how I accomplished them having Asperger's, this will give you, Ethan, a better understanding of everything that you and that many people with Asperger's are able to accomplish, even though you may not know all what you are capable of doing at this time in your life. I will show you how these important items can be accomplished. You can easily know if these milestones are to be part of your life, and you can know how to prepare for them by staying close to the Spirit of the Lord for guidance. I will show you how to do all of this, so that you can know about and achieve that which our Savior knows you are capable of doing. I knew that I needed to achieve all what I was capable of doing in my life, and you will discover that you are capable of doing much more than what you first thought you could."

Having this disorder, I have a very strong need to be connected and social with the more spiritual members of my family and relatives. Frances and Bob, my favorite aunt and uncle, are more easygoing, like I am. We used to do fun activities, like going on short hikes and having simple meals together such as hot dogs for lunch. When I got my own place later in life, they would stay with me as they traveled. When they came to visit, they excitedly said, "Hi Robert. How are you? We've come to visit you. If it's okay, we would like to stay with you tonight." I would say, "Sure. Thank you for coming." Then they mentioned, "Our son and his family are traveling and are planning to meet us here today. Would it be okay if they stayed here tonight as well?" I answered, "That would be wonderful." I was happy when relatives would come to visit. This provided healthy interactions and loving connections with other good people besides my immediate family.

There was a swimming pool in the little homeowners' community where I was living. Frances and Bob loved to swim, and they also taught me how to swim somewhat. I really appreciated their teaching me. I was close to them all my life, as well as with my own family. My family members were actually my closest friends, and I was able to talk to them openly about my concerns. Before knowing about any disorders, I remember asking my mother many times about why I did not have friends and why people would not want to associate with me much. I would ask, "Mom, why don't people stay around me and talk to me very much?" She would say, "I don't know. It is hard to answer."

Looking back on when I was a child, some of my Asperger's characteristics, such as literalness and concreteness, were not distinguishable from the other children. However, other ones like social unawareness were a bit more obvious. As I became older, my childhood characteristics didn't change as much as they did for other people. During all this time, I thought that I was normal, and I perceived the world through my eyes, which I thought was not harsh or very evil. I thought that most people were thinking the same way. Even though I didn't have many friends when I was younger, this also meant that I didn't have much anxiety from interactions with others. I found out much later that my sister and parents were feeling a great amount of anxiety about me as I was growing up, as they saw that my behaviors were very different from everyone else. I would exhibit very odd facial expressions, turn my head quickly, move my hands and arms in an odd, eccentric manner, and would not talk very much to people outside my family. I would act very shy and would look at the ground. My family didn't know why this was the case. They wanted me to fit in with society. I didn't know this was happening, that there was any problem at all, and they didn't know what to do about it. As I became an adult, some of my characteristics were becoming more obvious to me, like social unawareness and a lack of social skills.

"This was causing me more anxiety, not knowing

about Asperger's, as I will be showing you, Ethan. You have also felt this anxiety, and I will guide you through it."

All during middle school and high school, I just didn't understand the other kids' ways of socially interacting and associating with each other. When I tried to talk to them, many of them would show expressions on their faces which were unusual to me and which I did not understand. Many times I tried to enter into their conversations, but I would get only a brief response, if any. I just didn't know why they would look strangely at me, and their ways of communicating were not making any sense to me. I had no idea that I was making strange faces that were not making any sense to them. I was also unknowingly making strange body movements. I was the only one of all the students there who acted in this manner. My face looked much younger than my actual age, and they all appeared more mature. However, there were a very few kids who were more friendly with me and I felt more comfortable talking with them. I didn't act so unusual around them. The Asperger's person may need to know more about his disorder at this point in his life, to help answer questions about his way of functioning in this world, and about how to continue to improve his communication and to learn good social skills, so he can progress more efficiently and effectively, and mature more appropriately. I will be showing you this.

Around the time I had finished my teenage years, I was still thinking more as how a child would think in social interactions. Other people would start to talk to me in more of an adult way of communicating, asking me my opinion about the subject being discussed, and I would then start to realize that people perceived me as an adult. This thought pattern can commonly occur among those with Asperger's. I would then realize that I needed to change my thought patterns and start thinking of myself as an adult, and I realized that other people already had this perception of themselves much earlier. This was helping me to learn about the adult world, and was preparing me for life's experiences as I grew older.

"Ethan, have you thought that this possibly has been occurring with you as well?"

I was able to move from my family home and rent a place for myself when I was 31. One day, my parents came to me and said, "Robert, we have felt through the Lord's guidance, and our Church leader has counseled with us about this also, that it is time that you should move out to your own place. Your sister, Susan, knows a friend who has a basement apartment closer to your work where you can stay and be more independent. We know this will help you progress and will be much better for you." (Susan had been married for 11 years and had many friends.)

I was quite shocked, and responded, "Wait a minute, how am I going to be able to live by myself?" My father reassured me, "It will be okay, the Lord will help you. He also wants you to do this. You can talk to us on the phone and we will help you also."

I had enough faith and agreed. This was a whole new experience and was very hard for me at first. I didn't know how I would be able to live without my family around me. I was able to slowly adjust after many phone calls to my parents, my "safe" people. They would help me with emotional support, love, and connection, being the type of people whom I could talk to and trust, and who would understand me, which I really appreciated. They would say, "Remember to pray and call us whenever you need to talk or need emotional support." They helped me to stay close to our Savior. One time I was having difficulty preparing my dinner by myself. I was becoming very frustrated, as many of you can understand, so I called my mother for help. I said, "Mom, this is not working. This mix is not cooking like it says it should. What am I doing wrong?" She lovingly went through all I had done so far and found the part I had left out. I then gratefully replied with, "Thank you, mom." She responded, "I'm happy to help. Call me any time you have a question or if you need to talk."

Heavenly Father gave me wonderful, understanding parents. In any family situation, parents can be extremely helpful to their Asperger's child, more so than they first realize.

"Sarah, you know that you have been helping Ethan very well, and you will learn more about him and how to help him through this journey. You have a very loving, helpful relationship with your son, and you want him to be successful."

"I sure do. Robert, this is the most helpful information I have heard about Ethan. This is truly a very exciting journey."

"Ethan, although this type of relationship is not always the case with others who have Asperger's, they will find that there is a 'safe' person for them within their family circle. This person could also be a special friend. Your mother is indeed your 'safe' person."

Moving out from your family is a very major step for

someone with Asperger's. Each person is unique. In some cases, it is better for the Asperger's person to move out on his own, as it was for me. For others, it would be better if he stayed with a family member, friend, or in a group living situation if he has a particular need which he cannot completely meet on his own, in order to take care of himself. Staying close to the Spirit of the Lord will provide tremendous guidance in this situation.

About five years after I moved out on my own, I was diagnosed with Asperger's Syndrome. My mother, Mary, and my sister, Susan, had obtained some information from a relative about Autism Spectrum Disorders and Asperger's, which seemed to describe me. Also, a member of the Church ward where I was then living had family members with Autism, and knew I had a similar disability, which she mentioned to me. A little later, I obtained the diagnosis.

Now to back up a little. Right after I came home from my mission and before I found out about Asperger's, I decided to obtain employment. I applied at many locations, but nothing turned out anywhere. I had a Church calling at the time, working in our ward's clerks' office. I felt very impressed to work one 40-hour week there, as there was much paperwork to do then, in that calling. I felt that if I did, then everything would work out for me. As I was there, with the door open, a Church member came in to speak with me. He said, "I am impressed by the Spirit to come talk to you." He had walked past earlier and noticed me there. He was getting to know me when I mentioned, "I am looking for employment." He mentioned, "There is an opening for you, working right here in Church employment." He had felt right then that

I am an honest person, and told me, "I am involved in the hiring process." This person, named Tom, was able to get me hired there, doing cleaning and maintenance in the buildings in that stake of the Church.

I had been working for several years, cleaning and maintaining buildings with my good friend, Tom, who was also my supervisor. Therefore, a little after I had moved from my parents' home, I had enough funds to be able to get my own condo, close to where I worked. I was in that home for 7 ½ years. I found out that Tom also had a disability, but he was very intelligent, and knew how to keep me in my work, as others over us tried to dismiss me due to my Asperger's. He also studied about Asperger's, and knew that I had it at the time I found out about it. I was able to work very well, and it was good employment for me. I worked for 14 years in various Church buildings, taking care of the grounds, repairing sprinkler systems, cleaning carpets, waxing and buffing floors, etc. I was a good, honest worker, but the leaders were trying to remove me. I left for a year to continue some college education, and then decided it was better to continue working where I had been. Again, the leaders did not want to hire me, but Tom advocated for me to be hired again, the same as he had done before. He had to work with them even harder this second time to keep me hired during the entire 14 years. He understood me very well and was my advocate.

After I was rehired, the Church leader where I worked did not want me to continue in my employment there. He felt that he had been forced to rehire me. He called Tom at work to explain this to him.

He said, "Tom, I have been forced to rehire Robert,

who has mental problems. I do not want someone like this working for the Church in this stake. He needs to be dismissed."

Tom responded, "Robert is an excellent worker, is very honest and dependable, and completes his work very well."

"But he has mental problems and is a liability here."

Tom informed him, "To remove him would be discrimination and would be against the law."

The leader shouted, "He needs to be dismissed!"

Tom shouted back, "I will take legal action against you if you pursue his dismissal!"

The Church leader paused, and then indicated that he would not pursue it right then. Tom had been there for my defense, so I was able to continue my employment for many years. This was the same leader who did not think that I should go on a Church mission. I am very grateful to Tom for advocating for me in this way. People with Asperger's need someone like this, who understands about Asperger's and the needs of the person in his employment, to advocate for him or to be his employer. If this happened, more people with Asperger's could have fulfilling employment, and more could realize their true potential. Those with Asperger's are able to do very honest work.

"Ethan, you have probably noticed more discrimination and fewer opportunities for employment in your life than what most people would normally experience. Sadly, this is a trend among many people with disabilities. I am sure that you would agree that we need many more 'Toms' around us to advocate for us and to enlighten people about the true nature of many of us who are disabled. If you had good part-time employment, you would be able to greatly assist your mother with the family's financial needs."

At first, after moving close to my work and moving into my condo, my Church ward was very good with me. Later, members there would not understand me, they would get angry and start to punish or treat me as a troublemaker by ignoring me or angrily shouting at me. It was at that time when I discovered that I had Asperger's Syndrome and I tried to enlighten some of these people with this new information, but many would not believe me, thinking that I was making excuses, acting rude, and intentionally behaving differently to irritate them. Some even used this new information against me. One of them would say, in conversing to another, "Now he's saying he has a disability, as an excuse for his rude behavior. Doesn't that beat all? He should know better than that!" They didn't understand that Asperger's is an invisible disability. They said that I was intelligent enough to know better. One asked me, "Can't you use your intelligence to know when you are behaving badly, and then behave better around us?" They didn't understand that even though I am intelligent, I am very blind in certain areas, such as social awareness, social skills, body language, communication, involuntary movements like waving my arms or frequent scratching, etc., especially when I'm put in an uncomfortable situation. They also didn't understand that I was trying my best. They became angry to the point where I needed to stay away from them. This involved several Church leaders.

"All this made me feel very sad and frustrated, which may sound very familiar to you, Ethan."

I initially had a few callings in this ward. I was the newsletter editor, Sunday School secretary, and I was to keep the list of callings current on the board in the office. However, as people were starting to think that I was acting rude and trying to irritate them, it became increasingly difficult to fulfill these callings. When I became the ward newsletter editor, the previous editor in this calling was training me somewhat about how to do it. She misunderstood me due to my Asperger's characteristics and we each had a hard time communicating with each other. Many times she didn't know what I was saying or asking. I said, "I will just do it on my own." I learned how to do much of it myself, and through the help of another kind, understanding person there. I was then able to fulfill that calling well.

I had similar experiences in other callings there, such as when I was Sunday School secretary. It was better at first, but when the Sunday School presidency was changed after a few months, the new leaders did not interact well with me, and I was released.

During my 11 years in this ward, there were 5 successive leaders. One was called after he moved in next to me with his family. He and his wife did not understand me at all. There was a single person on the other side of my condo who also did not understand me, and was very unkind to me as a result of believing I was being disrespectful. For example, there were some planted areas in front of our condos with some groundcover in front of my porch. This person had suddenly planted a vegetable plant right by my front porch. My father and I had been planning to put a small landscaping bush there.

I had told this person about our plans, but he was

nasty about it and said that he would do what he wanted to do by my porch. When I saw the plant there, I asked my father to help put the bush there. We put the plant in the pot with soil and put it on this person's doorstep with a note that I wanted the landscaping bush by my front porch, and to please put the other plant somewhere else. The next day, I found that the plant and pot had been thrown over the fence into my backyard. The soil was widely scattered and the plant was by itself on the concrete, left to die. This scene was very upsetting to me. My father came and took the plant to his home to grow there. I had reaction episodes of PTSD and panic attacks, where I had to make loud sounds and walk heavily to help me feel better and remove some of the reaction out from me. This is very typical of Asperger's, especially when no other good person is physically present to provide comfort and prevent a panic attack. However, this is perceived as very strange behavior for others who are trying to comprehend this, who do not know about this Disorder. Their first impression would be that I was acting out and being angry, just to annoy people, not usually seeing people behave in this manner.

"Many of you who have Asperger's, as well as you, Ethan, can really relate to this."

At this time, I did not know that I had PTSD. The neighbor would start to bang on the common wall to disturb me more. I was feeling attacked, and my response was the only way I could help myself through panic attacks. I asked the leader for help and he got angry with me. I had to have my parents come and help me feel better. My father tried speaking to him, with no avail. I never had any more interaction with him. One time later, his wife was tenderizing some meat by pounding on it with a tenderizing tool. She was doing it on a counter which was attached to the common wall, not knowing how loud the sound was transferring into my condo. I had another panic attack, so she heard my reaction, called my phone, and left a nasty message instead of compassionately finding a way to help in this situation. I know that people react on their first impression without realizing the real reason for the person's behavior. This is especially true when the behavior is a characteristic of a lesser known disorder, and the person appears more normal in other ways. This is a great example of when an appropriate Christlike response would have been extremely helpful.

Later, this leader was changed and the new leader had the same attitude with me. I tried speaking to him about one of my concerns in a casual way in the foyer. To my surprise, he then started shouting at me with other members around. I felt he should know that his behavior was inappropriate and I mentioned it to him, but he would not respond. My father called him on the phone about this situation, and he yelled at my father about it. This was never resolved. Another ward leader responded to me about another concern in a similar manner. Many times, I was scared to go out my front door. I was feeling like I was being wrongfully judged, like I was not good enough or as good as the other members of the Church. I felt like I was not acting normal with them, that I could not be part of the group. I felt very alone and really wanted to have friends who understood me and could help me.

Many of you may have experienced this or maybe even worse. This degrading chain of events can usually be attributed to great misunderstandings, and a lack of desire to become any more involved in what these leaders perceived as gross misbehavior on the part of the Asperger's person. We know that they should be Christlike, and find out what the underlying problem is, but there are those who choose not to pursue it any further.

"Ethan, what would you do at this time?"

I know that there are those who would leave the Church and become inactive at this point. Many would have extreme depression. Some may even turn to doing something wrong as a coping mechanism, just to feel better and to feel accepted by others who are doing something similar. Some may act in revenge. I will explain what I did, and then I will show what happened, which made things even worse.

I would have to be on the phone with my parents every day to help me deal with all these combined, intense situations. They were my "safe" people who would help me feel more comfortable and secure. They would come and visit me often, as they knew of my needs at the time. I did not feel that I was in a "safe" place. I prayed often.

In order to help me recover somewhat from the PTSD, I could not return to that ward. I tried visiting other wards and my parents' ward. I was thinking and feeling that there were more loving people in the Church in other areas, away from where I was. At this point, I felt upset, with very little trust in these particular leaders whom I thought I could trust with my concerns. I really wanted to have these situations resolved and feel loved in the Church.

This is not just an isolated example of how a member

of the Church can feel. There are more members who feel quite like this, more than what anyone would ever know. At first, we don't know what pains lie hidden in people's hearts. We all know that our Savior has taught us that we, as members and Church leaders alike, should lovingly seek out these people and fellowship them in a kind, ministering way. Don't let them fall in the cracks.

At this time, my work was about to end because they were downsizing and I was basically being pushed out due to my disability. My work with the Church, cleaning meetinghouses, had been reorganized into a group program, where we had a director over the cleaning in several stakes. This was at the time when my parents were trying to get me to see my nephew, who was about to pass away.

When I told our director about my disability and showed him information about how to understand me and help me, thinking that this would improve my work experience, he had more animosity toward me and also thought I was making excuses. He just didn't like my behaviors due to my characteristics, which were not rude, offensive, nor aggressive. He was the one to evaluate the workers. He would evaluate me a little below average when I did excellent work, the same as I did when Tom would evaluate me above average, before the group program began. It didn't matter if I worked excellent or average, I would be rated the same. Then a couple years later, the Church was going to reorganize the group program with fewer workers. I had found that I was near the end of the list, where those workers would be involuntarily terminated. The Church was offering a higher buyout rate if I left on my own, so I took the buyout instead of being terminated without it. If the director had rated me higher, I could have stayed working. He intentionally rated me lower as he was trying to remove me, not wanting "disabled" workers there. In this program structure, Tom was not in a position to be able to keep me there as he had before, and he knew what our director was doing. I have not had an occupation like this since. I was able to get on Social Security Disability soon afterwards, which was helpful.

When all these situations were occurring with these people, I was more scared to talk to any people and I felt much more awkward in communicative situations. I could only talk to my parents and sister, who were very concerned and were praying for me.

During this time, I had very severe depression, where I wondered if my earth life were still beneficial. It felt similar to having very severe, long-term migraine headaches (as they have been explained to me). I no longer had employment and I still was not married. I did not feel welcome in my Church ward. I had been praying to know if the Lord still wanted me on the earth, or if He would take me. Many of you with Asperger's/ASD or other disabilities may have had these same feelings. This is extremely important, very serious, and can even be life threatening. Many Church leaders and members may not have any idea about all this going on in the life of the Asperger's member, if they even know about him having Asperger's/ASD, with its associated characteristics and behaviors, as well as its associated side disorders. I know that if they understood all of this, and if they were more caring, wanting to truly minister to him, that they would have a change of heart, apologize, and help the Asperger's individual with love and kindness. How I wished that would happen, but many people did not ever resolve the issues in these situations, thus increasing the PTSD. This really shows the extreme importance of truly being an understanding, loving, caring listener, and of being very helpful to the person in this type of situation. It does not matter if it is known that the person has Asperger's or any other disability, in order to give needed assistance.

Many people without disabilities can have these serious issues also. When there is a real need for help, people should be true, loving friends, where they can make a great difference in a person's life. This applies to bullying at school or other locations, and any other situation where the person has great depression and anxiety, and can receive life-changing assistance.

"Ethan, you know this has happened to you, and you may also know someone who has experienced this. Your mom and your sister have been and will be of great assistance to you during intense situations you experience. At times, your family may also need assistance from good friends and other good people, or maybe from a helpful support group, especially when these types of situations occur. This all shows that information about disorders and other intense situations you experience is extremely important for good people to know.

"Here is an example to illustrate this. It will be especially important to both of you, Ethan and Alexis. This is a true story I heard recently."

A student named Carrie had just started ninth grade, as a freshman in high school. She and her family are all active members of the Church. Her parents and her two older brothers are very loving and caring. Her brothers,

Ryan and Tyler, were attending the same high school as a senior and a junior, respectively. They were especially helpful in getting Carrie adjusted to a new, bigger school for her. They were quite concerned for her, as she has a touch of Down's Syndrome, giving her face just a little different, characteristic appearance. She is quite intelligent, and was able to be involved in regular classes at her middle school, where she had excelled in many of them.

Carrie had been teased at times during her earlier years in school, but there was obviously a greater concern as she started high school, given her appearance plus a decrease in her ability to normally interact with the other students. She was a bit shy; also, she communicated at a lower age level, using words and actions a pre-teen would use. She would say, "Mommy, I wanna watch my cartoons before I finish my homework."

Ryan and Tyler were prepared for this. When the school year had been going for a few weeks, Carrie told them that she was being teased, and it was starting to turn into bullying. She said that one boy told her as another stood nearby, "Hey, take a look at this. You don't look very smart." Then he laughed and walked away. This turned into bigger pranks, where she was set up as apparently doing something wrong, which she would never do.

Carrie had gone to her first class slightly early one day to work on her assignment. Two other students there asked her to go over to the teacher's desk, where they wanted to show her something. One of them picked up a stack of papers on the desk, apparently to show something to the other student and to her. He intentionally dropped them but made it look accidental. He asked Carrie to help pick them up and pretended to start helping as well, when his phone went off (the other student was calling him as planned), and he went outside the room to apparently talk. They were timing this close to the class start time, because as she was still collecting the papers, the teacher walked in and saw what looked like Carrie getting into his personal papers. He then reprimanded her and took her to the office. This was upsetting to Carrie, so she called her oldest brother, Ryan, to let him know what happened. He came to the office and straightened out this problem, so that the administrators understood the situation. He said, "I know these students and they are only taking advantage of Carrie. She is a very honest, caring person." They then knew that these students were pranking her due to her looks and her appearing very naïve, so that they could be controlling and feel superiority.

Carrie was very thankful for Ryan's help and she knew that her brothers would need to probably help her again. This turned out to be true, as a more serious bullying event then occurred. Again, due to her perceived disability and apparent weakness, another student took her phone when she was not aware, as she was being distracted by this student's friend, and he uploaded a very threatening message on it using social media to all the studentbody, along with a photo of a gun. He put her phone back so that she was never aware of what took place. The school administrators quickly got a tip about this from another concerned student unrelated to this threat. They very quickly traced this to Carrie's phone, and she was taken from her class to the school office, along with her backpack. This was taken as a credible threat of harm to the students in the school, and the police were called. Carrie was very emotionally upset, crying, when she was asking for both her brothers to come. "I want all my family here before you do anything to me," she sobbed.

When this was determined to be a prank, through information that her brothers uncovered, it was still considered a very serious violation. It took awhile for Carrie's brothers to settle her and to help resolve this major issue. Ryan explained to the officers, "I have uncovered messaging evidence on my phone about who was involved in this prank." He then told his sister, "Carrie, we will get this all straightened out. Don't worry. We're here for you."

Her parents arrived, and through much explanation, convinced the officers to not take her into custody. Her dad told the officers, "I will be responsible for this, and I will handle any further confusion."

Carrie was very distraught from this, along with the rest of her family. They decided to do something more about this growing trend. Ryan, who was involved with the studentbody leadership, came up with a plan. He first planned a school assembly, with the approval of the school principal and the help of his parents. He suggested some plans to incorporate new school policies to help curtail any of these threats. He also suggested some excellent resources to assist these problem students and their families, many of whom were having family issues, resulting in some of these students' bullying and threatening behaviors. The principal was very pleased with his insights. Those who continued to initiate threats would be severely punished. He also suggested a new curriculum to the school principal, which was implemented. This would effectively help all students be prepared and learn what to do, along with a quick reporting system, so that no pranks or even bullying could occur without a rapid response. No disabled or naïve student would be a target. His parents supported him in this, then other families rallied around the family to make these changes become a reality in the school. This worked so well that many other schools in the region wanted to utilize these programs, which they implemented with much success.

As a result of these great improvements in the community, Carrie and her family did a news interview, which put her in the spotlight as the one who was the reason for all these wonderful ideas. Her disability along with her honesty was looked at very favorably, and many people highly regarded her. Her brother Ryan was also interviewed, and put in the same spotlight, where he explained the new concepts and programs, and how they were easily implemented in the schools.

This story shows how a person with a disability can end up in a very bad situation, then have his or her life turn in a very positive manner through the help of other good people, and how many other people receive great benefits as a result. I will tell you how my life improved later, by what I did and by what other people did to help me. I will show you what wonderful surprises awaited me. Staying close to our Savior by keeping my testimony strong in the Lord and His gospel through prayer was and is a key factor in having a better life. I will show Ethan and all of you how this is done, and how it is able to work specifically in each of your lives. I will also show how these Asperger's disorders with their associated characteristics can be greatly reduced and how they can be barely noticeable in your lives. To introduce this, I will have Ethan first explain what major and even degrading situations happened to him and then what he and his family did.

ETHAN'S EXPERIENCES WITH ASPERGER'S

"Ethan, to help other people better understand how Asperger's Syndrome/ASD or other disabilities have a farther-reaching effect on people than is first realized, to show how there are many people who have little idea who you really are, and to show some intense, emotional experiences of an Asperger's person from another perspective, I will let you explain about the heartbreaking situations you and your family have experienced."

I am Ethan, and I appreciate this opportunity to share with all of you some extremely hard experiences I had. Some years ago, my parents were having a very difficult time in their relationship. Much of the time, I thought their difficulties were from my having Asperger's, but my mom reassured me that they weren't. I still had my doubts. To make things worse, I was being bullied at school sometimes, more often now than what it used to be. I'm very thankful for my mom's concern for me. She really helped me resolve these issues by talking to the school staff, who then took appropriate action. They were already planning to start some new programs to help with this too. This made me feel a bit more secure. But I kept having difficulties talking to the other kids at school. It seemed like they had their own language, the way they would talk and look at each other, and it was hard to make sense of it. I wanted to talk to them and fit in with them, but they would say very little to me and they would look at me in ways I just didn't understand. Apparently, I was talking to them and looking at them in a strange way, by their responses to me. I felt like I was misunderstood, but I thought that I was being as normal as I could be. I really wanted them to understand me and accept me. I felt sad this was happening and I felt left out.

I was also being misunderstood at Church, where other members and some leaders were treating me like I was misbehaving, when I wasn't. I was diagnosed with Asperger's Syndrome many years ago, and I had also had some early intervention assistance for Autism Spectrum Disorder at that time at school, along with some at home which has helped a little. My mom tried to help the ward leaders understand what I have. They just didn't seem to get it. There wasn't quite as much information available about Asperger's then as there is now. They were thinking that I should be behaving better, not understanding that I was really doing the best I could. I was told that I was quickly turning my head frequently and moving my arms around a lot. One leader told me, "Ethan, you need to behave better here at Church." That made me feel worse. They didn't understand that Asperger's is an invisible disability. I looked like a normal person, and they wouldn't think that I had any disorder at all. They kept thinking that I was just trying to get attention the wrong way. My mom has been my advocate, as my dad was not active in the Church, and didn't seem to have as much interest in me.

When I was at Church on Sunday, some of the other

boys in the youth program there would tease me when I would unknowingly make strange movements with my arms, head, and body, and when I made some odd facial expressions without realizing I was doing it. This happened even more when I was put in an uncomfortable situation, like when I was asked in class to explain about a story in the Book of Mormon. Trying to figure out body language was also very difficult for me. I tried to get the leaders to help me understand nonverbal language better, but they just kept thinking that I was trying to get attention by being disruptive. I knew I was being misunderstood.

After class the following Sunday, one of the young women, Aubrey, who was two years older than I was, stopped me to talk to me. She had been noticing my odd behaviors and wanted me to behave more respectfully around other people. So, as I was going down the hallway, she called out, "Ethan, I need to talk to you for a minute. There's something very important I need to tell you."

I asked, "What is it?"

She explained, "Ethan, many of us in the ward have been seeing your strange, sometimes disrespectful behaviors. We want you to stop doing them. My friend, Lindsey, was upset with you when you made a strange face at her while she was trying to talk to you. She was only asking you a simple question about your sister, Alexis, so that she could contact her. You apparently misunderstood what she was asking you. Then you made this strange, silly grin at her as you gave an unrelated answer, not knowing what she meant by 'contact.' This made Lindsey more upset and then you just smiled, not even looking at her. Ethan, that was just plain rude! Please, will you be more respectful around us?"

I was quite shocked and responded, "I didn't know that I was doing all that. I didn't know I was being rude. I never want to be rude around anyone."

"That is really hard to believe, Ethan. Please don't lie to me and don't make excuses for your poor behavior. Just act your age and treat us the way we should be treated, with respect. Will you make sure that you do this and stop being rude?"

"I'll try," I muttered. "I'm doing the best I can." Aubrey shook her head as she walked off with her friends. I felt very sad, almost to tears. My body was trembling. I quickly went to my mom and told her everything that just happened.

"I'm sorry this keeps happening to you, Ethan." My mom consoled me a little and said, "I will help you to be more aware of your facial expressions and gestures. I'll do everything I can to help you, so you won't be so miserable. I, too, want these unpleasant situations to stop. I want you to be happier. I love you and really care about you."

My mom always has a way to make me feel better. I like how she helps me. However, I don't want to have more incidents like this, so I just keep to myself at Church, so as to not create more problems. I really want to be part of the group too, but I was belittled and left out. I had a very hard time trying to explain, using the right words, what I was actually thinking and feeling. I've had continuing sadness and depression at Church and at school.

A month later, it was time for me to have an interview with my ward leader, which the leaders do with all the youth in my ward. He was a kind person, but he just didn't have very much understanding of my disability. I appeared very normal and intelligent to him. He talked with me about my progress in my life. He knew I was doing very well mentally and academically, but was concerned about me socially and emotionally. He understood that my dad was not active in the Church and that I would naturally be unhappy about that. However, he didn't know why I was so depressed. When he asked me I told him, "People are not very friendly with me." He responded by saying, "Ethan, you need to be more outgoing and talk more with them. You need to look them in the eye and communicate normally with them. Don't move your hands and arms so strangely around people or make strange faces. I was told what happened last month, how you were not very respectful around Lindsey. This is something that is very important, which you need to stop doing."

I was startled and a little upset. I responded, "But I don't know I'm doing that. I'm never trying to make strange faces around people to make them upset. I don't want to be accused of doing that. I thought that I was communicating normally. It's just too uncomfortable to look at their eyes. They can hear what I'm saying just fine without having to do that. I have a disability that affects me this way."

He told me, "Ethan, you don't appear to have any disability. Please don't make excuses for your bad behavior. You are very intelligent, and I know you can do what I have suggested just fine. Remember to keep praying."

"But I wasn't behaving badly. You just don't understand," I sobbingly told him. I was feeling more frustrated because I told him again about Asperger's, but he still didn't believe me. I said that I was always trying my best, but he continued to think I was making excuses for my behaviors. I knew that I could improve, but I needed the right kind of help. I could see that he didn't know the right way to help me. I left feeling sadder and hoping there would be someone besides those in my family who would understand me completely.

My mom has been the best comfort for me, and she would pray with me. I want to do what is right, and I haven't had any desire to associate with those who do wrong. I really want to reach out to others, but they just don't let me, so my only friends are my family and close relatives. I know my dad loves me, but he isn't as close to me as the rest of my family. He just seems to be more upset at things, and he doesn't want to go to any counselor. He keeps thinking that life is always giving him a bad deal. The rest of us don't know what to do. We keep praying for him and we invite him to Church. We were trying to show our love for him. How I wished that he would be more loving. We tried to help him understand that the Lord's way is the happier way.

My dad just wasn't cooperating, and things got worse with him. He just didn't understand our hardships, and it seemed like he couldn't be around me due to my disorder. This made me feel like I was the problem, but my mom told me that there were many other things involved. I sadly told her, "My dad doesn't like me because I have Asperger's. I'm having a terrible life right now, the way other people treat me, and this with dad is just too much for me to take!" I then started crying.

Mom comforted me, saying, "I know how you feel." She then put her arms around me. "You are not the problem. Your dad is having many issues. Just know that I truly love you." This really helped me.

My mom continued to try to help my dad and resolve the problems, but it didn't work. He ended up divorcing her, which was very traumatic to me. It was an extreme shock. I am very sensitive, and this has affected my whole life. It made me cry often, but I didn't let my family see it. I was very depressed. My mom did her best to comfort me during this time, which helped a little. Some members of my Church ward have helped us, but they still didn't understand my increased odd behaviors the next Sunday. I was unaware of my behaviors and I had thought that I was being as normal as I could. Of course, I was upset about losing my dad. I had very tender emotions of sadness about it. I was really grieving. A few ward members thought that my behaviors were a result of my dad leaving. Many others thought I was overreacting. I had a hard time talking to them. I felt more alone and depressed during the next few days, along with feeling more upset and scared. They didn't really help me to feel much better, after the divorce. I just needed some comfort from my mom. I sobbingly asked her, "Mom, why are more Church leaders and members treating me like they do? Don't they understand that this is a very hard time for me along with the rest of us?"

She answered, "Ethan, I know you are feeling many hard emotions right now. You are a great person. People in the Church all have their agency. Many don't quite understand you. Many of them may be having difficult problems themselves. We cannot change what other people say or do. We can't expect everyone, or even some of them, to understand you and know just the right way how to help you. We love you and our Savior loves you. What is most important is what our Savior thinks of you. He understands you completely."

"Thanks, Mom," I responded. "You are the best in the world for me!"

My two younger sisters, Alexis and Trisha, were also very upset with the divorce. They also wanted our dad to be kind and forgiving. All of us kids were born three years apart. I, being emotionally sensitive, tried to comfort them, which brought us closer together. Soon after the divorce happened, and after talking to my mom, I said, "Lexi and Trish, can I talk with you for a few minutes?" After they let me into their room, I explained, "I know this is a very hard time for all of us, but I know the Lord can help us feel better. I feel that we should all talk together right now. Lexi, maybe we could play your favorite game together while we talk. I know that would help us feel happier. Would you like to now?" They both agreed. They told me that they were feeling the same prompting.

We shared some very precious moments then, feeling family togetherness. We talked about the problems each of us were having, and we helped each other feel better. We were very open with each other and we knew that we could all confidently share some personal, emotional concerns, too personal for me to say here. We truly gave emotional support to each other. It was a very special comforting time together. We all had tears in our eyes, and we hugged each other very tightly. I know that my sisters would always support me and love me. I also love them very much. Having this experience bonded us as a family even more. We later shared our experiences with our mom.

Trisha was especially comforting to all of us, even though losing our dad was very distressing for her too. She just naturally seemed to have the Spirit of the Lord with her much more and appeared quite resilient, no matter what trials she faced. She was always smiling and would treat everyone in a very kind, loving manner. She was extremely thankful for her blessings. She helped me through this time, as well as sticking up for me whenever she could. Trisha was very understanding of me, knowing what I was going through, and would especially try to help me by helping others to understand who I really am, and why I have these different characteristics. Even though she was a young preteen of almost ten years, she was quite mature for her age and had great faith. She and Alexis would come to me, and she would say, "Ethan, can we have a prayer together? I know that will help all of us at this time." Trisha said the prayer, and included a blessing on our mom, asking our Heavenly Father to bless our mom and help her feel better, especially now, since our dad has left us. She also prayed that people would be more understanding of me. This prayer was additional to the times we would have our family prayers with our mom.

Alexis was also understanding of me, and would try to help other people understand me better. I didn't know it at the time, but my sisters told me later that they had heard me crying in my room and had great empathy for me. Alexis said, "We didn't feel that we should disturb you right at that moment, but we want to comfort you, too."

They had a lot of love for me, even more than I first realized. I felt very close to them and I told them, "Thank you for your love and concern for me." They both have comforted me many times and have helped me when I had difficulties with my Asperger's. They lovingly let me know when I was acting strangely around people and would make weird expressions. For some reason, I felt even closer to Trisha. Many times she told me, "Ethan, I love you so very much. I'm very happy I'm in the same family with you!"

As we were slowly getting over the shock of the sudden change of our dad being gone, another major trauma soon hit us. About two years later, Trisha, my youngest sister, had started developing really bad headaches. The new school year had just begun. She was starting 6th grade and would be turning 12 in a couple of months. However, she had to stay home from school more often. My mom had our neighbor, a close friend to the family, check in on her frequently while my mom was at work and we were at school. Her headaches were very unpleasant and distressing, very painful, and she asked my mom, "Mom, why am I having so many bad headaches?" My mom responded, "I don't know. If it keeps getting worse, we will need to go to the doctor, and have you checked."

We comforted her during this time and my mom gave her headache medication, which helped a little, but her headaches started lasting longer.

Her condition didn't improve, so my mom took her to the doctor, who then referred her to a specialist. We all then went with her. After extensive testing and scans, we were all told the shocking news that she had a large brain tumor and that she had only up to six months to live. Surgery was not an option. I, along with the rest of my family, was extremely devastated. I felt very numb, very scared. My body was trembling. Through our emotions, we all helped her to be as comfortable as we could, emotionally as well as physically. We hugged her and my mom lovingly said, "Trish, we love you so very, very much." Trisha tearfully responded, "I love you and I'm so happy for all you do and how much you care about me. Ethan and Lexi, I really love you, too." There was no treatment and nothing else could be done for her, only prescription medication to help her feel more comfortable. Alexis was also very emotional, and my mom was especially emotional during this time.

When we got home, my mom offered a prayer together with all of us. Part of what she said was, "Heavenly Father, please bless Trish to be comfortable during this time. Please bless her with thy Spirit, that she will feel peaceful and feel thy presence. Please comfort the rest of us and bless us with thy Spirit, that we will also feel at peace. We are thankful for all Trish has done to bless our lives." After this special prayer, we saw that Trisha was in tears. She sobbingly said, "I know Heavenly Father will help me." We all gave her a hug together. I, with my very tender spirit, couldn't contain myself, and I started crying right there. Alexis was also sobbing. This was a very tender, emotional time for all four of us.

Trisha was getting worse and was not able to continue going to school, so our close neighbor friend came and took care of my sister while the rest of us were gone for the day. About two months later, however, Trisha became worse, and had to be in the hospital to receive more care. She was taken there by ambulance when she started to lose consciousness. We went to visit her each afternoon or evening, in between school and my mom's work. Trisha was very weak, but was able to communicate, slowly and softly saying her words. She kept talking about how I will get better. She would tell me, "Ethan, don't worry. I'll continue to help you. I love you."

A few days later, two days before Trisha's birthday, the doctor called that morning and told my mom that Trisha's time was about up. My mom got us out of school and we went to the hospital. When we went into her room, we saw that she wasn't very responsive. She wasn't really able to speak, even after her mouth apparatus had been removed. We shared with Trisha how much we loved her. My mom explained, "Trish, you are such a joy in our family, and we are all very happy for everything you have done to help us. We really appreciate the light you bring into our family, and we love you so very, very, much. We thank you for all your goodness and love." Alexis and I also thanked her and told her how much we love her. I looked straight at her and tearfully said, "Trish, you have been such a tremendous help to me. I'm so happy you're in our family. I love you very much."

Suddenly, Trisha turned her head a little bit and looked at us. She appeared extremely weak. Then she slowly mumbled with an extremely weak, almost inaudible shaky voice, "I...love...you." These were some emotionally tender moments. A moment later, she started smiling very tenderly, and then she was gone as her spirit left her body. This was extremely hard for us to bear.

We all had tears. My mom hugged Alexis and me very tightly. She said that it was Heavenly Father's will. One of the hospital staff took us to a private room. My mom then offered a short prayer. Alexis and I let out our emotions, but my mom seemed to have a great peacefulness about her which helped settle us. I felt her Christlike love for both of us. However, I still had very intense emotions which I couldn't hold back. It was very hard to stop crying.

All this was just too hard for me to take. First my dad, now Trisha. When we got home I went right to my room, closed the door, and then couldn't contain myself. I started weeping and sobbingly cried out, "Lord, why this?" I felt like I had been through so many great challenges, and that they seem to just keep getting worse. I felt like the Lord had left me alone. Plus, many people had still not been treating me very well because I have Asperger's with its associated odd characteristics, which had especially increased lately with my stronger, intense emotions. I had a difficult time communicating with them, and many would avoid me. Most of them wouldn't understand, despite my mom's continuing efforts to try to explain my situation to them. They were sorrowful about Trisha's passing, but they thought I was strangely acting out even more because of it, just to get attention. They would see my unusual anxiety attacks and reflexive panic attacks.

I really needed to have a talk with my mom. I asked, "Mom, why are more people ignoring me? Why do they treat me as they do?" She told me that some of them told her they just didn't know how to communicate with me. This was happening to me, even though my youngest sister had passed away. Mom then had me sit on the couch with her, sensing that there was something else causing me great anxiety.

I asked her, "Why did Trish have to go? I feel that I'm partly to blame, because I'm told that I act so unusual around people. I really feel that the Lord didn't want Trish around my strange behaviors that people accuse me of having. I feel very bad about this."

She intently asked me, "Why do you feel that way about yourself? Ethan, you are a very wonderful, important person. Please don't put yourself down."

I was starting to cry a little. I repeated, "I feel this way because I have Asperger's, and I feel that I haven't been treating her the way I should. She was such a great, loving person who lived her life so much better than I'm doing, that I feel that the Lord took her so that she wouldn't have to deal with any more of my bad behaviors."

Mom was shocked at this and responded, "Ethan, that is completely false! Your behaviors have nothing to do with Trisha's passing." She softened her voice a little. "It is our Savior's plan for her that she left at this time." Mom took my hands in hers and softly continued, "Ethan, you are my very precious son and a very precious son of our Heavenly Father. You're doing very well, having Asperger's, and I know that you're doing your best. Again, please don't put yourself down."

These words meant a whole lot to me. She knew that I would have an extremely difficult time at the funeral, so she told me I could sit close to her. She held my hand most of the time during the talks. When my mom gave her talk, Alexis helped me in a similar way. I had just been through a very difficult ordeal with grieving during the viewing before the funeral service. At the viewing, my grandfather was there and comforted me a lot. I'm just so sensitive that I physically show my emotions more than they do. For this, I'm very happy for the help my mom, Alexis, and my grandfather gave me during that time.

During the following weeks I still felt very bad depression and loneliness, along with a lot of anxiety. I was very sad and didn't feel like doing much of anything. I would go in my bedroom and cry a lot. I really felt like everything was lost and that there was no hope. I was upset that the Lord was putting me through all this, and I would cry out, "Lord, why are you doing this to me? I'm really hurting! Please help me!" I was wishing there was somehow a way to help resolve my really bad problems and to ease my emotional pain. I truly wanted the Lord to take me from this horrible situation I was in, and take me from this earth life. I didn't feel that I should do anything to myself, because I felt that it was wrong to do. I wanted the Lord to understand me and to help me feel better. I was going through more intense, nearly constant grieving, crying many tears.

It was harder for me to do very well in school now, even though it was my senior year. Thanksgiving was only a couple days away, but I didn't feel very thankful. I was feeling more by myself, except for the presence of my mom and Alexis. I didn't feel like going to Church very much either. I didn't want to be treated worse there. Many things would bother me even more, especially irritating sounds. How I wished there would be a solution for this. I felt like I was getting worse. I had increasing depression and anxiety. I would hit my hands together,

and hit walls and cry out when a loud sound or something else started bothering me, and I couldn't do anything about it. I would frequently have panic attacks and
meltdowns, along with PTSD episodes, but I didn't want
to make my mom and sister feel bad. I didn't want to put
them through even more trials, just because I have Asperger's. I would try to make it up to them, never wanting to hurt them in any way. I didn't want them to have
more anxiety because of me.

Alexis then tearfully asked my mom, "What can we
do to help Ethan? It's hard to hear him suffer so much. I
feel very sad about all he has to go through with his disorder."

Later, I would tell them, "I'm sorry for making so
much noise, but it's the only way I can feel better. I need
you to talk to me and reassure me a lot more, to help me
feel better and feel more comfortable. How can I make it
up to you?"

Mom told me that it was okay and that they both
would talk to me more often. She said to us, "We need to
do the right things to bring the Spirit of the Lord into our
home, and we need to fervently pray." She also explained to me, "The Lord's Spirit is not in our home like
it should be, and you should pray to have that Spirit with
you." I felt a special feeling while she was saying this,
and I then knew that doing this would especially help me,
also because I am the older brother and I knew that I
should help Alexis and be a good example to her.

Still, having all these reflexive reactions plus social
difficulties made me feel very frustrated and inadequate,
so I couldn't completely be the kind of person I really
wanted to be with my family and others. My mom con-

tinued to try to help other members in the Church to understand, who just didn't know what to do. She explained to them that they could help me if they would show more kindness and love toward me. She said that this would make me feel more comfortable to go to Church.

Mom and Alexis comforted and reassured me the best they could, and we all prayed, but they also still had to continue to deal with our losses in our family. My mom reassured me that things would get better. She repeatedly told me, "Ethan, have more faith, and ask Heavenly Father for help with this and with your difficulties." She would go to the temple frequently, as she knew it would be a great help to all of us. She said that this would bring the Lord's Spirit more into our home. I had prayed that I would receive the help I need. She was then prompted that I should receive a priesthood blessing of comfort to help me at this extremely difficult time. She called a couple of brethren in the ward who were more understanding and loving, and who understood me a little better. Part of the blessing said that I will improve, that I have important work to do, that I need to have more patience and faith, and that the Lord will bless me as I pray for this. Mom told me later that Trisha was also right there, in spirit, listening. It was not very long after this blessing that I was told about something from another family friend who lives some distance away, which was completely, positively life-changing for me in a major way. It was a tremendous blessing which I knew was heaven sent. It turned my grieving, anxiety, and sadness into great joy. I then realized how much my Savior loves me.

OUR SAVIOR LOVES ALL OF US

I, Robert, having let Ethan relate his experiences, am able to briefly share another perspective as to the type of life and traumas a person with Asperger's Syndrome experiences, along with his family. I am sure you would have great empathy about their situation and what they all have experienced. You would want to reach out to them in love and try to help in any way you can. I will tell you later about what was really life-changing for Ethan and also for his family. Would any of you have more ideas and suggestions to help Ethan and his family at this point in their lives? Helping members to remember to be more Christlike would be a great start. Being a good friend would be very helpful.

Now, to continue with my story. I, like Ethan, was in a ward where I was basically pushed out, socially and emotionally, and where some people showed animosity toward me. I did not have any Church callings at this time. I did not have any employment. I was not married. I didn't know if I had anything more to contribute, and if the Lord wanted me to stay on this earth. I had been praying frequently, as well as communicating often with my parents. I was talking with them on the phone every day, and they came to visit me many times to emotionally comfort me. One day they suggested, "Robert, maybe you should move into our ward. We will help you." At this point, to manage these traumatic issues, I had to move and get another condo in my parents' ward where I already had friends, and where my parents could advocate for me in a positive way. Through fervent prayer, I felt the Spirit guiding me and confirming to me that this move was the right thing to do. All went quite well in selling my condo and buying the new one. Some other people helped me move, and it went very smoothly. I was extremely thankful for that move. The Lord was truly helping me and guiding me. I could feel His great love for me. I still knew that going to Church was very important.

This new ward was much better. Some of the members there had already known me through my parents and by my visiting there, and I received a few good Church callings. I was asked to be the financial clerk in our ward, as I am great at math. I had this calling for five years. I was called to work at the stake family history center and to be a consultant in the ward. I also fulfilled a shift at the temple baptistry each week, while my parents were at the temple. This shows how the Lord will bless us if we keep our faith in Him, stay close to Him, and continue to endure through our trials. This demonstrates the power of prayer. We have all heard before that we should "Never give up," and I know that it is very true.

These experiences I have listed and what Ethan has related are a sample of what can easily occur in the life of a person with Asperger's Syndrome/ASD, especially due to the fact that Asperger's is an invisible disability. The person can be very easily misunderstood and thought to not be Christlike, even though he is trying his best and might be experiencing some intense trials. This shows what to be more aware of, to help prevent such degrading behaviors toward people with Asperger's, and how to treat them in a more Christlike manner. Of course, we should be more Christlike and show charity toward everyone, but those with Asperger's and similar disorders will especially respond to this. This is due to the fact that they are very tender as well as being more misunderstood. They really need to feel worthwhile and accepted by others. As we focus on living the gospel in our interactions with everyone, and truly showing Christlike love, those with Asperger's will feel calmer, happier, more normal, more functional, they'll feel our Savior's love, and they will notice their Asperger's characteristics decrease. This is a blessing for everyone!

MARRIAGE AND ASPERGER'S

During this time, I had been more concerned about my situation of being single, as my parents were in their later years in life, and I could not emotionally be alone after my parents were gone. My sister was not in a position to have me live with her. I was very concerned about this when I asked my mother, "I think the Lord wants me to get married and have a companion when you and dad pass on. Could you pray in the temple about this?" I had been praying about it as well. On two separate occasions, my mother earnestly prayed that this situation would be resolved. Each time she felt very impressed that it would. She told me, "Keep doing what's right and you will not be alone. Things will work out." I strongly felt that if I continued staying at the family history center every week, and also if I continued to fulfill my other callings, I would meet the special girl I would marry.

This did happen, which I will later explain in detail. To summarize: A few weeks later, while at the family history center, I met my sweetheart. I was 44 by that time, but then I had progressed enough to be able to manage this new responsibility. That summer, Jeanene had been called to be a family history consultant in her ward in the same stake, and had come to learn about the center. She was very interested in getting to know me and I was very comfortable around her. One time, while at the temple baptistry, I received the confirmation through the Spirit that Jeanene was the one to marry. In the fall, I proposed and she accepted. Early the next year, we were married.

We had great support at our wedding and reception from many of our friends as well as our family. It was one of the larger highlights in our lives. Being married was also a very wonderful blessing which our Savior had planned for me and for Jeanene. There will be more to follow, where I will be describing my whole experience in detail with dating, becoming engaged, and being married while having Asperger's Syndrome, and how being married actually helped me with my Asperger's.

"Ethan, you may find this extremely interesting."

During our marriage, Jeanene and I have had great times together. She has helped me and I have helped her, especially emotionally, mentally, and spiritually. She has really understood about Asperger's Syndrome as well, which has been a real benefit. She helped me socially. Not too many people have understood me like she has. Meeting her was not a coincidence. She was guided to me. She has always been very understanding and caring about other people as well.

All my life, I have been more naïve, which is another characteristic of Asperger's. This made it easier for people to manipulate me and take advantage of me, which has happened and created some unpleasant situations. Some of these occurred with a few of my coworkers when I had my employment with the Church; however, Jeanene stood up for me. With my wife's help, I have progressed in many ways and understood social interactions much better, and I have been able to communicate and better understand what the other person is saying. She would explain social interactions to me in detail, what people are saying, and would tell me how I should respond. I have also helped Jeanene to progress and experience a more enjoyable life, within our marriage, a life which she has not previously had. She has been a lifesaver, along with being a companion for me. I know that she was definitely sent by our Savior to help me learn and progress even more in my life, by helping me with my Asperger's. I'm very thankful for all she has done to help me. She was also sent by the Lord so that I could help her with her mental and spiritual progression.

Whenever I had a stressful situation or moment, I could go to my wife, Jeanene, and receive emotional help from her. She has been my "safe" person I love and trust, to whom I can go and sit close together. She would put her arms around me and reassure me with comforting words. I would also hug her, which has helped both of us. This helps to settle me and reduce the effects of PTSD or depression. Calmness, love, playing good music, and other positive emotions help to suppress PTSD and panic attacks, especially when something is triggering an episode.

My wife, Jeanene, was especially helpful in comforting me when my parents passed away. There were three years between their passings. My mother went first, almost seven years after we were married. Just before she went, my mother told me, "Things will all work out and will be all right. Jeanene will help you. I love you both very much!" Three days later, when it was her time, we were all at the hospital. My sister, Susan, and her husband were also there. We had called my father, Ralph, on the phone, who said he was on his way. My mother stayed long enough for him to come in and take her hand. He said, "Mary, I'm here." She smiled at him, then she left her body to greet others in the spirit world, including her birth mother she had never known in this life. What a wonderful reunion!

Jeanene knew how to help me with my losses, having experienced the death of her parents and other family members. It is still very difficult to manage my emotions after their passing, and depression can easily occur. She reminded me about their progression, what they are doing, and about our joyful reunion with them later. She hugged me and told me, "Everything is all right." The answer to prayer my mother received before I met Jeanene came true in every detail. I received the comforting help I needed from Jeanene at these times, along with that from the Lord's Spirit during my time of grieving, which was more beneficial for me than anything else.

I will speak more of our marriage in a later chapter, along with how I got to know Jeanene, the whole dating experience, proposing and getting ready for the wedding, then the wedding and reception, and adjusting to married life. I will also explain how I dealt with issues in our marriage, with Jeanene's help, all while having Asperger's Syndrome. Wow! All of you with Asperger's Syndrome/ASD, along with your family members, will find this information very interesting, as it shows what can be accomplished through the Lord's help as you find out His plans for you as you mature in life.

"We will be entering some very exciting areas in our journey, Ethan, as I see the surprised expression on your face!"

"You mean that I could actually get married and have a more normal life?"

"That's right! There are those with Asperger's who can be married."

I know that there are many of you with Asperger's who would not be in a position to be married; however, there are options such as living with other family members. I know that many with Asperger's cannot live alone for a long period of time. They will need extra emotional support throughout their lives, to help them manage stress and all the social demands placed on them. They will need someone to talk to and give assistance, especially when something is triggering a side disorder. They will need help in meeting some of their needs, especially with transportation.

"However, I know that you, Ethan, will continue to learn and progress through your life, along with all of you with Asperger's."

Many of you will be able to live a nearly normal life. I will be sharing how to find out what some of our Savior's plans are for you and what you can actually accomplish in your lives. I know you all have very tough struggles in your lives, as I have. I have found many activities and other ways to help me with my life's struggles, which I would like to share with you. Doing these activities with a good friend or family member will be very helpful. Here are some examples of more ways that help me to deal with life.

DEALING WITH STRESS AND ASPERGER'S

Other ways that help me handle stressful times, along with those mentioned earlier, are prayer, attending the temple, going to Church meetings, exercising on the elliptical exerciser, playing some fun games such as board games and card games like Uno, putting together puzzles, going on walks, and enjoying time with my wife outside in the fresh air, in our vegetable garden and in the backyard. Doing projects together also helps. This has helped me and will also help you. If you are not married, spending quality time together with parents, siblings, or a good friend will work very well to help you manage stress. This person can talk to you, comfort you, and do some fun activity with you to help alleviate your anxiety and depression. Temporarily going to a safer place with him may be needed. One or more members in the Church can be a close friend. Playing some calming music also helps me to feel settled. It is very relaxing.

Another thing that helps me to feel calmer is living in a more open, country area where it is quieter with fresh air and water, and more of nature's sounds around. This is my "safe" place where I am comfortable. We live in an excellent ward in the Church where there are many spiritual people who really care about others and who understand my personality. This helps to reduce my Asperger's characteristics. We have taught a family history class at times as well. Helping other people really helps me to feel happier and more confident.

Jeanene and I have also been called as temple workers when a new Temple of the Church recently opened in the area. I feel that working there, doing the Lord's work and helping others, has helped me to progress much more, spiritually, emotionally, and socially. I have had some very wonderful experiences there. I am able to lead people in the work there, as well as leading the music in our meeting. Being in the temple has helped me to manage my unique Asperger's issues much easier. I feel the Spirit of the Lord and His great love very strongly there. I also feel Christlike love from the workers and from other people there, which is very beneficial to me. I receive answers and I get the help I need. I even notice that all of my Asperger's characteristics and associated disorders greatly diminish or completely disappear during the time I am in the temple. You don't have to be a temple worker or a volunteer to receive these blessings. You can be helped in the same manner by going there as a patron, doing the Lord's work. You will feel a "specialness" there. This applies also to the youth and others who go and do ordinances at the baptistry, or even just being at the temple, inside the main entrance, in the visitors' area, or on the grounds.

I have found that eating balanced, nutritious meals, having sufficient sleep, doing enough physical activity, and having a good schedule also help with Asperger's. Being involved with a good, enjoyable project helps as well. Helping someone else in ways where I am talented, such as building wooden shelves, is a real benefit. Jeanene and I have both noticed that all these mentioned items have helped to diminish the characteristics of Asperger's and associated disorders, and they will also help with dealing with issues.

"Later, I will give you, Ethan, some extremely important information concerning some simple things which you can do to diminish these unwanted disorders and characteristics more completely. This information will especially help you to deal with issues you now experience."

As a child, I had struggles from having Asperger's, but in a different way from other children's struggles who don't have this disability. I don't feel that my experience as a child was any worse than those of other children, except for not having many friends. This was from a lack of social skills and awareness. I was ignored and occasionally I was bullied. As an adult, Asperger's has affected me more, being that my childhood characteristics stood out more, as explained in the experiences previously noted. If I am around people who are more understanding of me, I am naturally able to function more normally.

When I found out about having Asperger' Syndrome as an adult, knowing about this information was not the cause for others to treat me worse than when I was a child. I just did not conform to the adult world as well. My Asperger's characteristics were more obvious. Social awareness is still greatly suppressed, although it is improving as I focus to manually learn important social skills through the help of other good people. My family and friends would tell me of what I should or should not say or do when they observed me in a particular social situation. Learning from them helped me prevent awkwardness and misunderstandings in my social interactions with others. This will help you too. I will be showing you this.

When I did find out that I have Asperger's, it gave many answers to the questions I had about the way my life had been. Many parts of my life came back to my mind, with the explanation that Asperger's was the reason for my behaviors and also why situations occurred as they did, many of which I have discussed here. Even now, I still perceive much in my life with an Asperger's mind, though not nearly as much as before, and I still miss some hidden meanings. I still perceive the world with a more innocent view than most people. Through the help of my wife, family, and friends, and with the Lord's help, I have been able to overcome many of the aspects of Asperger's Syndrome in my life. I will be showing you how to do this in the next chapter.

I grew up in a Christ-centered home with my sister, Susan. She helped me considerably, recognizing I had some unique differences. She would stand up for me in situations with other children, when they would not understand why I was the way I was. I really appreciated her doing that. Since there was no information about Asperger's at the time, she and my parents did the best they could. I found out much later that Susan had many emotional issues of her own, trying to deal with many of the social interactions with others when my differences were concerned. Many times she didn't quite know what to do. I absolutely had no idea at all that she was experiencing this, as with Asperger's my social awareness was suppressed, and I was unable to read any nonverbal body language.

"Ethan, Alexis has experienced some of this."

Susan will later give more information about these situations, how she was able to help me, and she will explain her feelings in dealing with my situations, along with how she handled them, in more detail in her own words.

"This will be extremely helpful to you, Sarah and Alexis, and to all family members and friends of the person with Asperger's, as Susan will be explaining all this information from her own perspective."

Now that Asperger's Syndrome is known and can be easily diagnosed at an early age, it will be much easier to manage the issues associated with Asperger's through early intervention. As noted, my family and I, as well as others involved with us, had absolutely no information about Asperger's or Autism when I was growing up, as there was no accurate knowledge of these disorders in the world at that time. We all just had to learn on the go, toughing it out, learning how to deal with unique issues the best we were able, through the guidance of the Spirit of the Lord. Information from our experiences will give you excellent help to handle similar issues you or your family are experiencing. I will be showing you how problems can be more easily resolved, and how all of you will progress as a result. Have hope, things will get better as you follow a few simple steps, which I will be showing all of you.

In the next chapter, as we continue on our journey, I will explain in more detail about dealing with unique issues I have experienced in my life, as a member of the Church.

"Ethan, I will also specifically give you a guide to help you resolve your problems, including those issues associated with your being a member of the Church, and those associated with the expectations in your life. This information has been proven and shown to work, and will really work to help you with your difficulties. I can see that you are getting even more excited about what you are learning and experiencing here."

"Wow, I can hardly wait to find out! It'll be really great to be able to resolve more of my problems, and be able to have a better life. I'm so excited!"

"This is awesome! Let's continue on this wonderful journey."

CHAPTER THREE
HOW I HAVE DEALT WITH CHALLENGES, HAVING ASPERGER'S SYNDROME/ASD

"Why is he ignoring me?" "I feel sad that no one sits by me at Church!" "Why don't people want to talk to me no matter where I go?" "I wish I had more good friends." "I feel very lonely!" "I don't feel needed!" These are a few of the very intense, real feelings which people with Asperger's/ASD and some other people experience, including family members of the Asperger's person.

"You have felt all these emotions very profoundly in your life, Ethan. At times your sister has also. You are not alone. There are many things you can do yourself to resolve these issues, besides what you have been taught at school. You will learn more Christlike attributes which especially will help you. I will show you what I know will work. This journey is becoming even more exciting as we continue traveling!"

This chapter in our journey will cover more details to

show you what I did to manage the issues and challenges I experienced. As I look back at how various Church leaders treated me, I can see how some of them can become very confused around someone with Asperger's. Each person is at his or her own stage of progression and each has his or her own unique personality. Of course, this is true for everyone, for Church leaders, for other Church members and other people, and for those with Asperger's. I have found that what is most important is staying close to our Savior. When we do, the Spirit of the Lord, the Holy Ghost will be with us more, and we will feel His promptings to help us. I have seen that if each person could be more Christlike, show charity, and live the gospel more fully, there would not be nearly the issues and challenges for members of the Church with Asperger's Syndrome. In this scenario, the person with Asperger's would function more normally. Focus on staying close to our Savior and your functioning will start improving.

As we know, everyone has agency, and we are all learning how to be more Christlike. Some leaders may be called to learn from different experiences. Whether they utilize these experiences to improve their lives is their choice. Some leaders may choose to not learn from experiences with those who have Asperger's, and may choose to treat them unkindly, as a result of not understanding Asperger's. We know that they are still progressing and are at a different stage of progression, still learning about being Christlike. As we cannot control another's actions, we can only control what our action and reaction will be. If the Spirit prompts us to move away from that person, to prevent the issue from becoming more intense, then that would be the best action to take at that moment. We could then pray for that person that he will be softened, that he will feel and do what is right. The Spirit can also prompt us with the proper response. We are to love everyone, but not all of their actions. As we take charge to improve ourselves and our actions, and be positive, staying close to the Spirit, we will have a much happier life. Sincerely praying really helps. Other people's unkind words, actions, and judgments will then not have nearly the negative effect on us as we do this. Our Savior's teachings, of course, will be applicable in any situation with anyone.

THE SOCIAL ISSUE

"Ethan, to help illustrate this, I'll share a true story of a shocking experience which happened to someone I knew. Here's the story."

Jason, a high school student with Asperger's Syndrome/ASD, had just come to Church one Sunday with his parents. He was trying to be more social, which he was learning from the help of his parents. He noticed an acquaintance from school who was still outside, and went over to greet him. He said, "Hi, Matt, how are you today?" Matt responded with, "I'm doing fine." Suddenly, Jason heard a group of boys talking rather loudly as they were walking near the building. One of them started using some bad, profane language which shocked Jason. He quickly walked away as fast as he could into the building, saying "Don't" and "No" to himself a few times and hitting his hands together a couple of times. His body started trembling.

Jason was having an anxiety attack, when he saw one of his Church leaders right there in the hallway. He quickly went up to him and said, very urgently, "There are some boys outside using very bad language." The leader responded, "What do you want me to do?" This question really confused Jason, and he started moving his arms around in a peculiar manner. He loudly said, "I want you to tell them to stop doing it!" The leader paused and then loudly responded, "I'm not going to do anything!" and then quickly walked away.

Jason was very shocked at this and felt quite hurt. He was already having an anxiety attack, which was intensified by this leader's response. He didn't feel comfortable being at Church with all this happening. He quickly found his parents and asked them to take him home. His mother asked, "What's wrong, Jason?" He quickly and sobbingly related all that had happened, then she calmly and lovingly responded with, "I know that you will feel better if you stay here. You can be with us today. Talking to that leader wouldn't be a good idea right now. He doesn't understand all that you are experiencing with Asperger's. Just let it be." She comforted him, which helped him feel much better.

A person with Asperger's Syndrome is usually very sensitive, and when problems in today's world are encountered, this person's first response is the "flight" reaction, where he needs to get away from the aggressive or overwhelming situation to a "safe" place and preferably to a "safe" person. I accomplish this by leaving the area and going to a calmer place as quickly as possible. This is a good thing to do. It's like doing your own personal "comfort timeout." It is not done to be disrespectful or rude, but to help prevent a panic attack. Some may characteristically make various soft or loud sounds as they leave.

Many with Asperger's have certain problems which are repetitious, where they cannot physically escape. These may be linked to communicative difficulties, social unawareness, odd behaviors, etc. Being socially unaware creates an extreme difficulty in knowing how to socially interact. The Church setting makes it more unique, as those with Asperger's along with everyone else are taught that members of the Church, along with Church leaders, should be more understanding and kind. They find that this may not always be true. Those with Asperger's tend to seek refuge with those who are more Christlike, where they feel more safe and secure, where they feel loved, and where they can receive help with their unique problems.

"You know what I'm talking about, Ethan."

Their social demands are also very unique in the Church, as their Asperger's characteristics can be more easily misunderstood when viewed with the teachings of the gospel. They can easily be mistakenly viewed as intentionally acting self-centered, disrespectful, and rude, as a result of their communicative difficulties, social unawareness, unawareness of involuntary movements and expressions, and having sudden reflexive reactions and attacks. They have problems responding and may not respond at all. They have great difficulty interacting in the normal, expected way. There is too much for them to understand, and they don't know how to do it correctly. They can quickly become overwhelmed when this occurs, combined with the great confusion which arises from the lack of social awareness with members of the Church, along with anyone else. It is just too hard for them to understand and deal with all the social demands, such as being reprimanded for apparently not responding to a member of the Church in a friendly manner, when they thought they were. They don't feel like they fit in or feel welcome. They actually need true loving attention in the Lord's way.

When Christlike behavior is not shown to them, a conflict develops in their minds about the Church teachings. This happens when some members of the Church do not appear to be following our Savior when interacting with them. People with Asperger's may have been mistreated; they may feel alone, overloaded, confused, and angry. They then have a strong tendency to put up a barrier and try to "escape" by becoming inactive, less worthy, or not believing what they were taught about the Church is all true. How can they trust what they were taught about the gospel and about leaders when opposite behavior is shown to them? Sadly, this also happens with many members who don't have disabilities or have other types of disabilities, but it is much more pronounced for those with Asperger's, as they are very sensitive and they perceive life in a completely different manner. It becomes much harder for them to trust what the members of the Church say or do.

"Ethan, you have personally experienced this. Your family may have experienced related issues as well."

This shows the extreme importance of a great example of a true, loving Christlike person in the Church, along with good works without any appearance or implication of hypocrisy. This power of example is extremely important for Church leaders and members to know.

The person with Asperger's also needs help from his family and good members of the Church to learn some social skills in order for him to be able to interact appropriately with other members of the Church. He can be helped to learn very important social skills and respectful attributes which focus on our Savior's teachings. He is very able to learn how to socially interact in the Lord's way. He will receive divine help as he is sincerely trying to learn what the Lord would have him know, to improve his life. For example, he could be reminded to smile more around others and he could give good handshakes to people at Church and in his community as he asks them how they are doing. He could say, "Jim, I've been thinking about you." He can remember to observe and learn from other good people about social needs and interaction, so that he can more appropriately interact with others. He can easily seek for this. He could genuinely show he cares about others by generally inquiring about others' wellbeing, or that of members of their families. He should call the person by name. A person's name means a lot to him. He could say, "Shawn, is your son, Tyler, recovering well from his accident?" He can be complimenting to others, showing interest, and say, upon meeting someone, "Jeff, I'm happy to see you." Be positive. Being of service to others and learning how to be more selfless will be tremendously beneficial. Many people around him will realize that he is really not disrespectful and rude, as he follows the counsels given here. They can start to learn about him and understand who he really is and the difficulties he is experiencing, and they will then be more welcoming to him and comfortable around him.

As his behaviors change, people will validate him and his good actions. He will then want to be more active in the Church, improve his worthiness, and learn more about the gospel. He will feel our Savior's love for him as he is loved by other good people. This equally applies to other inactive members of the Church, when they feel more loved and welcomed by others.

"Ethan, try practicing these ideas and you will start noticing improvement in your life you haven't seen before."

"Robert, this really makes sense. I'm excited to try this. I'm already feeling like I'm improving, by what you're teaching me. I know that I can improve much more, especially with mom and Lexi helping me."

"I'm excited for you too, Ethan. I now have some very important information to share."

A SAFE PERSON AND A SAFE PLACE

The Asperger's person has an extra need for a "safe" person, and a "safe" place, to feel loved and secure and needed, just as children do. Parents of a person with Asperger's Syndrome would be the first people to take the role of the "safe" person or "buddy" in his life to love him and to advocate for his true needs. He will need to feel very secure with this person, who will be a tremendous help to prevent emotional overload. To fulfill this role, the parents will need to be more Christlike; doing the simple things we have all been taught. Being temple worthy and going there often will help the child with Asperger's immensely. Why? Because a child with this type of disorder will feel the Spirit of the Lord much more in the home and will feel safe and secure. Priesthood blessings are very appropriate to give comfort and help to him, especially when he experiences anxiety and emotional overload.

"Here is some more important information for you, Sarah and Alexis, as well as for parents and family members of the Asperger's person to know."

Along with living the gospel, sincere scripture study and prayer together, as well as individually, also bring spiritual guidance to help with the many needs of Asperger's. Studying the Book of Mormon especially helps. It will bring the Lord's Spirit into the home. Some may find it harder to understand the scriptures, but reading together and discussing what is read will help them feel the Spirit and feel more peaceful.

Involving the Asperger's person in being of service to others will go a long way. Spending quality time with him will be an extreme benefit. A parent could spend some one-on-one time with him doing some fun activity or just talking to him about his feelings. The parents or other "safe" person will then be able to better interact with him and help him to feel calmer. Doing this will help him to feel that he is much more important than ever before, and he will really feel needed. He will then feel our Savior's love for him even more in his life. My "safe" people did this for me, which was very beneficial in my life. Other honest, kind people can also be "safe" people. Being a member of the Church helps him feel safe and secure, as he has the gift of the Holy Ghost. Living the gospel, to have this constant companionship is very beneficial to help him feel love, peace, and security in his life.

These important needs of love, safety, and security in a righteous, Christlike home, as well as living righteously throughout our lives, are referenced very succinctly in our hymn, "Home Can Be a Heaven on Earth." (*Hymns* #298)

"This is very important for you, Ethan, and especially for your mother. There are many things she and your sister, Alexis, can do to help you. Your mom and sister love you and are your 'safe' people who can comfort and assist you when the need arises. You see that they are able to effectively assist you in your life, having the Spirit of the Lord."

This information is also excellent for all young children as well as others who are in their tender years. Those who have Asperger's and similar disabilities will need this increased positive interaction throughout much more of their lives, even now.

A "safe" place is also extremely important in the life of a person with Asperger's Syndrome. This will help meet his increased need to feel secure. A righteous home where love and respect are always shown will go a long way to help him live a more normal life and to progress well. I know that no home is quite to that point, but we can be actively working on achieving a more righteous home by following the prophet's teachings, reading the Book of Mormon, and keeping the commandments. Concentrating on making our home more righteous, where the Spirit of the Lord can be there in greater abundance, not only makes life more comfortable for all who live there, but also knowing that you are helping the Asperger's person to have a better life makes this very worthwhile. The home can also be dedicated by a Melchizedek

Priesthood holder, so that the Spirit of the Lord will be there and that it will be a safe haven from the world.

The home's location also has a great influence on the life of the Asperger's individual. Being in a quieter area where there is less noise and having disturbing sounds be softer or farther away can help prevent or reduce various types of overload. If he is in a community or area where there is more aggressive behavior around, or in a ward that is not suitable for him, causing him great anxiety, then moving to a more suitable location would be very helpful, as guided by the Spirit of the Lord.

Adults with Asperger's can be close to faithful parents, siblings, an extended family member, or other faithful Church members who can relate to him well. They can be his "safe" people. Remember, boys and girls of various ages who have Asperger's especially need to feel loved and secure, just as little children have this increased need. Those who visit and minister to the family of a person with Asperger's who see a need where parents or a single parent or sibling are not in a position to be this "safe" person, can coordinate with leaders to find someone or to extend a calling, if those assigned cannot be this "safe" person themselves, to relate to the person with Asperger's in a genuine, Christlike way. If those assigned are not available, or not in a position to fully understand this need, then the family can coordinate with leaders in order to meet this need. The individual will need a "safe" person and a "safe" place to go when he has this intense need to feel loved and secure, when he experiences emotional overload, or panic or anxiety attacks, or when he has a need for extra comfort or reassurance. Having felt this, I personally know that people with Asperger's have an increased need to be fellowshipped and to feel needed, and to be included in activities. This is needed throughout his entire life. This will especially help one who has become inactive or is lonely and feeling neglected.

As mentioned, a person with Asperger's usually has one or more great talents where he has an intense interest, and can be very useful in some Church activities or programs. These talents should be encouraged, and there should be assistance to help the person develop these talents into great skills. Callings could be extended to this individual to utilize his great abilities, such as when I was called to be the ward financial clerk for five years. Where he can assist with the work of the Lord, he will feel greatly wanted and needed. Of course, everyone needs to be fellowshipped and to feel included, but for people with Asperger's, these feelings and needs are much more intensified, partly because these people have been painfully disregarded during their lives.

"You know very well what I'm talking about, Ethan. I'd like to tell you another story I heard about being included and feeling important. You'll enjoy it."

Megan lives alone with her single mom. She is a tender 13-year-old girl who was diagnosed with Asperger's ten years ago. Early intervention at school has been helpful, but she still has great feelings of insecurity. She doesn't have any close friends. Her mom, Christy, is her "safe" person to some degree; however, her mom has to work full-time and cannot spend sufficient quality time with her at home. Megan once commented, "Mom, I don't feel very safe here, especially when you're still at work." Her mom responded, "I know, Megan. I've been feeling that too. I will ask Stacy, our Relief Society president, for help."

The next Sunday, Stacy went to their home, where they had recently moved, to visit and talk more about the situation. Stacy commented, "So I understand that Megan has Asperger's Syndrome. Can you both tell me more about what it is?" They did, giving lots of information about Autism Spectrum Disorder. They explained also about Megan's increased need for a "safe" person in her life, along with being in a "safe" place when Christy was at work after the school bus had brought Megan home. Christy explained, "She has this increased need due to her insecurity and anxiety disorder, which accompanies her Asperger's. Having another 'safe' person would also help with her anxiety attacks." Christy inquired, "Stacy, do you know who would be a good person to help Megan in this way?"

Stacy answered, "As a matter of fact, I would be delighted to help Megan. I live quite close to your home, so she can come to my house after school. She can then feel secure while doing her schoolwork, and I can talk to her and help her learn more social skills. My teenage daughter can also help her and get to know her better and be her friend."

They were very excited about this fantastic plan. Megan went to Stacy's every afternoon, and Stacy and her husband invited them both over the next Sunday to have dinner together. For the first time in her life, Megan really felt included and felt important. She was learning some important social skills. She started feeling closer to her mom and was starting to be more sociable at Church. A few girls in her youth program at Church were feeling more comfortable around her and were becoming closer friends to her. This shows how being close to the Spirit of the Lord and following the promptings can bring about great results in many ways. Spending time to help people with their needs is very important.

Many people commonly think that there are too many extra items to remember and to do when dealing with people with Asperger's Syndrome, Autism, or any other type of disability. Many feel that it is too hard to keep dealing with this situation, so they tend to avoid it and may even end up shunning the disabled person. As we know in the Church, our Savior would have us do otherwise, and make the extra effort to understand and help these people. I know that people with Asperger's already have to deal with all the unique difficulties and side disorders they experience, as well as all the extra learning and extra effort they have to put forth in order to feel included and accepted by society, and to be able to function each day without frustration. No wonder they can very easily become angry or upset, and have anxiety attacks at smaller unpleasant situations. They need frequent reassurance to help them feel settled and to know that things will work out more positively in their lives, as they do their part. I have experienced all of this personally, so I know what people with Asperger's are feeling, and what those who interact with the Asperger's person need to know, so that they can really understand what to do to be able to help him.

The Lord would have all of us, including those with disabilities, be more Christlike, respectful, and kind to others. We should all learn to put forth the extra effort after learning what to do.

Church leaders especially need to be aware of the differences and needs of those with Asperger's Syndrome/ASD. They need to understand the problems these individuals have in understanding social situations. They need to be aware of the great difficulty these people have in dealing with the social demands in the Church. They should know that these people are not trying to act rude or provoke others. These people are very tenderhearted. They need to be treated in a loving, Christlike way. Leaders should assist in helping them understand social situations in the Church. As we all know, this should be done in a kind, loving manner. Differences should not be looked upon as a disability or disorder, but rather as less common differences. Many of these differences are very positive and are great gifts. Higher quality traits identify these people as extraordinary, and are part of who they are. As we listen to the Asperger's person openly, we could be surprised what we learn. We can be humbler, and be sympathetic and respectful of their information, which can help us understand more truths. Heavenly Father can teach us more as we do this.

With Asperger's, the ability of being able to view many situations very literally and logically, with great accuracy and detail, is a tremendous asset for these people. This is especially true when helping with the Lord's work. Church leaders should especially consider these points of gifts, talents, and abilities when they make inspired decisions concerning these individuals, as well as all others over whom they have a stewardship.

When those with Asperger's have their needs more fully met, they will have a much more positive outlook on life. There are always good "workarounds," which the

Lord expects us to utilize to help these people. We are not to enable them and do almost everything for them, but we should teach them and be supportive, loving, and kind. Maybe a formal interview at Church would be emotionally overloading for some people with Asperger's, so a more informal setting such as an appropriate area in the home for the meeting would be less intimidating and more comfortable. In addition, all of us should let people with Asperger's be more involved in the decision-making process together, where they can progress and assist in finding some solutions to problems they experience.

IT'S NOT MY FAULT

When dealing with challenges involving Asperger's/Autism Spectrum Disorder, the following subject is relevant in helping the Asperger's person, as well as his family. Having this important item concerning blaming understood and resolved, it will be much easier for all involved to manage and resolve the many challenges confronting the family where a member or members of the family have Asperger's or Autism.

"This story I'm about to relate is for you, Ethan, as well as for all of you, Sarah, Alexis, and your relatives."

"I don't know why we have a child with Autism Spectrum Disorder," Rachel lamented to her husband, Steve. "However, I've been feeling that I'm mainly to blame because I was 40 when Travis was born. I feel that I'm too old to have healthy children anymore. I don't know why the Lord is allowing this to happen to us. It is a hardship on our other children. I feel like I'm being punished. I also feel quite embarrassed around our friends."

"Please don't blame yourself, Rachel," Steve answered. "It's not your fault. I have prayed about this after we both did, and I felt inspired to explain that we are to experience raising a child with this Disorder because this is the Lord's plan for us. He has many plans which we don't fully understand yet."

"But Steve, honey, it is and will be very difficult for me. Travis gets upset so easily. I'm so emotionally drained each day while you're at work, trying to keep Travis settled. I must be doing something wrong. Many times our children are at their wits' end trying to not upset him. It's very difficult. How can I do it and how can I keep them happy?"

Steve responded, "It will be okay. I'll help you through this. I'll give more attention to you and Travis and our other children. We also need to keep fervently praying. Things will work out. We'll be blessed for it." Rachel finally felt a bit more comfortable after hearing these consoling words.

It is quite common for those who have Asperger's Syndrome or other disabilities, along with their parents or others involved in their lives, to feel a sense of guilt at times for various reasons. Parents and siblings frequently feel that they have done some things or many things wrong around the Asperger's child. They may think, "I don't know what I'm doing wrong," when he acts out or becomes angry for no apparent reason. Many think, "What should I do or not do," in order to prevent his negative reaction. They may think that they are "walking on eggshells" every day with him, and it becomes a tremendous struggle. They become extremely stressed. They ask, "How can I do this any longer?"

The first thing to realize is that it is not your fault that your child has Asperger's Syndrome/ASD, and it is also not your fault that he acts out the way he does. You should try to not be embarrassed about this. As a parent, you should know that even though there is information circulating about Autism Spectrum Disorders being genetic, more likely occurring in older child-bearing years, and possibly being caused by vaccinations or by being exposed to greater amounts of toxins, there is no reason whatsoever to blame yourself or your spouse or ex-spouse for having a child with Asperger's. You are not being punished. You did nothing wrong. Know that our Savior is in charge, and things happen according to His divine plan. His Asperger's may more closely match his spirit and his personality during this learning experience in mortality, which will help him during his life. By striving to live the gospel and following the prophet, the Lord will help you and bless you, and His Spirit will tell you with a reassuring confirmation that you are not to blame. Know that our loving Savior has His purposes for your present situation, for your progression.

The second thing to realize is that you should never give up. Our Savior loves you tremendously and has His arms outstretched to help you every minute of each day. He is closer than you think. Do not think for a minute that it is your fault that your Asperger's child acts out because of you, when you are not consciously, intentionally trying to overload him or make him angry. He acts out and displays various characteristics of Asperger's Syndrome as a result of having this Disorder and being placed, many times unintentionally, in a more aggressive or intense situation for him. The answer to this dilemma is to learn and to be aware of behaviors and situations which cause him more agitation and problems, and those which would help him to feel calm. Any kind of anger or threatening moves, or watching TV shows with violence and bad dialogue, etc., will cause more agitation and anxiety attacks, as these would in little children. Help him feel calm by speaking in a gentle, loving voice, with a sincere desire to help him have a better day. Truly be his friend and smile and appreciate his efforts. Help him feel safe around you. He needs this.

As mentioned earlier, preparing him for changes in a kind, loving way will help him feel settled. As a parent, talking in a kind, softer voice will make him feel more secure. I know these behaviors actually work, because they have really helped me. Basically, behaving as our Savior would goes a long way to help subdue his emotions, and over time, will help his Asperger's characteristics to decrease. This equally applies to siblings and others who have more interaction with him. When you, as a family member to the person with Asperger's, learn what causes overload and emotional upset in him, you can be more aware of your behaviors, aware to eliminate those behaviors which are upsetting to him, and you can incorporate more of our Savior's loving behaviors in your life. As you do this, it will become more habitual and natural to you, and you'll be able to do it without having to think about it very much. This will be a great benefit for both of you.

"Sarah and Alexis, you both know how important this is."

When something causes the Asperger's person to act

out, when you're able, go put your arms around him if he so desires, and speak to him in a loving voice. Talk to him about his feelings at that moment by asking him, "What are you feeling?" Listen to him. Show him that you care, reassure him, and show him that you are truly interested in helping to resolve the problems he is experiencing. He may not know how to resolve his problems, even though he wants to resolve them as soon as possible. He actually needs some assistance. Do these things to help him in an appropriate, Christlike manner, and he will feel much more trust in you, and you will become, in an even greater sense, his needed "safe" person. Remember to help him appropriately, only where really needed as directed by the Spirit, so that he will not become too dependent on you, but so that he will be able to participate with you in obtaining help with his problems and become more independent. You want to avoid having him become completely dependent on you for a solution to every problem, as he will not progress very well this way. You can help him by explaining what is viewed as inappropriate behavior, even though it may be a characteristic of Asperger's, and then by lovingly helping him to resolve it. Working together is the best way.

Also remember that all of us have "bad" days. Being aware of these times and then thinking about our Savior, and bringing Him more into our lives, will subdue the negativity of these days for us, as well as for the Asperger's person.

Another very important item to mention is that the Asperger's individual can feel guilty and blame himself for having Asperger's Syndrome and for manifesting characteristics of this Disorder, causing many misunderstandings and causing people to harbor ill will toward him.

"Ethan, you have felt this profoundly."

Blaming himself and feeling that he is being punished is actually a deception. He is absolutely not guilty because he has Asperger's, and should never blame himself for anything odd he still unintentionally, unknowingly does, as a result of this Disorder. He should never feel that he is being punished by having Asperger's. However, then comes the question, "Why do I have Asperger's Syndrome?"

"You, Ethan, should know that you were given this Disorder for a very important reason. The Lord knows that you have this, that you will have to work through your life with this, and that it can be very difficult. The Lord knows exactly what it feels like to have Asperger's, and has experienced all the difficulties and traumas you experience. I also know that our Savior gave this to you for your protection from the evils of the world, as you have more innocent childlike traits; for your positive progression and development in life, as you have a very tender spirit and have, or will have, more tender emotions about our Savior and the help He gives you; for your beneficial learning tailored just for you through your unique struggles; and for the positive progression of other people involved in your life. This is our Savior's divine plan for you. He knows what is best. I know the Spirit may be testifying to you right now about these loving truths I am telling you. What a wonderful, tender part of our journey. I urge you to develop the faith to know that this is actually more of a blessing for you, as strange as this may seem to you now. Our Savior has great plans for you. As you continue being faithful to our Savior through your life with Asperger's, you will receive tremendous blessings later, as well as now. Sincerely talk to your Father in Heaven about this and about your concerns. He, through our Savior and through His Spirit, will absolutely help you feel more comforted, you will feel His love for you, and He will help you so that your difficulties will diminish. If you have difficulties with prayer, and especially with learning how to pray fervently, I will offer you great assistance with some inspiring information to help you with this in the next chapter. It is never too late to start.

"As you know, Ethan, many times you unknowingly do things which appear disrespectful and rude to others, such as unawareness of your involuntary nonverbal communication, or having an undesired reflexive response or anxiety attack. You do not want this to happen, as you are really not trying to provoke or hurt anyone. You may feel very frustrated at their responses to you, and you may feel guilty that you did something wrong, especially when they indicate that you are in the wrong. Of course, when we actually do something wrong, we should recognize it and repent, but when you unknowingly do something odd, due to social unawareness and communication difficulties, or when you have a negative reflexive response, you feel awkward and may feel embarrassed. However, you should never feel guilty that you did something wrong, even if some people may misunderstand you due to your disorder and think that you are in the wrong. Don't take offense at this and don't oppose them, saying that you are not doing anything wrong. This may seem strange, but I'll explain. Instead, by thanking them for their thoughts when this occurs, you can utilize these moments to manually learn the social skill involved and learn how to communicate better in that particular situation. I will be showing you how to do this. Having a 'safe' person with you as a mentor to discreetly help you, or talking with him about the situation later to help you learn these skills will be a tremendous benefit. He can give you all the necessary information in detail to help you understand and function appropriately and correctly. This will also help you to not feel awkward in public, as well as helping you with negative reflexive responses."

For example, when I am in public and something occurs which is aggressive or emotionally overloading, my wife, Jeanene, has reminded me to take some deep breaths and to pray. I will be explaining a simple exercise later in this chapter that I do, which assists me tremendously. As another example, I had an experience where a neighbor jokingly said something to me, as Jeanene and I were out walking. I did not understand that he was joking, as it appeared as a negative remark, and I felt quite hurt. She then told me what he meant and that what he said was actually okay. I then knew that I did not do anything wrong and that he was not upset with me at all.

NEW SOCIAL EXPERIENCES

"I'll now tell you another true story of a person I knew, who had a new, good social experience after experiencing some anxiety. Ethan, you'll find this very interesting."

Nate, who is sixteen years old and has Asperger's

Syndrome, received a phone call from his ward leader one Sunday. "Nate, how are you today?" After responding, the leader continued, "I would like you to give a talk in Sacrament Meeting next Sunday as a youth speaker. I see that you haven't yet. You can pick a topic in the *For the Strength of Youth* pamphlet. It will be fine for you to talk for a few minutes. Are you willing to do this?"

Nate was stunned. "But, but I have never given a talk in Sacrament Meeting before," he stammered. "I don't know if I can do this. I wasn't ready to do it the last time."

The leader responded, "Nate, I have confidence in you. I know you can do it. There is a first time for any of these experiences. Ask your parents and sister to help you prepare. You can practice giving the talk with them. They will be proud of you, along with me."

"Well ... I guess I can do it, then. I'll be ready on Sunday."

"Thank you for accepting, Nate. I will see you next Sunday. Goodbye."

After the leader finished the call, Nate felt very nervous. "Wow!" he thought. "I hope all will go well." He quickly went and told his parents what had just happened. They were quite excited for him.

"Hey, this is going to be a wonderful experience for you," his mom exclaimed. "We will help you prepare your talk and be ready for it. We, too, know that you will do just fine."

The week went by as Nate prepared his talk with his family's help, and he practiced it a few times with his family. They were very excited that he was going to give a great talk about honesty and integrity.

Sunday came, and Nate was quite nervous. He was the first to speak. He read his talk, looking up at the congregation a few times. Even though his talk lasted almost four minutes, it went very well. Along with his family, the leader and a few members of his Church ward congratulated him on his message after the meeting. One of them said, "Nate, that was exactly what I needed to hear today. Thank you for your insights." This made him feel really happy about himself, that he was able to do something new which helped others.

"It will greatly benefit you socially, Ethan, to become involved in new experiences in the Church, and to have great, new experiences in your life. For someone with Asperger's, these can be very awkward and confusing initially, but with your decision to do them and with the help of other good people, these positive experiences can help you really progress, especially emotionally, socially, and spiritually. It will especially benefit you if you accept a calling in your ward when a member of the bishopric extends a calling to you. If you are asked to give a prayer or a talk in sacrament meeting, it will be very beneficial to you to take courage and accept the invitation. The Spirit of the Lord is involved in these activities. Pray about this. Your family and friends can also help you with this, especially in preparing a talk. Volunteer in areas of service which you are capable of doing, whether online or with other Church members. The Lord will help you learn more social skills, and He will help your involuntary behaviors to decrease. You will receive blessings as you pray for help when you become involved in new social experiences. This has happened for me. When I was asked to give the prayer in sacrament meeting for the first time, I felt quite nervous and very uneasy, but I knew that the Lord wanted me to have that experience, and that He would help me. I asked Him for His guiding assistance. I felt that happen, and felt good about doing it. Praying in the meetings after that first time became much easier to do.

"Here are some more examples of what I did and what others did to help me in awkward situations as I was growing up in the Church. For example, when I was ordained a Deacon in the Aaronic Priesthood, passing the sacrament was quite frightening to me. I wanted to have the easier assignments, but when asked to do a more difficult assignment, such as passing it to the center section, I would have someone explain it in great detail to me. I would need to know exactly which rows I would need to go to, in order to appropriately interact with the person passing it on the other side of the rows, as I knew people were watching me. This detailed explanation would need to be done in each more difficult assignment. I would explain that I needed the detail before I would understand, plus it would help me feel better. Taking fast offering envelopes around the ward worked much better if I went with another person who understood me well. I knew that I had to do new good things and have first experiences in my life, so I took courage and did them. This made me feel good. I also knew that I would make mistakes, but I knew, as we all do, that everyone else makes mistakes. This also helped me to feel better. Ethan, I know that all I have been explaining is helping you to feel better also. I can see your excitement from learning these concepts during our journey!"

"Yeah, this really makes a lot of sense. I'm so happy

and excited to learn more!"

These experiences indicate that someone with Asperger's needs more tender loving care by people who are very understanding of him, and who know what his needs are. They can then help him by giving him more instruction in a tender, loving way.

When I was ordained a Teacher in the Aaronic Priesthood, my father and I requested that we go home teaching together. If this is not a possibility in every case, the boy with Asperger's could be assigned with someone very kind and loving, who understands his needs in this area of ministering. He will need to be assisted in the social area of accomplishing this, such as how to greet the family in a friendly manner. Before and after meeting them, his senior companion can explain the social interactions with the family they visit, so that the person with Asperger's can better understand how to socially interact and be able to contribute in helping the family. He may not be able to pick up on a social cue, such as to change the subject when he has said enough about a particular item being discussed. He might need some help to answer a question he is misinterpreting. Of course, this should be done discreetly, in a kindly way. A positive conversation can take place after the visit, to help him learn of important social interactions. He will also need this help as he gets older, as I know that boys with Asperger's are able to greatly contribute in their responsibilities in ministering and teaching. They have a special, innocent spirit about them which can really touch people. These assignments for those with Asperger's, which are made by priesthood leaders, should be done with the information presented in this book in mind.

"Even though I didn't know about Asperger's at the time I was a Teacher in the Aaronic Priesthood, my father was guided by the Spirit to help me understand more of the social interaction with the families we visited. He taught me about being more friendly, smiling, and helping people feel more important by complimenting them and asking how I can be of assistance. This advice helped me socially, along with the many other times when my father was guided to teach me. By using this advice, he helped me understand how to socially interact with other students at school as well, along with other Church members."

Those who minister to a family of an individual with Asperger's can also be made aware of this important information. They can be made aware of his particular interests and needs, as well as his unique characteristics and why he exhibits them. Even though I and the rest of my family didn't know about Asperger's at that time, my father knew of my differences, and would let those assigned to visit us know, so that they could be very accommodating and understanding of the situation. My father stayed close to our Savior, so that he was frequently led by the Spirit to do what was most effective to help me. This is an extremely important point to remember. He let them know what kind of a person I really am, so that they would understand what was happening. I am very grateful to my father for doing this. This helped other people in the Church understand, so that my family would have a better interaction with them.

So how do you stay close to our Savior? Many of us already know that it starts with being obedient to His commandments. However, there are other things we can do to draw closer to Him and to feel His presence more in our lives. You can pray to have His Spirit with you each day; you can read the Book of Mormon each day; you can go to Church and partake of the sacrament each week, and keep the Sabbath day holy; you can also develop a closer relationship with our Savior by repenting frequently. Working on developing pure charity around others and being of service to others will also draw you closer to our Savior. Qualifying for a temple recommend and being there frequently will greatly assist you in feeling His presence more in your life. Doing these things are some of the ways to help you feel our Savior's love increase in your life. The Spirit of the Lord will be able to guide you much more each day. You will be able to interact better with other people, serve them, and help them with their needs.

Staying close to our Savior to receive His assistance through His Spirit is very important when needing to inform other people in the Church and community about the Asperger's family member, so that they can understand the situation when they see him behaving in a rather different manner. This information, when presented in an appropriate, loving way will also help them understand what the family is experiencing, including great embarrassment about the family member, so that these people will know how to better interact with the family. Many of these people will then be more understanding and sympathetic, offering appropriate assistance when they can.

The boy with Asperger's has often had a very difficult time in the scouting program, which has been within the Church in past years. Given that his gross and fine motor skills are suppressed, his coordination reduced, along with social awareness and communicative issues, his leaders, parents, and others involved have been very creative in assisting him in the scouting program. In the youth program, they can explain that he has a problem from birth, where he exhibits involuntary movements at times. There could be a "safe" person, preferably another boy or a leader, to be with him and assist him when he has difficulties. If this does not happen, another supportive individual can be involved to make the situation the best it can be. In some cases, maybe not achieving as much as other people have achieved would be better for him. The overloaded strain may be detrimental to him. Each situation is individual. Some may be able to achieve more. When I was a Boy Scout, the swimming requirements were beyond my capability, and we felt that it was better to not pursue higher levels of achievement, so that there would not be a severe emotional impact throughout my life as a result of inappropriate force. This is not to say to give up, but all that is appropriate should be accomplished, through the guidance of the Spirit.

The Church can offer great assistance for him. There are a great number of new programs and activities in the Church. These include activities such as going camping where there are no requirements, but rather, assistance in learning new skills like fishing, where more boys with disabilities can participate. Volunteering in service projects within the Young Men's program, where Asperger's boys can easily participate, especially when they become Teachers and Priests in the Aaronic Priesthood, will greatly benefit them. These appropriate activities will really assist the Asperger's boy socially and emotionally.

There are other new social experiences which occurred in my life and could occur in the lives of others with Asperger's Syndrome. I will go into these in more detail in the next chapter, as to how they came about, how I accomplished them, and how I dealt with the unique situations and issues they created.

Many times, Church leaders do not understand Asperger's, but there is more information being presented these days to make it easier to understand. Information presented here will help Church leaders understand much better what the person with Asperger's is really thinking and feeling, which is that he doesn't know why people misunderstand him so much and why some of them misjudge him. He may feel very lonely and depressed, with increased anxiety as a result. Many times he doesn't feel wanted or needed. He has very tender emotions. Much of the time the Asperger's person doesn't know how to properly talk to people, due to a lack of social skills. He then feels quite alone, wanting more friends, not knowing how to meet these needs in this area of his life. He has a strong desire and need to have other good people give positive feedback, communicate well with him, and show him that they truly care and that he is very important and worthwhile and needed.

"You especially know about this, Ethan."

As noted, Priesthood leaders and others can utilize this information, through the help of the Spirit, to better help those with Asperger's. I have received much spiritual help, the guidance to help me know what to do when I have choices to make, during which I have progressed and learned from my trials. This spiritual help is a two-way process, help from above as well as help from other people. There are those who have been spiritually prompted to give me helpful information during many times of difficulty. Our Savior has also provided me with many spiritual experiences, such as the great spiritual feeling I experienced when teaching a group of people about family history work and temple work.

"These and other 'tender mercies' were graciously given by a loving Heavenly Father when I needed them to assist me during difficult times, and He will for you, too, Ethan."

Dealing with the added difficulty of having Asperger's Syndrome, I have been able to learn much more about myself, including my importance to our Heavenly Father and our Savior, and my own self-worth. I am able to realize more of who I really am from a positive, Christlike viewpoint. I feel important, refreshed, and loved. I feel and know through His Spirit that there are great, wonderful blessings awaiting all of us with Asperger's, and that we are highly regarded. I know these feelings come from the Lord to help us feel better about ourselves. The Lord wants us to feel this way, instead of feeling worthless, rejected, and unable to amount to anything.

"Ethan, the Lord does not reject me or you."

When our Savior accomplished His atonement for me, I know He felt and experienced having my Asperger's Syndrome, along with all my struggles, panic attacks, anxiety, depression, etc. He also knows my great potential and knows me better than I know myself. I just have to put more faith and trust in our Savior, and realize that His atonement and grace is working for me and helping me every minute of my life, so that through my righteous efforts, I will become more sanctified and more like Him.

This is His desire for me and for everyone. I know that I have been given this Syndrome, this weakness so to speak, to help me learn to be closer to my Savior, to improve myself spiritually and in all areas of my life. This is beautifully mentioned in the Book of Mormon, in Ether 12:27, where if we recognize our weaknesses and have faith in our Savior, He will make our weaknesses become strong. Great spiritual strength is often developed by those with physical challenges.

"All of this is true for you as well, Ethan."

It's true for each one of you who has Asperger's Syndrome/ASD. I know that other people have been given various other similar disorders and various disabilities for this same purpose, which will help give them spiritual protection from the evils in life.

AGGRESSION AND ASPERGER'S SYNDROME

To review, the Asperger's response to verbally aggressive behavior is to want it to stop immediately. If it doesn't, then he will need to quickly leave the area. If sudden aggression or anything else occurs, such as a sudden, very loud sound which quickly causes a greater sensory overload, he usually has a reflexive, uncontrolled reaction, with an associated adrenalin rush. This causes him to have a panic attack, where he has uncontrollable, upsetting emotions which he has to release.

"Ethan, Sarah, and Alexis, here is another true story to show this, where you can relate."

Trevor's mother accidentally dropped a pan on the

kitchen floor as she was washing the dishes. It made extremely loud banging sounds as it hit the hard floor, and twelve-year-old Trevor, who has Asperger's, was at the dinner table. This sudden loud sound immediately caused a reflexive reaction and panic attack, where he quickly screamed loudly and hit the table before he knew what was happening. His mother loudly called out, "Trevor, stop doing that!" This caused him to hurry out of the room, stomping the floor as he went. He slammed his bedroom door and hit the wall a few times. He cried loudly during all this.

"Trevor, please stop your rude behavior," she called out again. "You're upsetting me and your younger brother. You need to be a better example." This didn't help, as he continued with his actions. He was really trembling. She then waited a few minutes before saying anything else. During this time, Trevor calmed down a little, so she went to his room and with a softer voice, asked, "Trevor may I come in?"

"Yeah, mom," he half-shouted.

She felt prompted to respond to him in a loving and soothing manner. "Trevor, I wasn't intending to make that loud noise, it was just an accident. I know how you are very sensitive to loud noises. How can I help you to not react in that way?"

He loudly responded with much irritation, "I don't know. It just happens, and I don't want it to happen. It's embarrassing."

She put her arm around him and comforted him with, "I understand. It's a part of your Asperger's, and I want to help you to overcome this reaction, but I'm not sure how to do it. You and I can pray about it, and maybe we will find something that will help you." She understood that Trevor was not having a tantrum, but was having a fearful panic reaction, a reflexive reaction in his brain, due to his Asperger's. He wanted a solution to this.

From this example, you can see that if an unexpected, very loud and irritating sound starts occurring, the person has a sudden, reflexive feeling of insecurity, along with a quick release of adrenalin, resulting in a rapid heartbeat and body trembling. He wants this stimulus to immediately stop. He has to release this very upsetting emotion, causing him to scream or hit his hands or something else, or slam a door. It usually takes several minutes for this to begin to subside after the noise has stopped. Anger from anyone else will only intensify this release. Loving, calming, and soothing actions will quickly settle him. This behavior is not to be confused with tantrum behavior, as a child would exhibit, but is a very common involuntary reflexive response for those with Asperger's. This reflexive, uncontrolled reaction is also not to be taken personally, but is only a characteristic of this Syndrome and PTSD and Anxiety Disorder. He is not being self-aggressive in this case. As the person with Asperger's is ready to improve by being more humble, and really wanting and trying to be better, with the Lord's help, these characteristics can and will diminish. He will not move his arms wildly, scream, or hit things anymore. Basically, this involuntary reflexive reaction can be completely eliminated from his life! This can really happen, just as Trevor and his mother intently desired.

"I will soon be showing you, Ethan, and all of you, experiencing Asperger's, how this has happened for me and how it can actually take place in your life.

"Whenever I faced an unpleasant situation, I would pray for help. I may not have been able to precisely in the same moment, such as when a panic attack started occurring, but earnestly praying quickly always worked. I would talk to my family and friends, my 'safe' people, when these situations occurred, and their faith, prayers, and hugs helped me additionally. They encouraged me to do the things which the Lord desires us to do. This encouragement and my responding to it made me feel more comfortable, calm, and secure. They especially encouraged me to pray, not only when we regularly pray, but frequently, when I needed the Lord's help with unpleasant situations or reactions. It is also a very good idea to keep your name on the temple prayer roll. Others can help you to do this if you need assistance. There is great power in this, along with your own prayers. I will speak more about the power of prayer and how it can really help you, Ethan, later in the next chapter."

Now to mention another subject involving aggression and ASD. This is about driving a vehicle. It is difficult for me to drive a car. Driving in too much traffic can cause sensory overload. Many with Asperger's do not drive at all. I did not actually learn to drive until I was a senior in high school. I just didn't have a great desire to drive a vehicle.

I took the driving course and test, and received my license when I was graduating high school. I obtained my own car a few years later, after going to Brigham Young University and completing my mission for the Church. Even then, I drove less frequently, as situations often caused major sensory overload, and more aggressive situations were beginning to occur. Some people with Asperger's/ASD will not be capable enough to drive a vehicle at first, but may be able to learn to drive to some degree when they become more mature. All this may seem quite strange to those of you who don't have Asperger's/ASD, as those with Asperger's also appear very normal; nevertheless, this is a very real, accurate description of what is actually occurring in the life of the Asperger's person, due to his brain development.

When I am driving and I encounter an aggressive driver or situation, such as when someone is driving too fast and passing unsafely or following too closely, I feel unsafe and may start shaking from a reflexive attack. I have to turn off onto the side of the road or onto another road, wait for reactions to subside, and pray for help. I then feel the help to safely arrive where I need to be, or to return home. I once had a driver start harrassing me. I just locked the doors and ignored him. This is the best thing to do. The Lord has helped me with many unpleasant situations with driving. He has helped me to have more confidence in a vehicle, either driving or as a passenger. Praying has always helped me so that I can drive more confidently, knowing the Lord will be with me.

When a Church leader or member becomes somewhat aggressive or harsh, I do my best to respond in a kind manner. If this does not work to help change his attitude, I excuse myself and leave the area. Assistance from friends may help to resolve the issue. I follow the guidance of the Spirit and the guidance of those close to me to help with any further response. I find that it is better to ignore the negative responses from members and other people, and not react to them, but to return a positive response and also to appreciate and respond positively to positive responses from others.

Everyone has difficulties in various areas of their lives, emotionally, mentally, physically, socially, and spiritually. Those with Asperger's/Autism Spectrum Disorder have varying increased difficulties in these areas, especially emotionally and socially. This, along with their very tender spirits, makes dealing with aggression and life's challenges an even harder task. However, everyone, including those with Asperger's Syndrome, can overcome these difficulties. This can most easily be accomplished through prayer and the Lord's help. Assistance can be received through other caring people as they are prompted by the Lord to help, but there is much that the person with Asperger's can do for himself, through the guidance of the Spirit of the Lord. Next is some very important information.

First, Ethan and all of you who have Asperger's, keep yourselves close to the Lord by desiring this closeness and by faithfully and sincerely doing the things which the Lord would have you do, like earnestly praying, reading scriptures, especially the Book of Mormon, and keeping the commandments. This includes attending Church every Sunday and partaking of the sacrament, paying tithing, and keeping the Word of Wisdom. You should believe that the Lord will help you as you feel more faith and trust in Him and as you sincerely desire this assistance through His grace.

Second, you need to be aware of the spiritual promptings you receive. A thought may come to you which you realize is a great idea to help you overcome difficulties. For example, you can manually, consciously retrain your brain that a sudden, loud sound is not going to hurt you in any way, physically, emotionally, mentally, socially, or spiritually. You can tell yourself, "This sound is okay." You may need to keep saying this to yourself many times to start the change, but improvement will occur. Unexpected or repeating, irritating sounds or other aggression will then not cause a PTSD or reflexive reaction, anxiety attack, or panic attack. As you get older, your brain continues to mature and progress in learning, and this type of exercise will speed up that process. You don't have to wait until you are older; this will start happening to you now. You will see some immediate results which will keep improving. You will be able to handle life's situations in a more appropriate, mature manner. These results will come to you quickly as you pray for help when doing this. You will then be able to help other people who have similar difficulties with reacting to stimuli.

It is important to note that having any of these disorders does not give you, a person with Asperger's, the excuse to intentionally act out more, as a result of others being accustomed to your frequent reactions or anxiety/panic attacks. Instead, you should consciously do this and other beneficial exercises to help these disorders decrease, which will help you improve. Other exercises could include saying to yourself, "I am happy when this happens," or "This is affecting me in a positive way." You could also repeatedly tell yourself, "I am in control of this reflexive response, and it will go away now." Do this immediately when a sudden, very loud sound occurs. By doing this, reflexive responses will decrease and then stop. This has changed my life for the better, and it will work for you too.

Many of life's difficult situations have greatly affected

my tender emotions, to where I cry inside, hit my hands together, and feel great anxiety and depression. However, when I do these exercises and follow other spiritual promptings, such as praying for comfort and guidance so that I will feel the Spirit of the Lord more abundantly in my life, the Lord really helps me feel at peace. Anxiety and depression decrease as well. I have also found that instead of hitting my hands together, a more appropriate form of release would be discreetly squeezing my hands together. This works very well, and allows the voice of the Spirit to guide me better. Talking to a "safe" person who can also give me guidance and comfort, being at the temple, and praying are things that help me feel great assistance from our Savior to help me with these difficulties. The Lord has given me great comfort and I feel more peaceful. My Asperger's characteristics, along with the side disorders, are actually controlled and managed, and some have even disappeared, such as involuntary movements, unusual facial expressions, reactions, and anxiety and panic attacks!

These methods have also greatly helped me with handling issues that come up as I interact with other people as a member of the Church. My responses are much more appropriate when dealing with a social issue, as I do not appear odd and my emotions are not affected nearly as much as they used to be. My behavior is and will be more mature and less affected by Asperger's and its characteristics. People see that I socially interact with them in a normal, mature manner, and they see that I really care about them when they witness me being selfless, showing charity, and showing genuine, Christlike concern for them. Some of them have indicated that I have helped them with their problems in ways I was unaware of, and that I have made their load lighter for them.

"This exciting information will definitely raise your trajectory in life, and your life will become more the type of life our Savior has planned for you. This will bring you much more joy and peace each day, and you will see this joy even more as you realize that you are helping other people in their lives. They will truly appreciate your efforts and your concern for them, as you endeavor to allow the Lord to help you progress and become more Christlike. You will see that you are leaving more of your Asperger's Syndrome behind you!

"Ethan, you have the realization of normalcy by doing these simple things for yourself. You will also be able to help others in more ways than you first thought. Wow, this is a very awesome part of our journey together! I can see your excitement and eagerness.

"I know that this wealth of information actually does work. Ethan, as you apply this information and do as I have suggested, your life will improve in a fantastic way, and you will feel much happier and more confident. You will have more friends who will think highly of you. Does that sound exciting? You will see even greater amazement in your progression as we continue."

"Robert, this is so exciting! I feel more hope now than I have ever felt before. It will be so fun to be able to live like you do, and not have these extra difficulties!"

CHAPTER FOUR
HOW I ACCOMPLISHED MAJOR EVENTS IN MY LIFE, HAVING ASPERGER'S SYNDROME/ASD

LIFE'S MILESTONES

I have noted that being a member of the Church of Jesus Christ of Latter-day Saints and having Asperger's Syndrome has made a unique, interesting life experience for me. I received my patriarchal blessing from the Church about two decades before finding out I had Asperger's. No information was available about Asperger's at the time I received my blessing. A patriarchal blessing gives the Lord's words and counsel applicable for the person's life, specific for the individual receiving it. The Lord's words to me said that I would be able to go on a full-time mission for the Church. All able young adult males in the Church are asked by the Lord to do this. The Lord also said that I would have good employment and be married in this life. I was able to have employment for

14 years. A small percentage of adults with Asperger's or high functioning people with Autism have been able to have employment; however, some have been able to have good employment, more so now than before. Also, a small number have been able to go serve as a full-time missionary or be married in this life. As Asperger's or any other Spectrum Disorder is now usually diagnosed in children, early intervention and planning can be done so that the person can lead a much more normal and fulfilling life. More of them could be employed and more could go on full-time missions; however, there are other options available for service for those who are not able to be a full-time missionary.

My patriarchal blessing has been a great help to me all my life, especially after finding out about having Asperger's. The Lord knows what I was able to accomplish before I knew that I had Asperger's, and what I am able to accomplish now.

"I would strongly encourage you, Ethan, and your family to receive patriarchal blessings, if you and they haven't already. Sarah, this blessing can be given to the person as early as his teenage years. It gives tremendous, specialized help and guidance in this unique situation involving Asperger's/ASD."

"Mom, I feel that I should get my patriarchal blessing right away. I know the Lord has great plans for me, and He will help me to accomplish them. I know that I can do more things in my life, after doing all that Robert is teaching us."

"We will do that, Ethan. We'll make the arrangements so that you and Lexi can receive your blessings. I know this is very important."

"Good. This will be a tremendous benefit for both of you. If you and any of you with Asperger's or similar disorders are not able to accomplish these important milestones, or if your patriarchal blessing does not mention all these important areas to be accomplished during your lifetime, this does not mean in any way that you are less important. Our Savior does not view you any less than those with Asperger's who are able to accomplish more in their lives. You are not viewed less than anyone else, for that matter. Our Savior has His very important plan for you in mortality, and you are able, through your faithfulness and by doing what you are capable of doing, to receive all the blessings which the Lord has for each of us in the life after mortality, as well as those He has for you in this life. You will not have Asperger's Syndrome in the life after mortality. I feel that many of those who have Asperger's and other similar disabilities in this life are among the more elect with the Lord, and that they have Asperger's to help them prepare for this. If they are not able to be married in this life, and they do what they are capable of doing, that which the Lord has asked of them to do, then they will be able to be married later, and have their own families. I know that I will be able to have my own family with my wife in the life after mortality."

I did not know why I was not finding the right girl to marry during the usual time in my life for this to occur. My patriarchal blessing did mention marriage a bit later in my life.

When I found out about Asperger's, I was wondering how this would occur, as a smaller number of us get married. I will later discuss how I dealt with the entire process of marriage, and how our Savior greatly assisted me to allow this to occur.

I will first talk about my experience attending Brigham Young University (BYU). I went there for two school years, comprised of eight months per year. I started the school year in the fall after graduating high school. Of course, this was before I knew about Asperger's. My father, Ralph, had been working there, and he helped me with applying, being accepted, and registering for my freshman classes. It was quite overwhelming for me to start attending school at a university, being that I didn't have the social awareness other freshmen have when they begin college. I registered for a little over half of the normal class load for freshmen. They were mainly general education classes. During the two years, I also had math classes, a bowling class, an introduction to astronomy class, and a couple of Book of Mormon classes, taught by Cleon Skousen. I was trying to find any meteorology classes taught there, but was unable. The counselor there didn't have the information.

Before I first started attending in the fall, my mother and I did a self-tour of where all my classes would be held. I needed this detailed information to help me feel more secure. I was living at home at this time, and I would go to BYU and back home later in the day mainly with my father, and at times with my sister or a good neighbor. When I started attending, I would visit my father often, in his office/workroom area. This was necessary for my wellbeing, and to help me to feel secure. He was my "safe" person there.

Within the building where he worked, there was a seating area where I worked on my assignments. This helped me feel more comfortable in those first years there. This was my "safe" place. I did very well in my classes, and was able to understand and complete the assignments. Several years later, when I went back to BYU to study elementary education, I was able to be more independent. This was after my mission, when I felt more comfortable. I attended BYU again for only a semester, as my plan to study elementary education didn't work. This was also before knowing I had Asperger's Syndrome, and their testing showed that I wasn't suited to teach a class of children, due to a lack of social skills and social awareness.

I will now explain about my missionary experience and how I dealt with issues I experienced there. Not knowing about Asperger's, I thought that I was just a normal young adult preparing to become a missionary. When I was 19 years old, the youngest age for missionary service at that time, I did not feel ready, mentally, emotionally, and socially. I also did not understand why I was not ready in these areas. I knew the Lord had told me that I was capable of going and that I would be going, so I did all I could to prepare myself, especially emotionally and socially.

I was prompted by the Spirit to go to BYU first for a couple of years, in order to have that experience, to receive more education, and to become better prepared in life. My parents and I then went to California, where my father sought better employment and I could study meteorology. None of this worked out as planned, and the Lord guided us to go back to Utah. After we were settled, my father and I had the distinct impression that I should be ordained an Elder and prepare to go on a mission. I had turned 21 and felt that I was ready to be a missionary.

I was ordained an Elder by my father, which was a very spiritual experience. Being close to the Spirit and receiving the Melchizedek Priesthood was a real highlight of my life. I knew that I was being prepared to do more of the Lord's work, helping others. I had the interviews to be a missionary with my bishop and stake president. Soon after, they were both released from their callings and others were called to fill these positions. I was informed that I would need to be interviewed again by both, so that my missionary application would be current. This all occurred in January. I was made aware that it would take a couple of weeks or more for me to receive my call.

About two months had passed, so my father and I asked our new bishop what was causing the delay. He responded, "At times it may take a little longer." We waited another couple of weeks, and then asked the stake leaders what had happened. We found out that the paperwork had not yet been sent. My father was extremely irritated at this and strongly requested, "Please send it in immediately." The Spirit had prompted him to say this to the leaders. This was divine intervention. The leaders were not planning on having me go on a mission, nor did they tell me. It had been noted on my application that I had mental problems. As Asperger's or its diagnosis was not known at the time, my different, odd behaviors could easily be interpreted in a manner such as this.

Later in the month of April, I did receive my mission call to Chile. I would be going to the Missionary Training Center (MTC) in two months and would be there for two months to learn Spanish, along with many other things to prepare us to be successful missionaries. My family and I were very excited. I had taken some Spanish classes earlier in high school, so I was somewhat familiar with it. I completed the checklist and got everything ready during those two months. Near the end of June, it was time for my mission to start.

My father gave me a priesthood blessing at this time. It is highly recommended that the father or other close Melchizedek priesthood holder give the missionary a blessing before he leaves on his mission. I had also received my temple recommend and received my own temple endowment. Going to the temple was an extra great help for me, as I felt the guidance of the Spirit even more prominently in my life. I was then set apart as a missionary.

Being in the MTC is difficult for many, and was a great challenge for me. I could not have any contact with my family or others, except through written letters once a week. It was becoming a real strain for me, but I knew the Lord was helping me. I was learning that I could do harder things with His help. I could get up earlier, go to bed later, learn and memorize every day, and speak more in Spanish with my companions. Before I was to leave the MTC, my priesthood leader there spoke with me and decided it would be appropriate for my father to give me another priesthood blessing to help me. There, the Lord said that I was to continue the mission, and that I would be of great service to others.

Leaving on a commercial plane was a new, exciting experience for me. I was with a few other missionaries on the plane. After two plane transfers, I arrived at my mission area, where the mission president would get us.

It seemed very strange at first, arriving in a new country. I stayed at the mission home first, and then I was assigned to my first area with my companion. We were to give a written report to our mission president every week. I knew that he was very much guided by the Spirit about who our companions would be and where we worked. I knew that I was in the setting that the Lord would have me be in right then. I felt comfort through the Holy Ghost all through my mission that everything was being taken care of through the guidance of the Spirit, and that I was being protected as I participated in the Lord's work.

When I encountered issues there, such as a companion being contentious or knowingly not obeying the rules, I would ask him about it. If he were still unwilling, I would then make a written note in my weekly report to the mission president, or in a more urgent case, I would call one of the leaders and explain the situation. I would do this to help remove obstructions from the missionary work, and to allow me to better function as a missionary. I was not trying to provoke or cause problems for people, as this has never been my intent all my life. I have always felt the calling to do the Lord's will. Hopefully, the person who was not being obedient would realize what was happening, feel the Spirit prompting him, and make changes so that he could have a happier, more productive life.

During my mission, I always felt that I had "safe" people around and that I was in a "safe" place. My "safe" people were any of my leaders with whom I had interaction during my mission. Most of my companions were also these people. I always felt comfortable in any place where I was working. This was because I had the Spirit of the Lord with me in great abundance. This was a result of being set apart as a missionary and by following the missionary guidelines, as well as intently praying for this.

When I was nearing the end of my mission, we were given the choice to be on our missions for 18 months instead of 2 years, as the Church was testing a change for 18-month missions for the Elders. It later was changed back to 2 years. I felt so comfortable and was having such great spiritual experiences, that I chose to stay the whole 2 years, as did the other missionaries. I felt at home there, and actually wanted to stay longer when the time was completed. This shows how the Spirit helps us no matter what disorder we have, if we fully put our faith and trust in the Lord. Missions or other appropriate service help people grow in many ways, and prepare them for their life's experiences. Our Savior continues to help us at any time during our progression, as we do our part.

DATING AND BECOMING ENGAGED

When I had been home from my mission for a few years, I had not yet felt comfortable dating girls, as it was very socially awkward for me, and I didn't know why. With my parents' encouragement, I went to a Church Valentine's activity with a single girl in my ward. I did not know what was happening socially, but she was apparently uncomfortable around me. She was visiting with numerous other people there during the entire activity. I could not figure it out, and I felt quite sad. I could tell later that she was not my type, but I was also apparently behaving in an odd, eccentric manner, not knowing about having Asperger's Syndrome. She could tell that I was very unaware socially, and immature.

A few years later, I was still living at home and my father was becoming more concerned that I was not dating much, nor did I seem to have much interest in it. He had been made aware of another girl I could date. Arrangements were made that I could take her to a smaller function at BYU. This turned out about the same way. She was not very interested in me. She met two other girls there whom she knew, and told me she was going to the restroom. All three girls went in and did not come out for awhile. I thought that was rather peculiar. I didn't know at the time that they would go there to talk in private about something important, at this time concerning me. In there, she could have easily said something like, "What is that guy doing? Have you ever seen anyone that weird in your life? I don't feel comfortable around him at all. Can I stay with you and have you take me home later? This isn't working out at all!" She later came and told me that she was going to stay with her two friends and they would take her home. I went home by myself and found out later that she was also very uncomfortable around me.

My sister also arranged for me to go on a double date with a girl she knew, but afterward found out that this girl had a severe learning disability and this would not be a suitable situation for me. A few years later, I found out about having Asperger's Syndrome, which explained much about the reasons these dates turned out as they did. I was then able to learn more about some social skills from my family, which would be useful when dating girls. They taught me to be aware to not move my hands all around. They taught me to smile more. However, I was still not feeling ready to do any serious dating. My father was feeling uneasy and embarrassed that I had this disorder, and that I was not yet comfortable dating. This was a normal feeling for him.

Several years later, after I had moved into a condo in my parents' ward, I was feeling more ready to be married. The Lord had told me in my patriarchal blessing that at the right time, I would be given a wife. As I then knew that I had Asperger's Syndrome, I knew why it would be difficult for me to find the right person, having difficulty with social awareness. I didn't have the skills to be socially outgoing. I also found out that I was much more innocent from the ways of the world, like a younger child, partly due to my lack of social awareness. I didn't understand much of how the world thinks, and I was viewing society in more of a spiritual way with sensitive emotions. The girls I had previously dated could see all this about me, which added to their perception that I was very odd and immature, and not able to conform to the normalcy which they expected in a person they would seriously consider for marriage. As a result, I was then thinking that the Lord knows the right person for me to meet, one who would understand all this about me and know who I really am. She would then be able to teach me and help me to progress.

When I was 44, I was enjoying working at the temple baptistry and also as a staff member at the stake family history center. This was when I was living in my parents' ward. As I did not have employment at this time, I had much more extra time to work on my family history information at the center. Two separate times, which were months apart, I had asked my father to give me a blessing concerning marriage. I was staying close to the Lord and was doing what He would have me do. I sincerely desired to have His guidance at this important time in my life, as I knew that the Lord knew I would need His help. After the second blessing, I felt very prompted to go to the center more often. I went every day, even when it was closed, to do my personal family history work. We staff members were allowed to do this. I felt that if I did this and continued working at the baptistry, I would meet the one I was to marry. This came from the Holy Ghost.

A short time later, a sister in the Church came into the center during a time when it was normally open. She told me, "Hello, my name is Jeanene and I have been called as a ward family history consultant. I just love doing family history. I live across the street, and I need to learn about the center and how to help others with their own family history work." I was quite familiar with the center, so I gave her much of the information she needed to know. I explained, "I'm Robert. Glad to meet you. I am a staff member here and I would be happy to show you around and explain how the patrons use the family history center. The center director will also be giving you more information."

A few days later, as I was showing her some information on the computer, she put her hand on top of mine as I was moving the mouse with it. I couldn't figure out why she was doing that, so I just continued on. I later found out that my mother had told her that I have Asperger's, and she was interested to see if I resisted touch. At the time, I didn't know her reason for that behavior.

Jeanene was becoming quite friendly with me. Not having much social awareness, I had no idea of the depth of that relationship, if she just wanted to be a good friend or wanted a deeper relationship. She had told me that she was single and was also a ward single adults coordinator. I asked my parents later at their condo about things that she said or did, and what they meant, so I would not be too confused.

One particular evening, I was at her place to have dinner. I was unaware of apparently doing some odd behavior, not knowing the proper social skill. She told me that she had to do something else right after dinner, and took me home. I did not understand what was going on, but later found out that I had unknowingly said something odd which made her uneasy. She had called me to ask me about it. She was learning more about Asperger's and then understood the real reason for my action, and that I was not intending to be rude.

However, a few weeks later, she told me that she was going with someone else. I felt sad and thought that apparently this was not to be and that there would be someone else for me. I went on doing my family history work at the center, getting names of ancestors ready for temple ordinance work. This was the process to follow at that time. Over a month later, I was at the family history center with my mother when I received a phone call from Jeanene. The Lord had prompted her to call me right then. She asked, "Can I come over this evening?" I told her, "That would be awkward if you are going with someone else." She explained, "I'm not going with anyone else anymore, and I need to be with you." This made me very happy and I felt even more certain that she was the one for me. She had developed a deeper, more sincere love for me than she ever had in her life.

Later, after we had talked at the family history center a few more times, she called me and asked if we could have a family home evening together. I said that would be fine. She came over and we discussed various subjects in each of our lives, to help us to get to know each other better. We talked about areas where I could help her feel better emotionally. She told me of some hardships and challenges she had been through and how she really desired a better life in the Church. She wanted a more spiritual life, but still didn't know me that well. I told her, "You can be comfortable with me. You are safe from the storm now." We talked awhile about life's experiences, and I said, "It is very important that we are headed toward the Lord." She was feeling more comfortable with me and desired that I give her a priesthood blessing. This really helped her. She indicated, "I am becoming quite attached to you." I then felt that she could be the one to marry. We had a great time dating, and I never felt awkward. We would go out to eat and I felt comfortable around her. This was the first time I had ever had a dating experience like this. She was very understanding of me and of Asperger's. She cared that I was always treated right. She wanted people to understand me better. She also knew how I could be so easily overloaded, driving in traffic, so we took turns driving.

Soon after, I was in the temple baptistry performing an ordinance, when I had an overwhelming spiritual feeling that Jeanene was the one to marry. This shows the importance of staying close to the Spirit of the Lord. I knew that meeting her was no coincidence, but that it was the Lord's plan. There are no coincidences with the Lord.

We were planning on becoming engaged, so one time when my father and I were doing a morning walk in the mall nearby, he and I found an excellent engagement ring. I purchased it and kept it in a safe place. Jeanene kept asking, "When am I going to get my ring?" She did not yet know that I had one. I said, "It will be later, when the time is right." She was going to have minor surgery; therefore, I planned to wait for a couple weeks afterward, so she could have time to recover.

On the night I had planned, we went out and walked hand in hand to the mall to have dinner. I felt very comfortable with her and had a very close friendship. It was a really fun and exciting, yet peaceful experience. Then we watched a movie, *The Parent Trap*, at my place. It was the more recent movie, which has the theme of love and getting married all throughout it. After the movie, it was getting a little late and Jeanene was getting tired. She said, "Thank you for this wonderful evening, but now I'm very tired. I need to go home so I can go to bed." I then said, "Wait, I have something for you." I went to get the ring and felt a little nervous, excited, and happy. I wanted it to be a complete surprise, so I had it in a gift bag in another room, instead of in my pocket. I went to get it and then felt that my knees were weak. I thought, "Wow, I'm about to do something that is one of the most major milestones in my life, which I have never done before. I'm 44 and I've waited all this time for this special moment." I felt very emotional, knowing that I could fulfill the Lord's plan for me. I went back to her, took the ring box out of the bag, opened it, and proposed. I said,

"Jeanene, will you please marry me?" She was extremely excited. She accepted very joyfully, and stayed a couple more hours. Jeanene was no longer tired. She had no idea that I was going to propose that evening. This proposal was not a very strange process for me, as the Spirit of the Lord was with me, and it was a very exciting, wonderful event. I felt completely comfortable.

Being truly in love gave me a very wonderful feeling of true joy, which I had not experienced before in my life. It was very fun to go together, making plans and selecting items together for our wedding reception. I was first experiencing in my mid 40s what many others experience in their 20s. I felt completely ready at this time. We spent time together each day, and at night we each went to our homes to sleep. We both knew that it was very important to follow the Lord's direction, and do things worthily and be respectful of each other before marriage as well as after. It was hard leaving her at night, but I was excited the next morning, being able to see her again.

I had decorated my place for Christmas, with a tree, and we exchanged Christmas gifts. We learned more about each other. I found that besides enjoying family history work, Jeanene loved pressing flowers and putting them on pillar candles. She had her own handmade flower press, and showed me how she made it work really well. Jeanene was learning about me too, and was learning more about Asperger's Syndrome. She was very loving, caring, and understanding of me.

We continued going on dates, many of which were going out to have dinners. I was very comfortable doing this, and my Asperger's characteristics were less pronounced. Jeanene also understood any characteristics I exhibited. I was very respectful of her, and would open the car door and hold other doors for her. I was starting to understand more how she was feeling, and she taught me more about understanding people's feelings by explaining her feelings in a more personal way.

Four months after we were engaged, after going around together purchasing items, reserving items for our wedding reception, and getting everything ready, the day came for us to be married. Jeanene had invited some of her friends to help get the reception set up, which was in our ward's Relief Society room. My mother had contracted the flu and had bronchitis a few days before our wedding day. She really wanted to be there for this great event. She had waited all these years for me to be married. She was 80 at the time. My sister was already married, so I was the last one. My mother had great faith and prayed that she could be well enough to attend. This did happen; her severe illness completely left her body for the day of our wedding and reception, then it came back later that night when she went home, and her illness ran its course for more than a week. This was a testimony to all of us about the power of faith and prayer. It was a special, wonderful feeling having my mother there, as she was also not very mobile due to her age.

The wedding itself was a very spiritual experience. Jeanene and I felt the Spirit really strong there. It was an extremely different experience to realize that I was actually married. It was also a very different but wonderful, spiritual feeling to know that I am sealed to Jeanene.

Many friends and family also came to our reception. It was great to see our friends who came to congratulate us and to show us how much they really care about us. It is difficult for people with Asperger's to see the true depth of friendship until it is shown in a much more obvious manner. Two of our friends even recorded videos of the entire reception, which they gave to us as a memory of this special event. Many brought wedding gifts, some of which were homemade and have special meaning to us.

We also had an enjoyable honeymoon. Jeanene had to help me feel adjusted and comfortable spending nights together, as this was a very new experience for me. We enjoyed having some romantic meals together. She lovingly spoke to me and helped me feel more comfortable. She was guided by the Spirit to know how to help me feel peaceful.

Being married and having Asperger's shows the fulfillment of the Lord's plan for me, as I stayed close to Him through prayer and my actions. This shows the importance of knowing the Lord's will for each one of us, and staying close to Him, so that He can help us realize it. This was a fulfillment of my patriarchal blessing about marriage. He helped me each step of the way. This is also true concerning the Lord's plan for all of you with Asperger's.

Living with a spouse required a great adjustment, as many of you know. However, having Asperger's requires an even greater adjustment, as Autistic people normally tend to think more of themselves, but not in an intentional, selfish way. This is just a natural characteristic of this Disorder. Jeanene knew that, and really helped me to think more of her and to refer to us together, instead of just thinking about myself. Through her help, I have been able to adjust to this new way of thinking quite easily. I would tell her, "I love you" many times, and I would show her consideration and respect, as girls naturally feel more of these emotions each day, and they especially appreciate frequent behaviors which make them feel happy, comfortable, and secure.

"Even though you, Ethan, might not be married in your life, there is still much you can do to change this way of thinking about yourself. You can put away the appearance of being selfish, even though you are not trying to be selfish, and start to think about the other person more, who has feelings quite similar to yours. Your family and friends can help you with this understanding of other people's feelings."

As in any marriage, being selfless and putting my wife first has helped with many difficulties. Of course, there were times when I didn't put her first, but then I learned from them with her help, realizing what I did, and made a change for the better. When we had disagreements, we found that taking a short timeout really helped with communication and with allowing the presence of the Spirit of the Lord. We were then able to communicate better. Jeanene was able to respond with the proper feedback, which really helped me with my communication. We were able to discuss the disagreement with the Lord's Spirit there. We could also talk to our counselor, Heidi, and receive great wisdom, which our Savior would have us know. Jeanene and I have been able to learn much about marriage and communication, as Heidi is skilled in Asperger's/ASD and marriage counseling, among other things. Jeanene has also experienced a true marriage in the Church, the way our Savior wants it to be. She has learned more about marriage, and we had the Spirit of the Lord attend us more in our relationship and in living each day, as we prayed for guidance.

Whenever I had a problem involving Asperger's, Jeanene lovingly helped me through it, and hugged and comforted me, which works very well. She continued learning more about Asperger's, which has also been a great help in our marriage. Asperger's Syndrome and Jeanene's disorder, which will be explained later, have become less of a factor in our marriage. I became able to help her with difficulties, and I gave her priesthood blessings when she needed them. Being selfless and putting her first really subdued any negative emotions. We both focused more on the Lord and we went to the temple often. This also helped us manage our disorders much more effectively. There, we received many answers to pressing issues, through the Spirit of the Lord. This brought an increased spirituality in our home, along with living the gospel, going to Church, praying, reading scriptures, and having family home evenings together.

PRAYER AND CHURCH

"Here is a great example from a true experience that shows the tremendous importance of communicating with our Heavenly Father and feeling the urgent need to attend Church. It shows the benefits a person with Asperger's, like you, can receive by doing this."

Gary, a 50-year-old adult with Asperger's, was a convert to the Church when he was 22. All those in his family were not members, but he felt that there was something missing in his life. He had one close neighbor friend at that time, a member of the Church who had fellow-shipped him and told him about the Church. He felt that this would alleviate some of his loneliness, as he felt very awkward around people who didn't understand him due to his odd behaviors and his difficulty communicating with others. (The following year, he was diagnosed with Asperger's Syndrome, which answered many questions.) Gary showed interest in the Church when his friend told him more about our Savior and His gospel.

"Being a member of the Church will be a great help to you," he told Gary. "Let's plan to have the missionaries meet with us, and I'm sure you will feel much better, hearing the messages they have for you."

They both met with the missionaries, and Gary became excited about being around loving people who were learning to be more Christlike. He also felt a good spiritual feeling as he was learning what the missionaries were teaching him. He was then baptized into the Church.

Gary met a few members at Church during the following months; however, they didn't seem to fellowship him very much. They seemed to shy away from him when he exhibited odd behaviors and had difficulties communicating. His friend tried to help him to feel better, but nothing was helping that much. He was also feeling more uncomfortable around large groups of people.

Then one Sunday at Church, a member asked him, "Gary, what are you doing here, acting the way you do?"

This really shocked Gary, to where he couldn't be around people like this at all anymore. He told his friend, "I feel worse being around people who act that way toward me. I don't think this is going to work out." He continued, "I have been praying these past months like the missionaries taught me to do, but nothing has happened as a result. Nothing has improved. In fact, things have become worse. I don't think that prayer is working, and going to Church is making it harder for me."

His friend answered, "Gary, you need to trust in the Lord more, that He will help you to know that things will get better. Please feel that what I'm telling you is true."

Gary felt that this just wasn't going to work out, so he became inactive. As he grew older, he lived with his sister and her family, who were not members of the Church. During these many years, his sister helped him to understand more social skills and be more socially aware, so he was able to interact somewhat better in public. His friend had long since moved away, so his sister was his "safe" person.

Just a year ago, they all moved to another state, into a town where the people were more friendly. Gary unexpectedly felt a strong prompting to check out the Church ward in this new town. He acted on the prompting and went there the next Sunday. To his amazement, the people there were very friendly and welcoming to him. He thought, "Maybe I should start going to Church here."

He went again to the Sunday meetings the following week. This turned out to be true. Many members of this ward fellowshipped him and made him feel comfortable. One of the talks was about prayer. Gary had not been praying, as he never saw any results from it. However, this talk impressed him and helped him to know how prayer really works. After the meeting, he told the speaker, "Thank you for your talk. It was a great help for me."

He went home and prayed for the first time in years. He felt a special feeling throughout his whole body that he was doing the right thing. He felt love from Heavenly Father and our Savior, which is hard for him to describe. It made him feel very important and worthwhile. He is now active in the Church. His sister and her family were so impressed about the change in his countenance that they are now interested in learning more about the Church, and are starting to have the missionaries come. They are also learning about prayer and have felt the special feelings during the lessons and during their prayers together.

Praying, reading scriptures, going to Church, etc., are very important in the lives of Asperger's people, as doing what the Lord desires of us to do will allow Him to be able to easily help us to accomplish the important milestones in our lives, and those mentioned in our patriarchal blessings, for those of us who have received them.

I know there are many of you who have Asperger's Syndrome, or are close to someone who has Asperger's, who have difficulty with prayer. Individuals with Asperger's are very literal, and they see life as it is. As with all of us, they don't see God in a tangible way, as a person who can be visited physically, as we do with any other mortal person. However, when a family member, relative, or friend passes on to the other side, you do not see that person as you did when he or she was alive. We know that person still exists and lives; we just cannot see him or her in mortality. This is the same with Heavenly Father and Jesus; they definitely exist with tangible bodies and they love us, and we can see them at a later time, just like we will see those people who have passed.

Through the Spirit, I have known since I was a young child that Heavenly Father and Jesus are real, and you can know they are real also. We all knew them before we were born.

"Not seeing them now may cause you, Ethan, to think that prayer doesn't work, that you are just saying or thinking thoughts and only seeing what is around us. You may also think this when something is prayed for repeatedly and nothing changes. You will need to be taught and understand that this is not the case. You need to lose your pride and become more humble. I say this out of love for you. You should also learn of our Savior, know of His love for you, and build your faith. This can be accomplished through your efforts, through reading the scriptures, through the prayers of others, and by putting your name on the temple prayer roll. You can be taught about the power of prayer. You can learn that you are actually speaking to the Creator and Governor of the universe, literally the Father of each of our spirits, who loves you individually with an infinite love, and who will listen to your feelings, emotions, and concerns individually. He is actually another 'safe' person for you. He knows you by name. By praying sincerely, you will know that prayer will unlock the powers of heaven for you. You can feel the blessings from our Heavenly Father and will feel happiness and peace in your life. You can also know that you can bless your family members and others through your prayers. Sincere family prayer will be a great help to you. You can be helped to offer the family prayer in a loving setting.

"I find it helpful to remember this: Before I start praying, I visualize Heavenly Father in front of me. I talk to Him about my feelings, like I would to another loving, caring, 'safe' person. When I do this, I know that He is actually close to me and is really listening to me. I truly know that He will help me."

As mentioned earlier, the person with Asperger's needs to feel much love and security in his life. Sincere prayer can bring this to you. Through the guidance of the Spirit, all of you can be taught through love and reassurance how to sincerely pray. You can see through testimonies of other people in the Church, and also in your family, how prayers have been answered. You will then begin to see this in your own life when you earnestly pray with faith for help regarding difficulties you experience, such as social awkwardness and being misunderstood. You will feel an increase in love and security just for you. It has worked for me, and the Lord has promised that He will offer the same help for everyone. This help is beautifully described in the hymn, "Did You Think to Pray?" (*Hymns* #140)

Reading the scriptures is the same way. We can find an interesting part to start reading at first, and then continue from there. Reading the Book of Mormon especially helps. The Lord has also told us that if we read the Book of Mormon every day, our homes will have greater peace and spirituality, and family members will be more responsive to our Savior and the promptings of the Spirit. If we read and ponder the scriptures consistently, it will help us to receive answers to our prayers. Doing this each morning will help us have more confidence during the day. It will also increase our faith in the Lord. Peace from the Spirit will assist with challenges we encounter.

"You will notice that the Lord is helping you with

your Asperger's, Ethan. You and other people will notice that your undesired characteristics are decreasing."

Going to Church can be quite a challenge for some who have Asperger's Syndrome. Many feel uncomfortable around crowds or large groups of people. They may feel intimidated. They may feel apprehensive or overwhelmed by the social demands at Church, not really knowing how to socially interact. They may have been mistreated by others in the Church. They may not feel welcome there. They may have been driven away. It all comes down to testimony and faith in our Savior and our Heavenly Father.

"You, Ethan, can work on becoming closer to the Lord. Members can see your positive progress and fellowship you through their loving ministering efforts and help you be comfortable in each meeting. You could sit by the door to help yourself to not feel overwhelmed. You are taught and helped to really understand the importance of taking the sacrament each week, to renew your baptismal covenants. You can be helped to know and feel that you go to Church to serve the Lord and receive the Lord's blessings, and to be spiritually taught, not to be seen by others. You go so that our Savior will be pleased with you, so that He can help you feel happier and help you feel His Spirit much more in your life. You should not think that the Church is not true with its teachings, and not go because of what someone said or did. You should not think that you are not worthy enough to go to Church. Going to Church is not a worthiness issue; almost anyone is welcome at Church, regardless of his worthiness standing. (Of course, very aggressive individuals exhibiting a mental disorder at Church would have to be dealt with in an appropriate manner. They would also be loved and assisted, so that they can improve too, and be welcome.) Having Asperger's does not make you not good enough to be at your Church meetings."

Anyone with any disability is welcome at Church, and Church leaders should be as welcoming to them as to anyone else who goes to Church, as this is how our Savior has taught us to be.

It is quite common for various people to think that they are not as good as everyone else at Church, so they feel very uncomfortable going there. People with disabilities or disorders may feel this even more. The truth is that they are, or are able to become, better than some or many others who are there, and they can help them in a Christlike way. I felt this at one time in my life, thinking that everyone in the room knew more than I did. I quickly found out that my thinking was not true, as I learned that some other people there were slower at learning what I was learning, and soon I was able to help mentor some of them.

"This gave me a much better feeling about myself, and it will for you, too, Ethan. You are much more capable than you think you are. Even now, you are able to help certain people in areas where you are more proficient. This will happen to you at Church as well.

"When you go to Church, you can then start to feel the Spirit through the talks in the meeting, and start to feel the Spirit helping you in your life more, as you have the gift of the Holy Ghost. I have always known of the importance of these things and doing them. When you sincerely and humbly do all of this, including praying, studying the scriptures, and doing the exercises mentioned earlier, your Asperger's characteristics will not be so prominent or recognizable to others, and the Lord will help to ease your burden. Social demands, especially those with communication, will no longer be intense issues for you, and you will be able to comfortably communicate better with other people as you show concern for them. Your facial expressions and other body language will be more normal. Our Savior will truly help you with this. I absolutely know He will.

"I know that you, Ethan, and all of you who have Asperger's, will feel the Spirit testify to you of these important items I have just mentioned. They can truly change and improve your life in a major, exciting, positive way. You will find that these items are rather simple to do, when you begin doing them as I have suggested. They have actually worked, and I share them with you so that you can achieve the results I have realized. I really care about you and your happiness. Again, you will be more confident, you will feel much more worthwhile, and you will have a much happier life without Asperger's being very prominent in your life. What an exciting place to be in this part of our journey!"

"So, Robert, are you saying that this is the way that you became the person that you are now, after having many Autistic characteristics earlier?"

"Yes. I experienced many trials having Autism Spectrum Disorder when I was younger. However, doing these things which I am sharing with all of you has made a remarkable difference in my life. After doing my part, our Savior has blessed me with these wonderful changes, more than what I could have accomplished on my own."

Many members of the Church do not know I actually have Asperger's Syndrome. Even though it is more of an invisible disability, my Asperger's characteristics are not as distinct as I feel the Spirit of the Lord more in my life now, and as I apply the principles and action items I have discussed here. I know that it is very important to teach people with Asperger's the gospel in a very clear, spiritual manner. This will help them know who they really are, and will help them to feel the Spirit, as these people have been sent here to earth by the Lord for extremely important purposes, including to help others.

It is very important that we do the simple things the Lord has asked of us, especially in these days, as the world is following more the ways of the adversary as has been prophesied. The adversary really desires to lead those with Asperger's away from Church teachings and religion, making them think that having this disorder will not let them be capable enough to live the gospel the way that the Lord has taught. This is false. Just the opposite is actually true. I know that people with Asperger's and others with similar disabilities are of the more faithful people who have been given disorders to protect them and to help them more easily progress toward the Lord. People with these disorders are special people—spiritual giants—who have been sent here to help others. They just need to realize this and apply the information presented in this book to help them achieve these great blessings of pure joy and all the gifts our Heavenly Father has for us.

You may have realized by now that the powerful gospel theme I have mentioned and have been referring to is becoming more Christlike, and returning to our Heavenly Father and realizing every gift He has for each of us and our families. This includes everyone, meaning those individuals who have Asperger's Syndrome/ASD or other disabilities, as well as those who have great trials in their lives. The way to accomplish this important goal is by turning toward our Savior so that He can help us progress and be better people.

It is my sincere hope that the information I have presented so far will be a great help and encouragement to all of you who have Asperger's Syndrome or are highly functioning people with Autism, as well as to your parents, family members, teachers, Church leaders, and other people associated with you. It is written out of true brotherly love, with a great desire that what I have shared as an individual in the Church will benefit each of you, so that all of you will have a much improved life experience.

"It has been a wonderful experience going this far on this awesome journey together with you, Ethan, and with your family.

"Now, my sister Susan will join us and continue this exciting journey, discussing her experiences growing up with me in my family, explaining the differences she experienced with my Asperger's Syndrome and how she dealt with them as she tried to help me. This will give you, Ethan and Sarah, a better understanding of Alexis' feelings and experience."

Susan will also explain how she helped me to deal with the unique issues I experienced, so that you, as a family member or friend, can better help the family member with Asperger's Syndrome.

Later, I will share some information about how my wife, Jeanene, was guided to me. This information will explain some of her experiences with me and how she has been helping me. I will then show how our therapist, Heidi, and another close friend (who are also members of the Church) have helped us. I will share their observations concerning Jeanene and me, along with my Asperger's factor. Included is some excellent information from Heidi, in order to assist families and others associated with those who have Asperger's Syndrome/ASD or other disabilities, and may or may not be members of the Church.

"All this information will be of great benefit to you, Ethan, and to your mom and sister. I will be accompanying you and your family as we join Susan. After sharing this information from these other people, I will then present some more extremely beneficial information for all of you, as we continue on this important journey."

my sister's perspective

CHAPTER FIVE
LIVING WITH MY BROTHER'S ASPERGER'S SYNDROME/ASD

My brother and I grew up through the years in several homes and locations. We shared a loving relationship with each other and with kind parents who both loved and cared for us. Our family was always open and honest with one another. We didn't keep secrets. We could express our thoughts freely, but like most families, we were not without our misunderstandings and quarrels. In our home we were taught by our parents to be kind, forgiving, and honest, as well as to love, respect, and serve our Heavenly Father and His Son, Jesus Christ. We attended Sunday School and Sacrament Meeting faithfully each week. At that time, we didn't have a two-hour block of meetings. Robert and I attended Primary on a weekday afternoon, usually Tuesday. Mom attended Relief Society once a week in the morning. Dad attended Priesthood Meeting before our other Sunday meetings. When Robert turned twelve, he accompanied Dad. The love for our

Savior was felt in our home as we learned from our parents' righteous examples. We knelt each morning and evening together in family prayer. Monday evening was reserved for Family Home Evening, which we consistently held each week, learning as a family about gospel principles and of our Savior, Jesus Christ. Robert and I have been blessed with many cherished memories as well as challenging ones.

Many of the challenges came as a result of my brother's Asperger's Syndrome, which is part of the Autism Spectrum Disorder. During the time he was growing up and also into adulthood, Robert's unusual behavior was not understood by others. Autism was not known at that time. As a family, we knew that Robert was different in some ways from other children. He was very intelligent, but struggled socially because of his actions and behavior, such as looking downward when we stopped to talk with neighbors. He made unusual facial expressions. He didn't play energetically like most little boys. He seemed to be overly fearful of certain situations. He was persistent when focusing on certain thoughts or ideas, dwelling on them longer than most people would.

EARLY CHILDHOOD

Mom told me that when Robert was a toddler, he began making sounds of words, as most toddlers do. Then he stopped speaking for a few years. Many prayers were offered on his behalf. The prayers were answered when, at age five, Robert began speaking using complete sentences instead of words, which was different from the normal development of a child. Most children will continue talking, learning, and adding new words, then speak using short sentences, gradually moving into longer ones. Because Robert had become silent, our parents knew that something wasn't right, and they began seeking help.

When Robert was about four years old, we received a long red cloth tunnel for Christmas. It was big enough to accommodate three or four children, and was bendable because of the round steel rings supporting the cloth. I loved crawling through it, making "S" shapes, circles, and other configurations. I encouraged Robert to do the same. He sat at the edge, peering anxiously through it. "C'mon, it's fun, Robert!" I encouraged. No matter how much I coaxed and pleaded, he wouldn't budge from his spot. Eventually, he overcame his fear of it, but by then he was older and wasn't interested in spending time inside it. He later explained to me that he thought it would collapse on him and he would suffocate. Robert understood concepts at a very young age without having to be taught.

A mother cat showed up at our home one day and stayed on the back patio. Robert and I spent the first two days safely inside the house watching her through the sliding glass door. We were both enthralled, but were also afraid. Mom used this as a teaching moment to show us we could trust our new kitty friend. The cat nestled on Mom's lap while Mom sat on the chaise lounge. We named our new cat "White Boots" since she was marked with four distinctly white matching paws. Each time I pet her, I discovered she liked it and was soon no longer afraid. Robert took longer to warm up to her, never feeling totally safe. I coaxed him the same as I had with the tunnel. "See, she won't hurt you, Robert!" I would say as I gently stroked her back. A week or two later, she delivered kittens. We brought them inside our home, where they stayed in my room until they were bigger.

To this day, Robert doesn't feel comfortable around cats and dogs. He was startled by a big dog when he was really young. That terror remains with him. Animals are unpredictable in his view and can, with no warning, instantly become threatening. Others with Asperger's may find the closeness of animals comforting. Each person will have his or her own special interests and variables. A young woman I know who has Asperger's enjoys being with dogs and especially enjoys walking the neighbor's dogs each day.

People with Autism feel comfortable with consistency. Sudden unexpected movement or change can be very unsettling to them. They need to be able to feel secure when faced with an unpredictable situation. They either panic and run or focus on a repeated behavior, which helps distract them from the situation and calms them down. That behavior may be unacceptable to others, who misunderstand that the person is actually experiencing extreme anxiety.

We had various cats adopt our family over the years, and Robert seemed more comfortable as he learned about their behavior by watching them. At one time, we had a loving dog in our home as well as a parakeet, both of whom stayed with us and became special parts of our family. In these controlled situations, Robert was not afraid of them because they were gentle and he knew he could trust them.

At age five, Robert enjoyed kneeling on both his

hands and knees on his bed, rocking back and forth while listening to classical music. Sometimes he hummed a little tune, which to this day I still remember, repeating it over and over while rocking. I joined in too, thinking it was fun to do, but soon grew tired of it. It seemed to me that he could go on forever. When I suggested that we do something else, he looked at me with no response and continued rocking. "Don't you get tired of doing this, Robert?" I asked. "No," he'd matter-of-factly state. He seemed self-absorbed and content, so I usually returned to my own room to play by myself.

Robert didn't speak clearly like most children his age. He was soft spoken; many of his words were difficult to distinguish, often sounding slurred to me, or with an incorrect pronunciation. I could usually understand what he was saying, but outside of our family, many people had difficulty understanding him. He acted shy around other people, but it was because he couldn't express himself and make himself understood, more than it was shyness. He looked to Mom or me for help in expressing what he wanted to say. He seemed to enjoy playing with other children and being with people; it was just difficult for him to communicate with others.

Since Robert was having difficulty speaking clearly, Dad bought a small reel-to-reel tape recorder to help him learn to speak correctly as recommended by a speech therapist. "Say, Lion!" Dad encouraged. "Ung-ion!" responded Robert. "No, L...L...Lion!" Dad corrected. "Nion!" my five-year-old brother joyfully exclaimed into the microphone. This looked like a fun game and I wanted to be included too. "Daddy, I want to do it!" I exclaimed. He allowed me to participate a few times, then kindly shooed me away. "This is to help your brother," he explained. I soon came to resent the tape recorder whenever it was brought out because it meant I had to leave Robert and Dad alone. I began to feel sad and that I didn't matter. Much of our parents' attention was centered on Robert during those early years. As a young child myself, I felt resentful that he seemed to be getting most of their attention. I was unaware of how much help and intervention Robert really needed.

I began to feel guilty that I was "normal" and my brother wasn't. Something was wrong and I wanted him to get better, but I didn't know how to help. I overheard our parents talking one evening after I was in bed. In my child's mind, I began to worry that something bad was happening to him. At one point I became so worried that I tearfully asked, "Is Robert going to die?" Mom hugged and reassured me that he wasn't, and I felt a huge sense of relief. It was a heavy burden for a child to carry alone. (Maybe Alexis has felt all this.)

It's helpful to explain things in simple terms to a child. Be aware of each child's needs in the family with relationship to the child who has Asperger's Syndrome or any other disability. Young children need to be reassured that their brother or sister can be helped. They need to be encouraged to ask questions and receive an honest answer. They need to understand that their sibling may need extra help and attention. This in no way means that they are loved any less. Each member of the family needs to know he or she is loved and valued. Children can be helped to feel loved and important by participating in helping their sibling. For example:

"That was very helpful when you played nicely with

your brother today!"

"I'm glad you are helping your sister. I noticed that you helped her sound out words. Good job!"

Compliments are always welcome and help the child to feel his or her worth in the family as they contribute. Children should not be forced to do something repeatedly for their sibling. It can lead to greater resentment and open hostility as they grow older. It can serve to distance them more from the family. Working together with loving encouragement is much more effective and helps build better relationships. No one should ever feel the burden of being forced. My parents showed love toward us and helped nurture us to be Christlike in our love for one another. True service comes from the heart, a part of being who we are as children of a loving Heavenly Father.

Children need to be taught in age-appropriate ways to understand how they can help, no matter how young. Children want to feel grown up, included, and important. Hiding the truth or not allowing the sibling to help can sometimes generate feelings of fear and isolation, as they try to sort it out themselves. I began to believe that I was selfish when I wanted to do what Robert was doing with Mom and Dad, and they wouldn't let me. "This is Robert's time, not yours." Sometimes I made a fuss and was sent to my room. There were times when I did deserve to be disciplined for bad behavior.

As I grew older, I felt guilty and selfish when I wanted to play alone with my friends, but Mom wanted me to include Robert. Sometimes we did, but my friends wanted to play with me. Sometimes they left my house to play somewhere else, leaving me feeling upset and rejected.

This, of course, is usually the norm with younger siblings wanting to be included with what the older siblings are doing. The older siblings don't always want a younger brother or sister tagging along. The younger sibling feels rejected. There needs to be a balance and understanding that there will be times when both can be together, but other times apart.

Learning to get along with family members is one of the principles we are taught in our faith. The strengthening of the family unit is among some of the most important work we will do in this life and through eternity. We are sealed in Heavenly Father's holy temple for time and all eternity as husband and wife with the sacred responsibility of raising children in love and righteousness. Our children are taught to love and serve one another by following the example of our Savior, Jesus Christ. Our parents worked patiently with us over many years, even into our adulthood, sharing their testimony and reminding us of these sacred covenants and obligations.

Robert also struggled with being able to run. It wasn't until he was about five years old that the doctors discovered he had a lazy eye, which made it difficult for him to see properly. As a toddler and young child, Robert's balance was affected due to his lazy eye. Mom explained to me that he was seeing two bars on a stepstool instead of one. He put his foot on what he thought was solid and it wasn't. He fell often and became afraid of moving and being hurt, so he was cautious when he walked. Once he had surgery to correct the problem, Robert was able to coordinate his movement better, but he still had a slightly halting gait when he walked.

At home, Robert felt safe and secure among those

who loved and understood him. He never hesitated in normal conversation with any of us, unless he was startled by a sudden request or demand. Then he struggled with an answer by looking downward and not responding. This happened time and again when he was reminded to say, "Please" or "Thank you." Becoming the center of attention with a demand caused him to feel overwhelmed and not respond. He looked at the floor, just as he would when meeting someone.

I recall Dad asking, "Robert, why is it so hard for you to say these simple words? C'mon, give it a try...please...thank you." When I chimed in mimicking my father, I was reminded to let Dad do the talking. I learned to respect my parents, but just as important, not to tease my brother. Teasing someone with Asperger's Syndrome causes greater confusion, which in turn creates greater anxiety, creating a vicious circle. Each one of us wondered why he wouldn't say these two words.

Robert, as an adult, was able to explain that he had trouble pronouncing certain consonants, such as the "L" or "R" sound. When as a child he didn't know how to express this to Mom and Dad, he looked downward, not answering them. As he grew older, he began to resent Dad always reminding him. He felt that he was being commanded like a dog to be obedient. "Say PLEASE!" "Say THANK YOU!" No child likes to be commanded to do something. As a parent, it's easy to become frustrated with our children when they don't respond to our wishes. Loving patience is the key to providing a safe and secure environment. I believe it takes most of us a lifetime to learn it.

Children need to be taught in age-appropriate ways

to understand how they can help those with a disability. They can be taught to show forth greater love, and not belittle or make fun of someone who may seem different from them. People with disabilities or differences need greater love and understanding; they do not need to be made to feel like social outcasts.

During all this time, we treatcd Robert the same as any of us. We were a family and we did everything together, as most families do. We didn't focus on Robert's differences, but on his strengths. When he was older, he brought rich insight into our home with the witty things he said. He could come up with a funny joke he made up on the spur of the moment, which would make us laugh. Dad was amazed with how smart he was and commented on it often. Robert came to understand how things worked by figuring it out mostly on his own.

An example of this occurred when he was four and I was six. Both of us were waiting in a station wagon (much like an SUV, only without the seats in the back) with three other children. Their mother and ours were visiting with a less active lady of our faith in her home. The lady apparently didn't like having a bunch of children in the house, so we were instructed to wait in the car. It was only for a short time, but it seemed like hours to us and we were getting bored. The other children, whom we didn't know well, were entertaining themselves. Robert remedied the situation by teasing me. He poked his right index finger into the soft padding of the car's roof.

"Stop it!" I hissed. "You're going to poke a hole in their car!" He kept smiling at me while keeping his finger in place. After several failed attempts alternating between threatening and pleading for him to remove it, I placed my hand on his arm and pulled it down. Robert promptly poked his left index finger into the soft padding. Now I was really annoyed. Being the older sister, I was concerned that I might get in trouble if he damaged anything, since I was asked to watch him.

"No, you're going to poke a hole!" I insisted. He kept smiling with a patient grin, switching hands as I pulled one arm down and then the other. By this time, I was feeling totally frustrated and out of sorts. He was teasing me and I didn't like it! He was certainly persistent.

Although he was only four years old at the time, Robert remembered this behavior and explained to me that he wasn't teasing me, but in his mind, because he wasn't able to talk, he was communicating through his actions. He was attempting to show me that it wasn't possible to poke a hole in the padding of the car's roof by the way he was holding his finger. He was persistent because he wanted me to understand. At age four, he understood how things worked, much better than I did, as a six-year-old.

ELEMENTARY SCHOOL

When Robert turned eight years old, he was baptized by immersion, because of his desire to become a member of the Church of Jesus Christ of Latter-day Saints. He was excited about the prospect but had never gone underneath water before. Neither he nor I knew how to swim. Dad carried a fear of the water into adulthood because he had nearly drowned as a young child. Mom, who knew how to swim, worked with both of us in our neighbors' swimming pools, but to no avail; we were too fearful of letting go. She didn't push us and Dad certainly didn't.

Secretly, I was worried about how Robert would react to going underneath the water when he was baptized. I asked Dad if they should practice ahead of time going underwater in a swimming pool so Robert wouldn't be scared. I kept having a feeling he would be, because I was when I was baptized. I wasn't afraid of the sacred baptismal ordinance, just being underwater. Dad brushed my questioning off with, "Oh, he'll be fine." Often times while we were growing up, I knew something more needed to be done in advance to help Robert overcome his fear of something that lay ahead. Many times my concerns were dismissed with, "He'll be fine," but it wasn't always fine. These times needed to be addressed, perhaps more slowly, so that Robert could develop a greater confidence in what he was capable of doing.

Robert, after going under the water, came up choking. Because his foot had come up while going under, he needed to be rebaptized in order for the baptismal ordinance to be done correctly. Robert began to panic, saying, "No, I don't want to do it again." The more he resisted, the more embarrassed I became for him. Dad continued to softly reason with him as a growing uneasiness filled the room. "Please, please, PLEASE, Robert," I whispered over and over, "Don't be afraid." The room became deathly silent as Robert continued to have his meltdown. "No, no, no! I don't want to!" he kept crying over and over. It was heartbreaking and I could feel the embarrassment of others for us. I silently prayed that he could find the courage to do it again.

Dad was finally able to get him to calm down, and this time all went well. A huge sigh of relief swept the room as everyone collectively let out their breath. If only we and they could have known why Robert had been so afraid, it would have made sense. When he was an adult, Robert explained that because of his balance issues, he was terrified that he would drown the next time he went underneath the water. He was, in his mind, fighting for his life. No one should ever have to live with that kind of fear.

I had believed that my hunch was right and I wondered then, as I do today, what would have happened if Dad or Mom had worked with Robert ahead of time, getting him used to being under the water. The more conditioned a person becomes reacting with fear toward something, the worse it becomes. By confronting the fear over and over, slowly breaking it down, the trigger becomes less frightening and eventually stops. The fear is replaced with confidence. Over time, our uncle and aunt whom Robert loved and trusted were able to patiently persevere in teaching Robert how to swim. He enjoys the water more now, and is able to swim a little better with confidence.

During our elementary school years, Robert and I played a marble game which we made up by ourselves. Together we would line up rows of marbles across his bedroom floor, each marble about 3 inches apart. We sat opposite each other and took turns trying to knock out each other's rows, a marble at a time. It was fun and challenging to eliminate each other's marbles, down to the remaining few, until one remained. I had begun to notice that Robert liked things to be orderly and in patterns. This is a trait of people who have Autism/ASD.

My brother and I enjoyed making our own special plans whenever our parents informed us we would be taking a vacation trip out of state. Or at least I thought we both did. Robert recently informed me that he felt anxious when we talked of going on a trip. It wasn't part of the normal cycle he was used to living each day. I wasn't aware of his anxiety as we confided in one another. We both looked forward to visiting our grandparents, who loved us very much. I must have really encouraged him about all the fun we would have because he seemed to be in agreement with me. I helped him by sharing my excitement and making small plans ahead of time. These included what time we would get up, what clothing we would take, what we would do each day of our trip, and when we would come home. We didn't talk about all this at the same time. Instead, we focused on one or two things and then played, acting out getting up early and traveling in the car for awhile. For me this was normal fun play, but for Robert it was a diversion from receiving too much information at once. An overload can cause anxiety for my brother, and I feel that actually acting it out helped Robert to prepare and accept change in our daily summer routine. Breaking the information down, step by step, helped him understand the concepts behind the vagueness of "we're going on a vacation."

At home, we looked forward to our grandparents' visits. One time Robert showed me how to make detailed intricate cutouts of paper snowflakes he had learned about in school. He loved tracking the weather and snowfall. Our grandparents didn't have snow where they lived, so we decided to let them wake up to a snowfall inside the house. It was fun planning and anticipating covering them with lots of paper snowflakes! Robert had a sense of humor, which showed up often. We patiently made dozens and dozens of them, which Robert never seemed to grow tired of making. Once we felt we had enough (our fingers were sore from cutting), we stored them in a box. We quietly and quickly placed the paper snowflakes over our grandparents, who were sleeping on the downstairs sofa bed. Grandmother was secretly awake though, and pretended to be asleep, not wanting to spoil our fun. Our sweet grandparents loved us so dearly! They accepted Robert for who he was without judging him, showing only true love and kindness.

A funny experience occurred when Robert was looking for his pencil, a special one, because it had finally shortened to where the lead almost touched the eraser, without getting lost in the pencil sharpener. We hunted for several minutes at his urgent request that we find it. He had waited a long time for his pencil to sharpen down to this amazingly small size, and he wasn't about to lose it! We questioned him, trying to help him remember where he possibly had it last. Several more minutes had passed when he said, "Oh, I found it!"

"Where on earth was it?" Mom and I exclaimed after hunting everywhere for it. Humbly and a little embarrassed, Robert replied, "It was in my hand." He was so intent on finding his pencil that he didn't realize he had been holding it the whole time we were all looking for it! A mistake anyone can make, but what was interesting was the purpose for which Robert intended to use it. I thought he just wanted to find it because he couldn't and it was irritating him. Robert explained to me that he had planned to fit the pencil into a small toy top so it would draw designs as it was spinning. It was just the size he needed and had taken a long time to get down to its small size, which apparently worked. He has the ability to see how things work together and remembers details as though it were yesterday, things others may have long forgotten!

Robert, while in elementary school, went through a short phase where he pretended to be sick and actually missed a few days of school. He had been experiencing a few problems there, due to his Asperger's, and was uncomfortable being at school. A doctor pronounced that he couldn't find anything wrong and he was sent back to school. When Robert tried to get out of going to school, Dad, trying the best he knew how, encouraged him to go to school. "Otherwise," he said, "We'll have to take you back to the doctor." He did it in a teasing way, mentioning blood tests and needles, maybe more out of desperation. We have discovered that it isn't wise to tease children with Asperger's Syndrome. They take comments so literally; and although Dad's ploy worked during that time to keep him in school, Robert became terrified of needles, doctors, dentists, and hospitals. Dad had never meant for that to happen and felt bad about it later.

While growing up, Robert was often content to play alone in his room. He especially enjoyed his reel-to-reel tape recorder, movie projector, and phonograph (electronic equipment of the 60s and 70s). He was fascinated by the intricacies of jigsaw puzzles, math, music, and grammar. He enjoyed keeping track of weather patterns and learning how things worked.

When Robert began attending M.I.A. (Mutual Improvement Association) known now as Young Men/Young Women's activity night, he felt uncomfortable. It wasn't with the opening exercises or gospel-centered ideas, but with the scouting activities. Participating in sports, camping, or other outdoor activities didn't interest him and caused him to feel anxious due to his lack of coordination and change of schedule. The leaders were at a loss about how to include him; how to help him feel welcome and accepted with the normal activities most boys enjoy. The normal majority of scouts, boys from our ward, began to ostracize him because of their differences. Robert loved the gospel of Jesus Christ. He loved the Lord and wanted to do the things he was asked to do.

Because his interests were so polarized from theirs, and his anxiety continued to worsen, he chose not to attend these activities. How could his differences be accepted by the group? He was thought to be inactive because he quit attending Scouts. People would ask me why he wasn't coming, and I would tell them that he felt uncomfortable there. They couldn't seem to understand why it was so difficult for him. Couldn't he learn to like what they were doing? (Can all persons with disabilities be healed in this life?)

For his birthday one year, Mom bought a box of cash register paper rolls. He found satisfaction in unrolling it all over his room until it looked like a paper jungle, then re-rolling the paper back onto the spindles. He was entertained for hours because it was soothing and brought him contentment. As a child, I accepted Robert's play as not unusual. In my eyes, he was learning about how things worked. He enjoyed having kids his age come over to play, but as they grew older and became interested in sports, he didn't follow their interests and he never seemed to have a really close friend.

JUNIOR HIGH AND HIGH SCHOOL

"There goes Robert's mom! She sure comes here a lot!" I overheard this one time at the junior high school.

Due to sickness, Robert was frequently absent from school, but this time it was all legitimate. Robert feels that much of his sickness was brought on by a weakened immune system due to the overwhelming stress and anxiety he was feeling so much of the time. It has been proven that a little stress in one's life can be motivating, but an overabundance of it can contribute toward many types of illness over the years.

I was with Mom, who had come to pick up his homework. A boy was pointing at us as he mentioned this to his friend, obviously thinking it was funny. It bothered me that kids were noticing. I felt like my brother's issues were a reflection on our whole family. I felt uncomfortable and unsure of my own self worth.

"It's none of your business!" I wanted to yell, but did not. I kept it quietly hidden inside. It was times like these when I thought, "Nothing will ever change."

I felt miserable and trapped. There was no way out. I felt that there was no explanation for Robert's peculiar behavior. I felt helpless because I didn't know how to help him or deal with some of the situations that arose. Many times I felt sad and alone, like I was being judged, too. Would others think I was the same as he was because I was shy and quiet? Sometimes I wondered if this was some kind of punishment for something I had done wrong. When I felt resentment toward others, I also felt guilt. I was the "selfish" sister who was embarrassed to be seen with her brother, because she didn't want others to judge her too. I loved him, but at that time in my life, I didn't have enough confidence in myself to not let it bother me. If I happened to be nearby, I would politely but firmly tell the kids to "lay off him." (Alexis, you have also felt all this.)

"He can't help it sometimes," I'd reply in deference to their mocking. If I kept my tone even and didn't take offense, some would ask me questions about him and I would answer honestly and directly. I felt empowered when people respected what I said and took the time to listen. Sometimes I wanted to shout to the world that my brother was smart and capable and that his differences didn't matter. He just wanted to be included and accepted.

YOUNG ADULTHOOD

I became aware, especially during Robert's transition into adulthood, that loud sounds really bothered him, especially if they were sudden, startling, annoying, or shrill. It could be a loud, noisy motorcycle thundering by, the driver suddenly revving its engine. Like a sudden jolt of electricity, his reaction to a stressor launched him into a full-blown panic attack, causing both him and me to have instant anxiety. He covered his ears and moaned, "No, no, no!" rocking back and forth, often pounding his fist on whatever was handy; the floor, bed, or car door. During this time, using a soft, low voice, I helped calm him by reassuring him he was all right, repeating over and over that he was safe and everything was okay. As he became less agitated, I continued to calmly address what had happened and explain that it was not directed toward him. I had to repeat this until he finally calmed down and was able to act rationally again.

Friends and others would ask me, "What's wrong with your brother? Why does he act the way he does?"

I didn't have an answer for them. My parents had taken him to doctors, seeking an answer. Different or unusual behavior was not widely talked about in the early 60s. There were some health care professionals who believed it was the parents' fault through child-rearing, although it has been proven this is not the case. It was difficult to explain Robert's behavior to others because he wasn't mentally handicapped and he appeared normal.

Robert once told Mom, "I feel like I'm wearing an actor's mask, but I can't take it off!" He realized something was different about himself, but he didn't understand it. There wasn't a name for what Robert had and we weren't aware of anyone else with his unique set of problems. He appeared to be shy and quiet when interacting in social situations.

Robert was teased and uncomfortable enough that Mom and Dad intervened at times, excusing him from school or a Church activity, so he wouldn't have to deal with the anxiety of conforming to the normal majority. I felt that at times Mom was enabling him too much, and others in our neighborhood and Church thought my parents were spoiling him. It seemed like everyone had an opinion, but they had no idea of what it was like because they weren't living with someone who had Asperger's. How little they understood what was happening in our family life. Opinions, no matter how well intended, can be hurtful at times. In the Church setting, this should not have been happening because we were being taught to love everyone as the Savior does. Granted, each one of us makes mistakes and we are all working on overcoming our own faults and shortcomings.

Communication, greater awareness, and understanding at that time would have been helpful. Some people did understand and acted with kindness, tolerance, patience, and love toward Robert.

I worried about what effect this would have on Robert as he became an adult. I worried that he wouldn't be able to function well on his own, that he would always be dependent on my parents or me to "fix" the situation at hand. When I became an adult, I was reluctant to step in to help as often as Mom did because of my own anxiety issues. I felt that Robert was certainly intelligent enough to live alone when he became an adult, but I feared for his ability to handle stressful situations. This was where the greatest fear lay for me. I couldn't take on more than what I was already dealing with in raising my own family, as I was experiencing anxiety and depression issues too.

Our mother was a great example in helping Robert to remain calm in difficult circumstances and I learned by watching her. I learned what worked and what didn't as I interacted with my brother growing up. The Spirit we felt in our home also helped communicate to me how I could help Robert each day. Being in a close-knit family, I was sensitive to his needs, which helped me to become more patient and tender toward him. It helped me to understand those with physical and mental difficulties better. Even so, it wasn't easy, and it took time learning to become patient, to listen, understand, and show compassion for him. Many times I felt angry or out of sorts because I didn't want to listen to what he had to say. After I could remove myself from the situation or have time to think about it, I could go back and listen to him with greater understanding. Once I understood, what he was saying made sense and I knew that he was right. However difficult it was at times to do this, I could always love him as my brother, an individual of great worth in our family. Asperger's Syndrome does not define Robert, it is only a condition of this mortal earthly state. He will be completely healed at a future time and will not have to endure this through the eternities.

I discovered what Robert had through our cousin, who is a few years younger than I am. She sent me some literature regarding her own son's behavior, as I had a concern with the behavior of one of my sons. As I read, it soon became apparent to me that this sounded much more similar to my brother's issues than my son's. My parents and I, as well as Robert, were relieved to finally find a name for Robert's unusual behavior. He has suffered socially all these years, but the mystery about his behavior is diminishing now that more is being discovered about Asperger's Syndrome and Autism Spectrum Disorder. It's much easier to explain about these disorders now that I feel supported with information. I have more empathy and compassion toward Robert, others, and families who are dealing with similar issues.

When my children were young, they didn't notice that Robert was much different than anyone else, but as they grew older and entered their teen years, it was a challenge to involve them with him. They were normal teenagers, busy and involved with friends, activities, or work. It was difficult for Robert to understand why they didn't interact with him more. Robert loved being a part of my children's lives. His joy was evident whenever I saw him interacting with the neighborhood children and my own. Even as a young adult, Robert adored children who could interact with him without being critical of him, because they didn't treat him unkindly, like many adults did. He felt loved and accepted on their level. The scriptures refer to childlike love, the kind which doesn't judge, which is the pure love of Christ.

People with Asperger's want to be treated normally like anyone else. They don't want to be talked down to or belittled because they don't react to situations the same as other people. They are extremely intelligent. When others listen to what they are saying, even if it takes time, it is helpful to the person with Asperger's to be heard and understood.

ADULTHOOD

It is often difficult to talk with Robert because he will talk longer than most people do when making a point. He misses the polite social cue of when to stop. He isn't meaning to be selfish; he wants to make sure others understand what he has to say, and he may repeat it for clarification. If he dwells on the same subject too long, those in conversation with him want to move ahead, often interrupting him and switching to a different topic. It upsets him to have a sudden shift when he wants to finish what he is saying. It's difficult for him to focus on something new while he is still thinking about where he was. This can be very frustrating to others and they can quickly become annoyed with him.

On the flip side, being cut off in the middle of a sentence can actually cause him to become anxious and upset, causing him to react by saying, "I wasn't finished yet!" It helps to validate him by saying, "Okay, we're listening. Please finish what you were saying, and then we need to let Lori have a turn." This helps him to be able to make the shift by being told ahead of time what to expect. It helps him to learn the social norm that is expected of him.

It is best to name the person wanting to talk rather than to be abstract by saying, "Others want to talk too." People with Asperger's understand better when we use literal terms. If I were to name an object and say, "It's over there," while pointing, Robert wouldn't know what "it" or "over there" meant. To help him understand, I would instead say, "The paring knife you are looking for is on the kitchen table." This helps him clarify a concrete thought.

Because they take things so literally, the many idioms we use in our English language do not make sense to people with Asperger's, until they learn the actual meanings. If someone said, "Oh, save your breath!" they would interpret it literally and wonder how to do that, when what was meant was, "It's not worth bickering over." Teasing that person by saying "great!" while using sarcasm when he accidently spilled a glass of water is confusing to him. Calling them pet names, such as "Sissy" or "Stinker," can also have a confusing negative effect.

When Robert was with me and I introduced him to someone, he usually looked downward, unable to meet the person's gaze. He never looked directly at a person. When he was asked a question, it took him a long time to respond with an answer. If the silence grew uncomfortably long, I quickly intervened, answering for him. I didn't know how to respond or want to try to explain my brother's behavior to others, especially when I didn't understand it myself. I didn't want him to feel lessened or belittled; I truly wanted him to feel validated and important, but it was embarrassing for me at times.

Robert was very intelligent, but couldn't seem to connect with the expected social norm. As a child, I covered it up by saying, "He's just being shy." People readily accepted my response because he appeared shy but looked normal, and we were ready to move forward in our conversation. As a young adult, I would remain silent longer, waiting for his response. Due to the awkward pause that occurred in those situations, I felt more comfortable with him when we were alone rather than in public.

Ironically, my brother enjoys being with people and out in public. He enjoys celebrating most of the holidays and participating in outdoor celebrations, especially the 4th of July. He enjoys inviting friends and family for dinner and an evening of games. When he is relaxed, happy, and feeling safe, he acts much more normal. The difficulty lies in how others treat him when he doesn't respond the way he is expected to by society. He looks normal, but his facial expressions do not always convey the proper emotions when conversing with someone, especially when he is startled suddenly, anxious, or afraid.

We learned years later that he was missing the awareness to connect what he was feeling with what he was conveying. When he was happy, he might not have been smiling. When he was anxious, his face would manifest a silly-looking grin, one he had no control over. He had no idea he was looking that way. It appeared as though he was pulling a face when in reality he wasn't. Because of this, he was often misunderstood and mis-judged. It was frustrating and confusing to him for years because he was unaware that his emotions didn't match his facial responses. We wondered why he was acting in an unusual way, even though it was the norm for him. If he looks at himself in a mirror, then he can connect the correct facial expression with what he is feeling.

As an adult, certain things that people did, especially while we were driving, would set Robert into a panic mode because of the suddenness or aggressiveness of their actions. This could be as simple as someone cutting in too close to us and slamming on the brakes. It would take several minutes to talk Robert out of his fear, espe-cially if he were shaking and pounding his fist. It was like a knee-jerk reaction as his emotions would seize his power of reasoning. I tried during those times not to show my own anxiety because it would only make mat-ters worse, but I could feel myself shaking on the inside. If he were the one driving, I would try to calm him down by saying, "Robert, we're okay, we're all right. Calm down!" several times, until he did.

Over time, he quit driving on main busy roads. He

drives only on a few back roads when absolutely neces-sary and is mostly dependent upon others to take him places. With more drivers on the road, it has become dif-ficult for him to remain calm, even when he is a passen-ger. At times his perception of impending possible danger is so keen, it's best to tell him to close his eyes and not watch what other drivers are doing, so that he doesn't flip into panic mode. If he does, it may be necessary to pull over to the side of the road and wait until he can re-gain his composure. An increase in undesired behavior may indicate that the person's stress level has increased.

Misbehavior, such as pounding a fist, is a way of sur-viving an experience that is overwhelming or frightening. Many people without Autism/ASD, when confronted with something frightening in a movie or in real life, will close their eyes, scream, or grab someone near them for reas-surance. For the person with Autism, the feeling lasts much longer and is more terrifying. The best way to re-solve the issue is to remain calm and speak softly but firmly, breaking down the cycle until the fear dissipates.

If Mom were with us, she would talk softly, gently, keeping her voice calm and soothing, even as Robert re-peated over and over what had just happened. "I can't stand it when someone does that!" he would exclaim. "Oh! Oh! Oh! I can't stand it!" She was his anchor, his "safe" person. She could help him calm down better than anyone in our family and I am grateful she was blessed with that amazing ability. If she ever felt anxious, I was unaware of it. I would feel my own anxiety mounting and then become frustrated, because I wanted to calm down, forget about it, and move on. If I were driving, it made things worse for me, as I had to concentrate on keeping

Robert calm and not becoming distracted while driving. Once his mind was set on something, it was difficult for him to change it. When he flared up with a severe panic attack, I had to remain calm; getting upset would only worsen the situation.

When I was eleven years old, a couple moved into our ward and the wife had epilepsy. I had no idea what epilepsy was until one Sunday, when she had a seizure. I was scared and frightened by her behavior, over which she had no control. Afterwards I spoke with my parents about epilepsy. Once I understood what it was and what to expect, I was no longer frightened by it because I knew what to expect. It is the same with Autism or any other condition. Once we begin to understand someone's unusual behavior, we lose the fear and want to help support that person.

Although it helps to be tolerant of others with disabilities, I believe that hiding Asperger's from the general public serves no purpose. Once people understand a person has Asperger's or epilepsy or cancer, it can be of greater help in promoting understanding rather than judging or being fearful toward that person. Any disease, autistic disorder, an accident which disfigures, or anything which affects an individual, does not define who that person is. It is only an earthly condition that is happening to the person, not who he truly is. The Savior loves each one of us unconditionally and equally, no matter our body size, mental capacity, or outward appearance. We are precious in His sight, no matter what we are called to pass through in mortality.

A friend who has a severely autistic son explained why it is difficult for people to understand Asperger's

Syndrome. With her son, it is very obvious he has a disability. He can utter sounds, but cannot speak or use sign language. People know and accept him as someone with a disability who will never lead a normal life. With my brother, Robert, it is different. He is married, can lead a mostly normal life, but his challenges are not visible like those of my friend's son. Because his autistic traits are barely perceptible, others often misunderstand his intentions. He misses verbal and body cues. His facial expressions are involuntary. He has no idea that he is smiling when someone is angry. They take offense at this, while he wonders what he has done to provoke them. This presents a very interesting and unique situation among Church members. Because he is extremely intelligent and speaks matter-of-factly, people become irritated when they realize they are wrong, or continue to think that they are right. Robert is persistent only because he wants them to understand, not to provoke them. I learned from the time when Robert was young, he understood reasoning and logic very well and I was reluctant at times to admit that he always seemed to be right.

Robert can be fun and witty, but also easily startled and uncomfortable in new or threatening situations. He has difficulty standing up for himself, which unfortunately has caused many people to take advantage of him. When people wonder why he doesn't look them in the eye, it's because he has a sensory overload. He doesn't like to see all the movement in a face. It's much easier for him to focus on an inanimate object, which helps him to concentrate on what the person is saying.

Due to these differences, it has been difficult for Robert to hold a job. He is capable, dependable, and honest, but people misunderstand his intentions. He has been harassed, taunted, bullied, and discriminated against, all because he has a disability that is barely perceptible, that others don't understand. As his sister, it is heartbreaking for me to recall these times. People with Autism make very dependable employees. They are consistent, punctual, and very detail-oriented. They perform their jobs well.

Robert was discriminated against because he had a social disability which his employer, ironically his stake leader, couldn't accept. Even though other employees stood up for him, Robert's employer didn't exhibit kindness toward him. Robert diligently followed his supervisor's instructions, executing them to perfection. He couldn't change the fact he had Asperger's Syndrome. His employer had not originally hired him and was told that there could be a discrimination suit filed against him if he fired my brother just based on his disability. There was nothing wrong with Robert's work performance. It was hard for me to forgive this person, who was in a leadership position in the Church, but I realize he must have had issues in his own life which were troubling him. How I wish my brother could have felt loved and appreciated for what he could do. Everyone needs to feel his or her self-worth no matter what the circumstances.

In public places, such as a restaurant, when Robert expressed himself, he wasn't always understood. His voice was low and soft, and it was hard for him to make eye contact. If he couldn't make himself understood, the waiter would become impatient and ask too many questions. Too much overload at once can cause an anxiety attack. Robert, becoming anxious, would pause, and wonder the best way to respond. I would feel his anxiety, the uncomfortable pause, and speak up for him. I did this most of the time as we were growing up, and was often reminded to let him answer for himself. He was capable and smart enough, but others didn't understand that he processed things in a different way. I would become uncomfortable and want to protect him and myself from further unpleasantness.

MY PERSONAL CONCERNS

As a young child, and even into adulthood, I felt the heavy load of responsibility to set a good example and to make my brother happy. Because I was the oldest, Mom reminded me of this often. I didn't know how to make him happy, especially after I was married and had many responsibilities of my own. I even began to wonder if I had the right to be happy, since he struggled so much. (Sarah and Alexis, you have indicated you have also felt this.)

"Why should I have, when he cannot?" I often asked myself, yet I knew that this kind of thinking was wrong. I had my own set of problems to deal with, learn from, and grow.

Once I was married, I was concerned about having a healthy marriage relationship, should the need arise for him to live with us. As an adult, his needs and demands were much stronger than as a child. His panic attack episodes when he lived alone were terrifying for me to hear about, either from him or my parents. His fear and anxiety seemed to be growing worse and more frequent.

An autistic person is not trying to manipulate, but is

egocentric. How could I balance his needs and my family's needs? How would it affect my children? The list of worries was endless and I didn't have an answer, only deep-seated guilt, feeling torn between my responsibilities of raising my family and helping him with his needs. Dad and Mom were getting older and it was harder for them to help him through the rough times he was experiencing. I tried to comfort him by talking with him on the phone for an hour or more at a time when he was experiencing overwhelming anxieties. It involved our talking over and over about the same fear, what he could do to calm down, and encouraging him to not give up. It was a heavy weight in both our lives, but we both continued to pray, show faith, and ask for help from a loving Heavenly Father.

As I raised my family, I often struggled to maintain a balance with my family, work, and health. We had a son diagnosed with leukemia at a tender young age, and I developed the onset of a painful health condition. Both of these caused me to have intense emotional and physical pain. At times, I could barely cope with my own life's challenges. In addition to these, I felt concerned about how I could help my brother cope in a normal world when his senses were ultrasensitive. I could not change the world, make it fit according to his needs, but I could help him understand ways to help him cope on hard days, by listening, encouraging, and giving advice. Just knowing that he had a "support person" he could turn to was helpful for him.

One time, I decided to make a change in my family's plans to accommodate Robert. It was advantageous for him, but not for my three married children. They were unable to participate, but wanted me to follow through with my plans. I soon discovered that I couldn't please everyone, especially when there were so many variables. I felt pressured trying to help my children understand my brother's needs, while meeting my mother's wishes, when they had their own lives and commitments. I was afraid to explain it to Robert because I didn't want to hurt his feelings. As it turned out, only he, my husband, and I got together. We had a fun time, but it would have been more fun with everyone there too. If I hadn't changed the time, then all my children would have been able to come as planned, but Robert would have felt left out. I love them all and didn't want to have to make a choice like that. I have since learned that it is best to make a plan and whoever can come that day is welcome; no regrets for those who can't make it. Life is always changing and moving, which is difficult for people with Autism to bear, as they like things to remain the same predictable way.

Robert often refers with fondness to the way things used to be while he was growing up. He compares the present to the past and feels safer living in an environment which reminds him of those times. It helps him to have many of our parents' things as a source of comfort, drawing them near, now that they have both passed on to the other side of the veil. It is a connection to the past of when he was young and felt secure in our loving home environment.

Mom would express concern for Robert when things didn't work out as planned and wondered when and if we might be able to make it up to him. There were many times when I felt that her concern and loving devotion for my brother overshadowed everything else. I felt the pressure of falling short, that I wasn't good enough, caring enough, and capable enough. She meant well and was concerned, always watching out for his best interest, loving as only a mother can. In time, I discovered I was putting too much pressure on myself to be a perfect mother, sister, and wife. Sometimes I just wanted to blurt out, "No, I'm sorry. I can't do this anymore!" without feeling the repercussion of guilt I heaped upon myself. At that time, I felt like I was running on a treadmill, but couldn't get off. I needed nurturing too. I didn't know how to show love to myself by setting boundaries. I was too busy running around putting out everyone else's fires, but not my own.

It was and is hard to plan on getting together only to have our plans fall through and then to see him be disappointed. I have learned over time to plan on a specific date to meet, but also remind him that it is contingent upon how I am feeling physically. If I am able to come, I will. If I can't, then we will reschedule. This helps me not to worry so intensely about letting Robert down, and it helps Robert to know that he can readjust his schedule too.

It is times like these when we need to step back and take a good look at ourselves and slow down. Our Savior's atonement is for everyone, lovingly given, as a gift to help us through this life and to return to our Heavenly Father's waiting arms. He doesn't expect us to run faster than we have strength, or do more than we can physically or emotionally handle. He wants us to place our trust in Him, and our Savior, Jesus Christ, to help us along the way. Our loving Heavenly Father will open ways for us and others that we may also experience joy in this life.

(This is very important for both of you, Sarah and Alexis.)

Robert met the woman of his dreams and was sealed in the temple for time and all eternity. They have built a special relationship, and they've been keen on helping each to grow and learn. Dad and Mom always kept the faith that one day Robert would find an eternal companion who loved him and whom he would love. The Lord has blessed them both in wondrous ways as they leaned on each other for support and strength. They have been able to serve as temple workers and found great joy and peace in doing so.

Although I was not always available to physically help him, I desired Robert's wellbeing and happiness, but I couldn't keep him happy all the time. Where did my responsibility for him begin and where did it end? I have had a difficult time defining where the boundaries should be, but I am learning that he is capable of caring for himself and that he is in good hands. He is moving forward in communicating and has been married to a beautiful, supportive wife. They have also had the support of close friends and neighbors. The Lord is providing ways for Robert to learn and grow in his earthly and eternal progression.

My mother, not knowing what condition Robert had, was inspired to help him as only a mother can. I am sure she felt the same overwhelming feelings of childrearing that I did at times. She had a heavenly connection and it came naturally to her to rely upon a loving Heavenly Father. She received counsel and inspiration through daily prayer. She was concerned as any parent would be about what would happen to Robert as an adult, especially when she could no longer physically care for him. She was also concerned about how he would be able to act on his own as she remembered the time he was living away from home.

THE CHOICES OF OTHERS

One of his Church leaders in the ward where Robert resided in his early adulthood thought Robert was intelligent enough to "overcome" his autistic behavioral tendencies. He was not tolerant of Robert's unusual behavior and didn't understand that Robert was experiencing full-blown panic attacks. Rather than listening and understanding, it was easier to ignore it. Each leader is different and each struggles with his own problems. For this good brother, it was difficult for him to know what to do or how to handle this unique situation when Robert resided in this ward. Perhaps it is possible to learn how to change certain responses, but to me, telling a person with Asperger's not to react is like telling someone with epilepsy not to have seizures.

There is so much we don't understand yet about Autism Spectrum Disorder, what causes it, and how to effectively treat it. As more children are being diagnosed with this disorder, I believe people's awareness and understanding will also grow. Early intervention seems to help a child diagnosed with Autism move forward better than one who doesn't receive this support. This includes special therapy programs parents can do at home on a daily basis. Education, patience, and understanding are the keys to moving forward in embracing our differences.

High functioning persons with Autism need to be a part of the community to learn how others act by watching and interacting with them. If it is possible for them to explain what they are feeling and others are willing to listen, it can be a breakthrough for both. Some people experiencing Autism want to be alone, but others do not. When in the company of loving understanding people, where that person feels safe, that person has a better chance of living a relatively normal life. Asperger's awareness needs to grow. When we begin to understand what they are experiencing and seeing, it can be quite amazing and enlightening.

On an intellectual level, Robert was way above average, but on a social level, he was childlike and innocent. Especially when he was living alone, it was the unkind remarks of others which caused him much emotional pain and sadness. It hurt me when others made accusations of things he would never do. When people don't understand a disability, they can be quick to assume the worst when in reality it isn't true at all.

A few times it got so bad that Dad had to intervene on Robert's behalf because Robert couldn't handle the anger and yelling of others at him. When Dad tried to explain the problems Robert was dealing with, he was met with anger and criticism. I knew my brother far better than anyone outside our family. At this time, it caused me to feel hostility and resentment toward the unkindness of others. I came to realize that they were unaware, oblivious, or disinterested. These were the people with whom Robert associated on Sunday in Church. Robert continued to remain faithful, attending his and other wards, even when he felt unwelcome.

These were good people who didn't understand Asperger's. They were quick to assume, judge, or not accept differences. They didn't understand that sudden loud noises would send him into a frenzy of anxiety, causing odd undesired behavior. They didn't understand that they needed to speak with him calmly, not in angry confrontation, which would only make matters worse. They needed to be patient listeners, letting him express why what had just happened was having an effect on him.

It would have been better if they could have been patient, learning empathy and understanding. We each have our own weaknesses to overcome in this earthly probation. None of us is perfect and I do not condemn them; I only wish they could have understood him better and been more sensitive to his needs. We had hoped that Robert would have an enjoyable life away from home, learning to become independent, but he was having a difficult time adjusting to being alone.

WHAT CAN BE DONE?

"I'm sorry, I didn't realize the loud and sudden noise I made caused you to have anxiety. I will be aware of it in the future. What can I do to help? Are you all right now?"

These are words of comfort and kindness that could have been used when Robert pounded on the wall of his condo, reacting with overwhelming fear to a sudden disturbing noise. Kind words are what are needed in today's world, especially with this disorder on the rise. There is such a wide variety of symptoms and behaviors in the

Autism Spectrum Disorder that there is no set rule for persons suffering from this. Each individual with Asperger's Syndrome has similarities and differences, a special uniqueness, that is his or hers alone. Robert feels that there are so many differences with Asperger's Syndrome that it should be called "The Asperger's Spectrum Disorder within the Autism Spectrum Disorder." Because each individual suffering with Autism is different, it is difficult to treat this with medication. What may help one person may not help another.

Mom, as a loving mother, always wanted Robert to be happy, as Dad and I did. As I grew older, I realized I wasn't responsible for Robert's happiness and I felt bad for him when he was teased. I was also teased, but for different reasons. I knew how it felt to be teased or laughed at for no particular reason. It's easy to want to avoid others by not having to confront them, as Robert was inclined to do by staying home from school and sadly, Church activities. It's important for us as adults to teach our children at a young age to respect differences, no matter what they may be. It helps to explain in simple terms to be kind and loving to others, especially those with disabilities. Children are careful observers of their parents. We, as adults, with the greater responsibility, need to set an example of goodness and love. How do we treat others?

Robert's self-confidence was lessened many times when he was bullied or teased. I wasn't always around to defend him. There was a time when a friend of my brother's friend noticed a cookbook on the floor of Robert's bedroom. He exclaimed, "You like to cook? That's for girls, sissies!" (At that time, gender roles were much more defined as feminine or masculine.) It was years before my brother picked up another cookbook. He refused to cook or look at a cookbook because of the pain he carried from this single remark. He has come a long way since then, and in fact, is quite talented with preparing delicious meals. I was happy and relieved when Robert found friends who played with him and didn't judge him harshly. I felt like I was always justifying his behavior to others, by defending it, to validate him and myself.

When problems arose and Robert needed support if his wife were not home, he could call me and we could talk about what he was experiencing. He has learned how to cope with new situations such as when his wife was in the hospital for several days. It was difficult for him to be alone at home because of the anxiety he was feeling for her. We talked about what he could do to fill his time and not let despair get the best of him. I reminded him to do what he has always done, and that is to put his faith and trust in Heavenly Father and our Savior, Jesus Christ. Then I reminded him of very specific things he could do to invite the Spirit to lend him comfort and strength. It's difficult when anyone experiences severe anxiety, and I understand how crippling it can be.

There are programs and medications that can help with controlling anxiety; however, a person with Autism may have a difficult time with a full dose of medication due to his condition. This should be discussed with a medical professional, as each individual responds differently to medications. A friend has discovered that a quarter dose of a certain medication has helped her severely autistic son remain much calmer without adverse side effects.

Now that I am a parent, I can see more clearly how a mother loves her children, especially the sick one or the one who has a difficult time fitting in with friends. I believe that Dad and I didn't fully understand Robert's differences, especially when he was a child. Mom seemed to have the greatest awareness of how to help him. Only now, as I talk with my brother, who has progressed in communicating what he is feeling and why, do I have more of the answers.

How I wish we could have understood Robert's perception while he was young! We are sharing these experiences with the hope they may be of help to others. We shared struggles as a family, but we also shared joy.

"We hope that you, Ethan, and also you, Alexis and Sarah, may gain some more insight about Asperger's, and also some insight into the life of someone you know who has Asperger's Syndrome."

Dad would come home from a long day at work and want to work outside in the yard to unwind. Yardwork and landscaping were his passions. Mom would be sympathetic with Robert's needs and mine during the day, and be exhausted by evening. She needed a break, but there was no one outside the family who would understand her concerns about Robert. There were no organized therapy or support groups that dealt with this type of situation. I applaud her for continuing on day after day, finding the strength to raise us and the courage to stand firm in her support of Robert. It took a lot of dedication, love, and determination to not give up, no matter what others said or believed, even within our own family.

Mom and Dad had a heavy load to carry, dealing with many of Robert's emotional issues as he reached adulthood. At one point in his life he was desperately depressed, wondering what purpose there was in living life alone with Asperger's. There wasn't an easy answer, but we continued to rely upon the Lord and His goodness for strength and guidance. Robert was given many priesthood blessings as he too, moved forward with faith.

MARRIED LIFE

Robert has been blessed with a special woman in his life and is happily married. She has helped him in many ways, and I have watched him grow and learn more socially than I thought he was capable. He is blessing us with a precious gift by being able to explain what he is feeling and perceiving as a person living with Asperger's Syndrome/ASD.

It's interesting to me that Robert's view of my world is that it is harsh. He explained to me that his world is not one of harshness. He thought everyone perceived the world and normalcy as he did. One of the things that set us apart was our perception. With Asperger's Syndrome, Robert felt comfortable with constancy, not with change. Change was difficult for him, such as making impromptu spur-of-the-moment plans. Robert would respond, "Hold on, wait a minute, I thought we were going to do this...now we are talking about something else and I don't understand!" It was disturbing to him when we changed plans midstream in a conversation and it caused him to have a physical reaction of shaking his hands, which he is now able to control better.

His wife has been a source of strength and comfort as

she has taught him how to understand socially. This isn't always easy, and has been a long, slow process, but they've been progressing together well. People with Autism feel comfortable with consistency, safe places, safe people, and predictability.

Since Robert has been married, he and his wife have seen some remarkable changes take place in him. A big factor that has contributed to his progress is related to her listening to him. If she felt too frustrated, then she would take a timeout from the situation. When she felt calm again and returned, he would explain what he was feeling and experiencing. Then she could explain how she viewed the situation differently. This has helped Robert to understand both sides.

Over the years, I truly yearned for Robert to be like the normal majority, and normal for me meant to get married, raise a family, have fun relationships with others, and to have what I had. He has always been extremely intelligent. He has great spiritual strength and knowledge. He understands things that many people do not. He has always been very spiritually sensitive and finds it extremely difficult to be around swearing, evil-speaking, raised voices, or emotional upheaval. He can remember many details about years when he was growing up.

It is impressive that he was able to serve a mission for the Church in a foreign country, given the circumstances of what he was experiencing. I know that the Lord truly blessed him and helped him during that time. When the time approached that most young men his age were already serving missions, people began asking me, "When is your brother going to serve a mission?" I knew socially he wasn't ready to serve at 19, the normal time most young men from the Church were called to serve a mission for the Lord at that time. I didn't feel comfortable explaining all my brother's issues. The one time I did attempt to explain it, the person was totally oblivious to what I was saying. I lost his attention several seconds into my explanation, as he was already formulating what he wanted to say. After we finished talking, I consoled myself.

"After all," I thought, "It's none of his business what my brother does." After a while, I simply said, "He'll go when he's ready!" This answer seemed to satisfy people's expectations and curiosity.

When the time was right, he did, but not without reservations from his stake leader. Dad expressed his faith in the Lord and in Robert, that Robert could serve a mission and should be given the opportunity to serve the Lord, as it was his desire. The stake leader was finally convinced, and Robert received his call to serve in a Spanish-speaking country. He was loved and appreciated by the people there who were of humble means, great pillars of love and spiritual strength. Through serving his mission, Robert grew spiritually and socially, helping many people "to come unto Christ and be baptized." He was blessed by the Lord to persevere, in spite of any problems he faced while there.

My brother has emotional feelings and awareness. He knows that he has something that sets him apart from others. He is concerned about what others think of him. He also cares deeply and is concerned for others. He enjoys being around people in certain settings, in others he fears people's criticism and responses. When people get

to know him well, they are impressed with his intellectual capabilities and his genuine caring spirit. They understand and accept him as different, but totally capable,
intelligent, gentle, and caring. They are his friends who
can look past the surface and see and love the real Robert.

CONCLUSION

"These words are given only from my perspective to
help all of you gain a better understanding of Asperger's
Syndrome, and how it affected our family's dynamics.
These are totally my own opinions from what I have
learned and experienced over the years associating with
my brother and others with disabilities."

Those in a family that include someone with Asperger's Syndrome should realize that he or she is loved,
that nothing you did caused your family member to have
this disability, and that you don't need to feel at any time
that you are not enough. You are here to help, but not
enable. You are their cheering section, their support. You
are not alone. Don't be afraid to share your story and
reach out to others.

The more people can learn about these amazing differences, the more assets we will discover in working together. Being able to share experiences and talk with
others who understand Asperger's is both informative
and comforting. Joining a support group, going to counseling, especially if the counselor understands the dynamics of Asperger's/ASD, and sharing what you know
with others is a great way to be supportive in your com-

munity and on an individual basis. Their family will thank you too.

Now that Autism Spectrum Disorder is on the rise, we are hopeful that more people can become familiar with its behavioral challenges and learn how to respond in positive ways. We hope that through this information, we can convey the importance of early intervention, treating people with Asperger's with kindness, love, and patience. Learn to listen, watch for anxiety triggers, be attentive to their needs, give them encouragement, and know that they too are precious sons and daughters of our Heavenly Father. We are all in this life together to learn how to get along with one another, to accept our differences, magnify our strengths, serve one another, love each other, and return home to our Heavenly Parents with honor.

"Thank you, Susan. The messages that follow, written by three wonderful people, will also give important insight for you, Ethan, and for your family. First, my wife, Jeanene, has written this inspirational message to all who are struggling with challenges in this life, showing how the Lord can help us, no matter what our present situation may be. She wrote this a few years ago, during some happy times in our married life."

My sweet wife's wonderful assistance

CHAPTER SIX
ROBERT AND JEANENE'S
SPECIAL LIFE AND JOURNEY TOGETHER

Years ago, I, Jeanene, went to my bishop when I had been having a very hard time in life and just wanted to give up! He slapped his hand down on his desk and said that there was a very special man "waiting for me with his arms wide open, and it wasn't the Savior!" That helped me feel hope, that Heavenly Father loves me and there was a special man waiting for me, to share our lives together.

At the time, I was living in Oregon and had been reconnected to my half-sister over the phone, after being split up when Jennie was only a baby, when our birth mother died. I was eight at the time that we were separated. I drove to Oklahoma to go see her. As I was traveling south in California, and went east to Oklahoma, I looked north towards Utah, and wondered if that special man was still waiting for me? I had decided after months of talking on the phone to my half-sister, Jennie, I'd go back and rent their trailer. Jennie said it would be fine. Jennie and her husband, Dan, had just built a home. When I got back there, I was told that Dan wanted to sell the trailer that I was going to rent. I didn't feel like that was going to be my home out in Oklahoma, which made me really sad.

I got on my knees and prayed. I asked Heavenly Father where I was supposed to be. I was told very clearly, "Utah!" I said, "Utah" out loud and looked up as I said it again! I packed my van; it was winter. I said a prayer and off I went. I don't know what I was thinking, moving so far from a temple.

I had been emailing a friend in Oregon named Julie; she had a friend also named Julie in Orem, Utah. She invited me to stay in Orem with her. I got a job in Orem and wanted to be close to my job. I met a person who had rooms for rent in an apartment. I felt very prompted to fill out the renter's agreement, but felt inspired to ask if he had any other places. He said, as a matter of fact, there is a downstairs apartment right across from a stake center in Provo. This is where I was guided to meet Robert.

MEETING ROBERT

As Heavenly Father was guiding me to Robert through many prayers of a righteous daughter of Heavenly Father, it was then that Mary, Robert's mother, also went to Heavenly Father in prayer. Mary and Ralph, her husband, were getting older and were worried that Robert, their son, needed a wife so he could progress. He was in his 40s when we met.

Robert loved family history, and so did I. Robert and I were in different wards. He really felt like he would meet that special mate if he spent time at the Family History Center and continued being a baptizer at the Provo Temple. I was called in my ward to help as a Family History Consultant at the FHC. That is where Robert and I met on this earth. He greeted me and welcomed me there. I told him my name and explained why I was there. He started teaching me about the various sites for Family History work, to connect families together forever. Robert's mother was there also. She loved putting her family history together, with him helping her.

I had some training in this as well, but Robert had so much knowledge and was very gentle and kind with me. As I kept going there, he was very kind and helpful! We were both single and I was emailing some guys on singles' sites, and going to singles' dances. One day, while at my computer, the Spirit told me to stop emailing these guys. I also felt like I didn't need to go out to the singles' activities any longer. I turned my computer chair around from the west to face east. The Spirit said, "What about Robert?" I looked up and said, "What about Robert." I called the FHC and Robert answered. I talked with him a few minutes. He asked me to have family home evening with him and said he would make us some homemade bread. We had a wonderful time. I was excited to have someone in the gospel with whom to share family home evening. I felt happy and joyful inside my heart. I didn't notice him having any Asperger's symptoms at all. The bread was very good! He was so kind, a real gentleman!

We started going to the Provo Temple together.

Robert took me to the stake Pioneer Day celebration right across from where I lived. They had all kinds of good food. When over at Robert's condo, he asked me what I wanted to eat. He opened the freezer and showed me TV dinners. He said, "Would you like chicken, chicken, or chicken?" We still laugh about it now, years later.

One day, before we were married, while Robert and I were at the Family History Center, we ordered a chicken garlic pizza to eat because we didn't want to leave. Later, he and I started talking and talking until 2 a.m. It had started raining. I was in the van and Robert was standing outside. I was so engaged in the conversation, I didn't even think about inviting him to come in and sit in the van while we talked. We had very important things to talk about. I felt very comfortable talking to him. I felt like I could share almost anything with him. I was telling him about my life. He said it doesn't matter where you are on the path, it matters which direction you are headed. I felt peace and comfort, that Robert accepted me for me, and he wasn't judgmental.

OUR LIFE TOGETHER

Robert has Asperger's and PTSD. I have Bipolar Disorder and PTSD, so we are quite the team! We each have a great sense of humor, so we laugh a lot. We play Uno and Skip-Bo games often. This really brings out our personalities. We laugh at each other about what is going on in the games and what we are doing about it. Sometimes we get frustrated how the cards are playing out.

Robert's thinking is literal, which means he means exactly what he says—it's solid and concrete. You don't have to read between the lines with him. It is really good for others who are around people with Asperger's to believe what they say. They say exactly what they mean. Robert doesn't always get the nonverbals, so I need to tell him how I'm feeling in words. Over the years of being married to him, I wish I could have understood his way of thinking more clearly. He has a pure heart and mind, and wouldn't hurt anyone. Due to my Bipolar, I sometimes misunderstood over the years what Robert was saying. Sometimes we needed to start saying the thought over. One thing that really helps is to ask questions, or "Could you please tell me again."

We have been going to counseling. We found this counselor, Heidi, with the Lord's help. She understands both of us with her training and schooling over the years. She is really helping us understand each other. She gives us examples of why Robert does what he does. When he gets upset, he grabs his hands and pulls on them. He also will grab the seatbelt and pull down on it if a car goes fast around us or honks at us. He may raise his voice or slap the dash in the van.

Our counselor also talks about my having the fight or flight. I will speak loudly or just run away to another area. Since I have been going to her, I think things out or get really quiet. Sometimes Catherine, a good friend, will go to town with me and we talk about ideas to help me help Robert. When Robert starts to have a panic attack, if I'm able, I can hug him. I'll say, "Robert, it's all right, nothing is going to hurt you," or I will say, "Why don't you close your eyes or look up at the mountains." That helps him.

Robert and I have had many good years getting to know each other. Now our lives are so much better because we can communicate, listen to each other, and trust each other fully. One thing that helps Robert understand when I'm talking is I use more nouns, names of people, places, and things, and I complete my thoughts. It is better to never use words like "over there" or "things," because it doesn't make sense to people who have Asperger's.

Robert has a great sense of humor, but does not always understand sarcasm. When others are talking around him, fun thoughts or jokes will come up and he loves to share them. He is very brilliant and intelligent. It's like living with a dictionary/encyclopedia. This is great, but can be difficult at times because he seems to know everything and wants me to also know what he knows. I just get overwhelmed to try to process all of it in my brain. I try to be understanding and calm, and sometimes I try to change the subject. Or I say, "I really need to take a nap."

At first, when I asked him to dance with me at home or in our business, he felt uncomfortable. Now he encourages me to dance with him, which helps us stay bonded. He was not as familiar with physical affection. He also loves to have his schedule, but allows me my own.

Throughout the years, whenever Robert and I have been around aggressiveness or bad language, or even when I raise my voice, it would cause him emotional overload. The situation would need to stop, or he would have to leave the area. Sometimes he gets upset at raised voices, even when people are not angry. Robert is doing much better in traffic, but for years it was overwhelming for him, and sometimes it still is. He has very sensitive hearing. Sometimes when I am chewing food or gum, it bothers him. The smell of some gum can really bother him. Many times for those who have Asperger's, when they get something in their minds, they do not want to change it, until they truly understand the need for the other person.

We are living in the country now and there are not any part-time jobs we might be able to do to make some extra money. We live on a half acre in a house with two levels. Since we have been married, we have moved three times. Looking back, sometimes I wish we would have stayed where we were. Our first move was to a larger condo. The owner at the time said it was really quiet, which was not the case. We moved so Robert could have a transcription job at home where it was quiet. The second move was so we could have a business and bake bread. We had two kitchens there. Each time we thought it was our last, so we made it our own with colors, etc. For the third move, we moved to the country where we can sit outside in our backyard, and look up and see the wonderful universe God made for us to enjoy! We continued our bread business, making other bakery items along with pizzas and hamburgers. Robert did a good job making food with special sauces in our business, but was a bit slow. He wanted every food item perfect, which slowed him down. He was good at greeting the customers, and working the credit card machine and cash register.

SPIRITUALITY

Heavenly Father guided each of us so we could find each other. We both love Heavenly Father and Jesus Christ and the Holy Ghost, who help us in our lives! We both love spiritual stories and going to the temple. Robert and I have spent many hours in the temple. We sit in a special room there, praying and listening for the Spirit to guide us. We talk softly to each other sometimes. I'll lay my head on his shoulder. I feel comfortable, safe, and content in the temple, sitting on the white couch next to Robert. He and I have had many spiritual thoughts and feelings while there. We have sealed many families together.

Robert loves to read the scriptures and our lessons on the prophets to me. Praying, reading the scriptures, and having blessings have caused us to become closer. I have not ever been totally connected spiritually, mentally, emotionally, socially, and physically before in my life, except when Heavenly Father guided me to Robert. I know He guided us each step of the way, through the Spirit. Robert is very close to the Spirit and wants to honor God in all he does.

He cannot understand why others struggle with addiction. It just isn't logical at all. He wonders why or how that could be.

Sometimes it really bothers me when others aren't willing to listen to Robert or get to know him. He is very sensitive. He loves Heavenly Father's children, young and old, and has a lot of wonderful knowledge to share with others. He also has much spirituality within him, where he enjoys showing happiness and joy in this world. I wish people would stop and take the time to listen to what Robert says. He is thoughtful with our sons and grand-children, who were here as part of my family before I met Robert. He talks to them and then listens to them. They love their Dad and Grandpa!

Robert and I have been serving in our current temple for the last couple of years. We have truly loved being in the House of the Lord. We have had many wonderful spiritual experiences there, and have become friends with these wonderful saints. When Robert served previously at the temple, he was basically working in one area. Now that we are at our present temple, he does all the ordinances. I'm really proud of him!

My wonderful husband has taught me to stay calm and talk about many parts of life, rather than being frustrated. It takes time, one step at a time. Sometimes we just sit close and watch a movie together. We take walks, and we both love being in the temple. It brings great peace to our whole beings. We both need each other, to walk beside each other and to hold hands. We comfort each other and learn through the Spirit how to communicate. We need to be willing to let go and trust Heavenly Father, and pray that He will help us through anything.

Many times I have seen who Robert is becoming, but not totally. Heavenly Father has allowed me to see who Robert is because I needed that help. Just by listening to each other, over time we are doing so much better. We are putting each other's needs before our own. Trusting in Heavenly Father is the key!

"Jeanene surely has a wonderful way of expressing what is truly important and what is everlasting for us. During this part of our journey, you can all see how our Savior's hand is involved, and can be involved in each of our lives. You see how our Savior loves us and helps us in our lives each day. Let's continue on our journey together as I share some important insights from two close friends, Heidi and Catherine, who have written their messages to help you and other people with disorders."

perspectives from our counselor
and another close friend

CHAPTER SEVEN
MERCURY AND JUPITER
Heidi K. Rodriguez, LCSW

I first met Robert and Jeanene in 2013. Jeanene came into my office seeking treatment for a mood disorder compounded by PTSD related to an extensive history of trauma and abuse as a child, teen, and young adult. After sharing some of her personal history, Jeanene asked that I meet with her husband as well, who was waiting in the lobby. As she returned to the office with Robert, he appeared cautious and somewhat uncomfortable. Jeanene went on to explain that while she struggled with Bipolar Disorder and PTSD, her husband had been diagnosed with Asperger's Disorder with some history of related mood and PTSD issues as well. They then proceeded to tell me the story of how they met and how they strongly believed that Heavenly Father had led them to one another. As they each shared their belief that they were meant for one another, I remember thinking, "Well, God definitely has a sense of humor!" After working as a therapist for over 25 years, having had significant experience with these issues, I knew this would be an interesting challenge.

Over the next several months, these two began to both impress and humble me on numerous occasions. One of the first things I noticed was how often when Jeanene was feeling emotionally distraught and Robert was feeling overwhelmed by all of her emotion, they would both step back from the situation and turn to their Heavenly Father. Their strong faith repeatedly helped them to overcome seemingly unmanageable challenges. When Jeanene wanted to run away and Robert just wanted to hide out, they would each turn to prayer until they were eventually able to work it out. As I learned more of their history, it became apparent that their faith was a major factor in helping them stay together over the years. Their Church and Temple attendance were major levelers in the relationship. It was this mutual love and spiritual faith which eventually allowed them to move from a place of opposition to a place where they were increasingly able to balance and complement one another. This spirituality was particularly apparent to me following the death of Robert's father in 2013. Robert's mother had preceded his father in death, making Robert an adult "orphan" of sorts. After years of unconditional love and support from his parents, he was left bereft without their physical presence in his life. However, his sweet parents were very much a spiritual presence for several weeks and even months after their passing. It was during that time that I began to truly get a glimpse of who Robert really is, and of how much he was loved by those who had passed on the other side. These glimpses into his eternal nature were truly precious and humbling for me, both as a therapist and as a person.

All of that is not to say it was easy. Many of Jeanene's issues would trigger Robert's issues and vice versa. In a myriad of areas they were at opposite ends of the spectrum, particularly when it came to emotional challenges. They had different ways of perceiving and dealing with the world, which made it particularly difficult for them at times. Communication patterns were a major factor as well. We sometimes joked that instead of their being from Venus and Mars (as the saying goes), they were from Mercury and Jupiter! Yet through it all, I continued to see their mutual love, trust, respect, and constant commitment to one another and to their faith. Having worked with other individuals with Asperger's, I was aware that many do not marry. Of those who do find spouses, they often have difficulty maintaining long-term relationships. I began to see the uniqueness of their relationships and the ways they could potentially help others dealing with the challenges of Asperger's Disorder/Autism Spectrum Disorder (or ASD). During our time together, I was also able to meet with Robert's sister and with a mutual friend. I realized how helpful these unique perspectives could be as well, especially for others who had friends and family members struggling with similar issues.

ASPERGER'S CHARACTERISTICS

One of the most important parts of their family therapy was ongoing education about the symptoms of Asperger's Disorder (ASD). Most individuals with Asperger's have above average intelligence, but may have difficulty with empathy or understanding another person's point of view. They often have particular difficulty in social situations and many Asperger's adults have experienced some history of bullying by peers. Individuals with Asperger's often have difficulty understanding nonverbal communication and tend to have poor eye contact, which may be misinterpreted by others. They may have difficulty expressing and dealing with emotions and can become easily overwhelmed as a result. They tend to prefer strict routines and feel a high level of anxiety regarding change or uncertainty. People with Asperger's are easily overstimulated by sights and sounds, thus making it particularly difficult for them to deal with large crowds, traffic, or with the public in general. They tend to be concrete and literal in their thinking patterns, with a highly visual (as opposed to verbal) view of the world. People with Asperger's are sometimes mistakenly perceived as being cold or unfeeling, when in fact they are quite sensitive and often lonely. They tend to be blunt and factual, which can be misinterpreted as being rude or insensitive when this is absolutely not their intention.

In discussing the special challenges of Asperger's, it is equally important to point out the strengths and gifts which can come with it as well. For example, Robert has an amazing ability to sense who is trustworthy and who is not. He was given a strong sense of discernment, which has been a great help to him and to those closest to him. He remains clear on what he believes and is not swayed by "peer pressure" or public opinion. Even as an

adolescent and young adult, he was never tempted to ex-
periment with drugs, alcohol, or anything with the potential for harm or addiction. Robert is completely genuine. He is one of the few individuals I have met who is
"without guile." He simply lives his integrity without
question. He is very sensitive to all things spiritual and
will not abide anything dark or angry. He simply cannot
be around it. Robert has gifts in meteorology and genealogy, as well as in other areas of science and math. Like
many individuals with this disorder, he is excellent with
numbers. His IQ is above average, yet he does not believe
he is "above" anyone. Robert is loyal, kind, and a truly
gentle soul. While he is sometimes misunderstood, he
does not judge others. It's easy for him to differentiate
the person from the behavior—although he does not always understand why people sometimes do the things
they do. He does not question his faith. For him, it is
simply a fact and an eternal truth.

It has been an honor getting to know both Robert and
Jeanene. It is my hope that their story will help others in
their personal journeys as well.

"What our therapist, Heidi has presented here has
been enlightening to many of you during our journey together, along with you, Ethan, and your family. Here is
some information from Catherine, a close family friend
who gives all of you her own personal perspective of observing a person with Asperger's. Additionally, Heidi will
offer more solutions to problems we all face, as we continue on this great journey."

CHAPTER EIGHT
MY DEAREST FRIENDS

A VERY CLOSE FRIEND'S ASSOCIATION
WITH ROBERT AND JEANENE

I, Catherine, am a very good friend to Jeanene and Robert. I have known them for over five years. I have had close personal contact with them, seeing them on many occasions. Therefore, they have asked me to state my opinion of their lives and the strides Robert has made to overcome Asperger's Syndrome.

"So I gladly write this to all of you who have Asperger's Syndrome, for I have seen great growth in the short time I have known this couple."

They are very good for one another, for Jeanene has had many upheavals in her life, and Robert says she has come out of the storm and is safe now, for he trusts in a Supreme power, even a power greater than his own to direct his path.

The thing I have observed most often is his sense of right and wrong. His thoughts are straight as a die, and he does not deviate from his devotion to principles of personal purity and devotion to the precepts of the Church. In other words, there is no gray area in his thinking between truth and error. Robert knows what he has been taught and what his truths are, and he does not deviate sideways. Once, I said to him that his Asperger's Syndrome is to be studied, not pitied. I still feel that the way for a person to stick to his way of living is very commendable, and the only way to change is for his higher power, even a power greater than himself, to change his mind.

I really am impressed with his senses and abilities being heightened, because he is lacking in other abilities, such as being able to socialize. The amazing thing is, over the last four years, Robert's abilities have changed greatly in socializing, for he loves parties and he loves to hear the laughter of others, and for each and all to have a great time! Robert talks and discusses and enters into conversations more and more than ever before! Robert must feel as if he is needed or wanted in order for him to feel confident in being around others. He has a great sense of humor. He takes an ordinary conversation and turns it very wittingly into great humor. Some examples are: As we were one day talking about driving to the park to do something, Robert said, "Isn't it interesting that we drive on a parkway and park on a driveway!" I said something about my husband having a "bee in his bonnet," in other words, being very concerned about something, and immediately Robert quipped, "Oh, he wears a bonnet now?"

We were talking to Robert about tacking pictures of animals to a wall and so he said, "Oh, I am going to be a taxidermist!" There are many, many other examples of his quirky sense of humor which are all spontaneous, and yet he talks of ordinary everyday things that are turned into laughter. His dad and mom started it, and he continues to use great wit and good clean fun and humor, for Robert does not have a devious thought ever.

He is very spiritual and a deeply humble man, and is very teachable and Christlike in his thoughts and actions always. I think that he came that way as a protection from the evils of the day, so that those who would persuade Robert in another direction cannot. In other words, they cannot deceive Robert, for he has a built-in filtering system, and so he shuts off the TV or turns the channel, or does not read filth or sleaze. He recognizes it for what it is and does not wink at the appearance of evil, but shuts it out from the very beginning.

Robert is a very positive person, always looking on the bright side of life, and not ever wanting to witness or discuss evil intentions of people. If his wife says the word "crap" or if she talks too loudly, Robert has to get up and go out of the room. Of late, he has been watching the news, and of course there are drive-by shootings and deaths by car and cop to report, etc. Robert skips over the drive-by shootings and talks of killings by muting or skipping over them. When there are wildfires or other weather situations, Robert watches. He reported the weather to the media for a number of years, and he still enjoys watching and monitoring the weather. Serious situations such as tornados or other eventful weather conditions Robert will watch, for he is familiar with those situations and they do not alarm him anymore, since the actual destruction is not usually shown, but the results after the fact. However, Robert does not want to see mangled bodies, as we do not want to either.

Loud noises and sudden jerks in traffic winding in and out still set Robert on edge. Jeanene has to drive carefully and turn smoothly and put on the brakes slowly, because his body is highly sensitized to motion. It is magnified and intensified many more times than usual. I have been with Robert and Jeanene when oncoming traffic moved into the turning lane in front of our car, putting Robert into a panic for fear of what might happen if the car got hit. He put his head down on his wife's lap in panic and she comforted him until he had his composure again. Of late, Robert can see cars passing and has no adverse reaction. However, if a car comes too close, his reaction is many more times intensified than ours.

Robert is very, very loving and kind and forgiving. Robert is very knowledgeable on a huge variety of subjects. He retains everything he reads, and synthesizes it all and has a marvelous opinion about everything he reads. Then he explains the concepts and tutors others who are willing to hear from his vast store of knowledge. Robert surprised me and Jeanene when he stood in front of the congregation and explained that if a husband and wife will have God as part of their triangle, as the couple draws nearer in compromise and love, they also are elevated higher and closer to God. He put his hands together in a triangle and showed that with husband and wife at each end of the triangle and God at the top of the triangle, the couple draws closer together as they move upward on the triangle and to their God. Because Robert,

Jeanene, and I belong to the Church of Jesus Christ of Latter-day Saints, we have brothers and sisters who are home ministers. I have enjoyed that relationship with them. When called upon, Robert gives very beautiful and powerful blessings when someone needs to return from sickness to health, or to be comforted in times of sorrow or calamity in their lives.

I believe that Robert has truly been compensated for his disability, which seems to be disappearing in many areas, such as the inability to personally interact with others. However, he still has some <u>unawareness</u> of others' facial expressions. Because of Robert's confidence and the confidence of his wife and friends to get rid of and get around the syndrome, Robert <u>is</u> overcoming parts of this syndrome magnificently!

If someone saw Robert on the street or at Church, he would fit right into the crowd and no one would know he had Asperger's Syndrome.

This was written by a very dear friend.

CHAPTER NINE
A THERAPIST'S PERSPECTIVE
Heidi K. Rodriguez, LCSW

Robert has asked me to address some of the dynamics of Asperger's/Autism Spectrum Disorder (ASD) from a therapist's perspective. In addition, he would like me to identify some of the coping skills used to help individuals and their families deal with the challenges associated with this type of disorder. Specifically, I would like to share the concepts which have seemed to be particularly helpful for Robert and Jeanene. As I prefer to use a holistic approach to therapy, I will divide these coping skills into the areas of physical, emotional, mental, social, and spiritual. Also, I will incorporate a Latter-day Saint perspective into several of these concepts.

WHAT IS ASPERGER'S/AUTISM SPECTRUM DISORDER?

Autism Spectrum Disorders are often referred to as hidden disabilities. Since they are not necessarily visible, others often are not even aware the individual is struggling with these issues. The diagnosis of Asperger's is still relatively new, at least in the United States. I remember when, as a new therapist in the early 90s, a dear friend of mine who was living in Norway wrote to tell me her son had been diagnosed with this disorder. At that time, I had never even heard the term and had quite a bit of difficulty even finding information (at least in English) about Asperger's. While we have learned quite a bit about this disorder since that time, there is still a great deal we do not understand. Asperger's, named for the German scientist, Dr. Hans Asperger, was initially defined as a high functioning form of Autism. As per the NIMH (National Institute of Mental Health), "Asperger's is a neurological condition. It is thought that the brain is wired differently, making this disorder a lifelong condition. It affects communication, social interaction, and sensory issues."

In addition, on ChurchofJesusChrist.org in an article entitled, "So Near and Yet So Far: Living with Autism," Autism is further defined as: "A severely incapacitating, lifelong developmental disability that usually appears during the first three years of life. The symptoms include: 1) Slow development of physical, social, and learning skills; 2) Difficulty with speech; 3) Abnormal responses to sensations; 4) Abnormal ways of relating to people, objects, and events; and 5) Distinct skills in music, mathematics, science, and/or in visual-spatial concepts."

Currently, the term 'Asperger's' is being replaced by the term 'Autism Spectrum Disorder' (as per the *DSM 5*) since it occurs on a continuum of level of functioning and intellectual ability. Prior to the diagnosis becoming prevalent in the U.S. in the late 90s, it was typically classified as a Pervasive Developmental Disorder (or PDD). For example, it is my understanding that Robert was not diagnosed until adulthood and that his initial diagnosis was PDD. Then in later adulthood it was amended to Asperger's due to his high level of intellectual functioning. Currently the diagnosis of Asperger's is rolling over to Autism Spectrum Disorder (or ASD). However, for the purpose of this writing, I will primarily use the term 'Asperger's Syndrome' (AS).

PHYSICAL CHALLENGES AND COPING SKILLS

One of the challenges of Asperger's (or AS) is an intense sensory sensitivity. This refers to the way people with AS respond to taste, texture, smell, sight, and (especially in Robert's case) to sound. People with AS are not able to compartmentalize these sensations nor are they able to tune out "less important" stimuli. The person with AS may get into a type of defense or panic mode due to over-stimulation in the environment. To others, this may seem like an overreaction to a seemingly minor irritant, as we are able to tune out these extraneous sights and sounds. However, to the person with AS, the sound of someone chewing may seem to be nearly as loud and invasive as an individual yelling in his face.

In NIMH's pamphlet on Autism Spectrum Disorders, it states: "Many AS children are highly attuned or even painfully sensitive to certain sounds, textures, tastes, and smells. Some sounds...may cause these children to cover their ears and scream. In AS, the brain seems unable to balance the senses appropriately. Furthermore, once this happens, the rest of the day the individual is often on high alert."

Unfortunately, this issue does not go away as the person becomes an adult. In Robert's case, sound is particularly challenging. For instance, if Jeanene is chewing or tapping a pencil or even yawning out loud, he sometimes becomes visibly frustrated and will lose his train of thought completely. This, in turn, may trigger Jeanene as she feels he is being overly critical of her for no apparent reason. Given her history of abuse, this is understandably upsetting for her. One of the things which helps in this situation is simply to point out what is going on. Jeanene chewing on a piece of candy is not in any way inappropriate, it is simply Robert's oversensitivity to sound which is making him uncomfortable. It is not "her fault," nor is it his intent to be critical or hurtful. It is simply a symptom of his AS.

This issue becomes more problematic as the stimuli become more intense. There are many situations where this occurs for Robert, including: loud or aggressive sounding music, fireworks, ATV riders driving by his home, loud or screaming children, a helicopter overhead. An example of this is the way Robert becomes particularly upset by aggressive drivers on the road. Due to his anxiety regarding driving, he rarely drives himself, a common issue for individuals with AS issues. However, he still struggles at times even as a passenger. If he perceives an aggressive driver or excessive traffic, Robert moves into a defensive posture of panic and may yell out or begin hitting the dashboard. This, in turn, can be upsetting for Jeanene as his aggressive behavior triggers her own fears about aggressive men. Robert is not angry in that moment, he is terribly frightened and overwhelmed; however, it looks very much like rage to Jeanene. Telling him to just "knock it off" is similar to telling a blind person to quit bumping into walls. This physical reaction is a very real part of his disability. As we have tried to problem-solve this issue, we have come back to the importance of:

1) First, identifying what is really going on. For example, in this scenario he is not angry, he is afraid and his increased adrenalin is causing a state of genuine panic. Also, it is not Jeanene's fault nor is it a criticism of her driving ability. It is also important to identify specific triggers, to try not to personalize his reaction and to try to remain calm. However, the longer he continues to hit or yell, the more likely it is to trigger Jeanene's panic, which then moves them into a negative cycle of fear. It may be necessary to pull off to the side of the road (where possible), breathe deeply, say a prayer, and just take a timeout to try to calm down.

2) The next step is to talk through the event after both have calmed down. What was the trigger? What did we do right? What didn't work so well? What can we do next time to maybe stop things before it gets to that point? For instance, if a car is coming at high speed, pull off to the side of the road until it has passed, or try to

stay on back roads and avoid major highways altogether.

3) Next, identify possible coping ideas. For instance, it may be a good idea for him to sit in the backseat, with headphones on and his eyes closed. This is particularly important if they are driving in a larger city with increased traffic. Also, it may be helpful for him to hit a pillow instead of the dashboard or the seat, as this would be less intimidating for Jeanene. In fact, given his issue with loud sounds, it would be a good idea to have headphones available in any situation. If bright lights are a problem in another situation, make sure to always have sunglasses on hand. These ideas will not necessarily "fix" the issue, but they can make it slightly more tolerable for all involved.

4) A final step is to identify any possible hidden reasons for this particular trigger—in addition to the AS. For example, as we processed his severe reaction to aggressive drivers, Robert eventually shared an experience in which he was directly threatened by an aggressive driver personally. This man literally came up to his window and threatened to harm Robert when he was a young adult. Robert was literally afraid for his life and personal safety. Thus, his panic reaction makes even more sense, especially when added to the high sensitivity to external stimuli of the AS individual.

Some additional issues as far as the physical symptoms associated with Asperger's/AS include poor coordination, an awkward gait, hygiene issues, sensitivity to certain fabrics or seams in clothing, and sometimes discomfort with hugging or physical affection. In addition, recent research indicates that individuals on the Autism spectrum are at higher risk of seizures. This is not always apparent, especially if the seizures are minor. If the person with AS tends to "space out" quite a bit, it's something that should be mentioned to his doctor.

EMOTIONAL OVERLOAD AND COPING SKILLS

Individuals with AS are easily overwhelmed emotionally and struggle daily with feelings of anxiety as well as periods of genuine depression. It is sometimes believed that people with AS are similar to Spock from Star Trek—completely intellectual and void of any emotion. However, this is blatantly inaccurate. While they have difficulty expressing their emotions or understanding relationship issues, people with AS tend to feel emotions very acutely. These individuals have much more going on beneath the surface than it may appear. It has been compared to almost constant internal screaming and being bombarded by anxiety triggers. Individuals with AS often struggle with feeling inadequate and different. They often report feeling lonely, sad, scared, frustrated, confused, overwhelmed, and sometimes even ashamed of who they are. Robert has experienced this. Far too often, children and teens with AS are punished for having emotional meltdowns. These episodes of panic are generally chemical reactions of fear, not a tantrum or attempt to manipulate. It is important to clarify what is going on internally for that individual and help him learn ways to cope more appropriately. Some coping skills which have been helpful for Robert (and other clients struggling with AS) when feeling overwhelmed emotionally include:

1. Deep breathing, relaxation, and visualization in a quiet, peaceful setting if possible.

2. Calming music or hymns, (visual) pictures of the Savior or of the temple, or time in nature.

3. Spiritual comfort through prayer, scriptures, meditation, or the temple.

4. Taking a personal timeout away from any stress to write in a journal or record personal experiences and perceptions.

5. Learning "feeling" words in order to try to express emotions versus internalizing. It can be helpful to take time to list one specific stress at a time.

6. Distract through pleasant hobbies like cooking, gardening, genealogy, art, etc.

7. Burn off the excess energy (adrenalin burst) through exercise or physical work.

8. Problem solve (usually afterward) by brainstorming a list of things which may be helpful. Keep the written list somewhere visible to refer to when you become overwhelmed in the future.

While anxiety is often the most apparent emotional challenge for people with AS, depression can also be a common side effect as well. Elder Holland has said of depression:

"I am speaking of something more serious, of an affliction so severe that it significantly restricts a person's ability to function fully, a crater in the mind so deep that no one can responsibly suggest it would surely go away if those victims would just square their shoulders and think more positively. No, this dark night of the mind and spirit is more than mere discouragement." (Jeffrey R. Holland, "Like a Broken Vessel" General Conference, October

2013)

One of the most important aspects of coping with depression is to challenge thinking distortions and to move away from negative (often even abusive) self talk. Feelings of inadequacy can be frequent in the person with AS, as he is often reminded he is "different" and can become easily frustrated and overwhelmed. It is essential at these times to remember who you truly are... from Wordsworth, "As we (all) come trailing clouds of glory from God who is our home." Shakespeare also penned the words, "We know who we are, but not who we may be." This type of cognitive therapy is just one way a professional can help a client get through the challenges of depression. Just as an individual with pneumonia or diabetes should seek medical help for his issues, so should anyone struggling with depression or other mental/emotional challenges. There is help available through private clinicians, County Mental Health Centers, and via the Church Social Services in your area. In some cases, medications may be needed to help the body regain its chemical balance, as well. There is absolutely no shame in seeking mental health treatment. Robert and Jeanene's willingness to seek help both individually and as a couple has resulted in their making significant progress in several areas of their lives.

Another major trigger for emotional overload for the person with AS is any type of change. People with this type of disorder tend to feel much more comfortable with schedules and consistent structure. Any type of major change is particularly upsetting for them, and in general, people with AS do not like surprises. This can be difficult for a spouse (like Jeanene) who enjoys a higher level of flexibility and some adventure in her life. It's important to make it clear that while the individual with AS can set specific schedules, meal plans, and time frames for himself, this does not mean those around him must follow his schedule as well. This has been a challenge for Robert, as he would prefer that he and Jeanene both be on the same schedule as much as possible. It is also particularly upsetting for him when she expresses a desire to move or at least go on some kind of extended vacation. The need to compromise on these types of changes is especially difficult for Robert, and previously has been an ongoing point of conflict and anxiety.

MENTAL CHALLENGES AND RESOURCES

Individuals with Asperger's are often intelligent people. In Robert's case, he is significantly above average. High functioning people with AS often excel in the areas of math, science, computer science, and/or engineering. They sometimes fit the old stereotype of the absent minded professor, in that they are clearly highly intelligent, but seem unable to pick up on simple social cues or norms. People with AS tend to be highly visual and as such do much better with visual learning models. They also do particularly well with metaphors and can be highly creative, but in a somewhat less traditional manner. They often have very specific areas of interest like computers, trains, online gaming, or in Robert's case, meteorology. They often dislike distractions, because (as explained above) they have difficulty tuning out external stimuli. The challenge for people with AS is that the social side of education and employment makes it extremely difficult for them to function in these environments. Unfortunately, a low percentage of individuals with AS graduate from college, and an even lower percentage are able to maintain long-term employment. With community education and support, these percentages are improving. Vocational rehabilitation can be a great resource, as can the Church Social Services, as long as the career counselors in these settings have a strong understanding of the challenges of AS.

Unfortunately, Robert did not have this type of community support as a young adult, as there was very little information about AS at that time. While Robert enjoyed the intellectual benefits of college, the social aspects made it overwhelming for him. At the time, he did not have a college advisor who could help him cope with these challenges, as he did not even have a diagnosis at that time. Robert's efforts at employment were similarly difficult—not due to his job performance (which was stellar), but due to his difficulty with social cues and social understanding. When he disagreed based on what he perceived as factual evidence, it was sometimes viewed as being argumentative or even disrespectful. His employment through the Church was threatened due to this type of misunderstanding on several occasions. His job was secured due to a supportive individual (whom he refers to as Tom) who understood the nature of his disability. This individual was able to advocate for Robert, as he was not able to do so for himself, due to his communication and social challenges.

It is important for those dealing with AS individuals to respect their intellectual abilities while not misinterpreting their social limitations. This has been an area of significant emotional pain for Robert, as he has struggled throughout his adult life in the area of employment. He takes the Church standard of being able to provide for his family very seriously, yet had struggled to maintain employment. While it is important for Robert to continue to look for employment opportunities that are reasonable, given his disability, it is also (in my opinion) important for society to gain education regarding the potential these individuals have to make positive contributions in the job sector given adequate support. There are many who believe Albert Einstein likely struggled with Asperger's. Look at what the world could have missed if he had been discounted for his social deficits or for his odd, somewhat eccentric behavior. How many individuals are we currently overlooking for higher education and/or employment due to AS issues, who could make similar contributions given the chance? Individuals with AS may come across as odd or different, as being "too OCD" or rigid in their thinking. These are all simply results of the innate thinking patterns of AS and are not some type of internal character flaws.

Currently, most individuals on the Autism Spectrum can qualify for disability status. Resources have come a long way over the last 25 years. One of the first places to start is at your local Department of Vocational Rehabilitation. Ongoing support can also be found online at Autism Spectrum Disorders, at NIMH (National Institute of Mental Health), via NAMI (National Alliance on Mental Illness), and at various other websites including myaspergerschild.com and medicinenet.com. Diagnosis and testing can sometimes be done at a local college (typically through their psychology department) at reduced cost. Also, there is help through the Church of Jesus Christ of Latter-day Saints via their website at disabilities.ChurchofJesusChrist.org.

SOCIAL DIFFICULTIES AND COPING SKILLS

Individuals on the Autism spectrum often struggle most in the area of social difficulties. People with AS often have problems with maintaining appropriate eye contact, being overly blunt, reading non-verbal social cues, understanding subtle humor (particularly sarcasm), taking things too literally, facial expressions, physical affection, and empathy. Sadly, most people with AS do not date much, have many friends, or marry. If they do marry, too often it does not last. While they are uncomfortable in social situations due to their limited social skills, people with AS often feel lonely. In addition, people with AS are often confused when others are offended; they may come across distant or odd, exhibit some repetitive patterns, and may appear obsessive or socially awkward.

Robert has made significant strides in his lifetime, in terms of his social development. He is definitely logical and intellectual, but is also emotionally quite sensitive. This sensitivity is part of what makes him so sensitive to the Spirit. When he has a "meltdown" due to external stimuli, he is best calmed down by Jeanene's calm voice and her presence. It is often thought that people with AS should be left alone to get through a meltdown, but the reality is that they often need the love, support, and patience of those they trust. It is important to note the difference between a tantrum or angry outburst versus the fear and panic of a true AS meltdown. Again, this is particularly important for Jeanene, given her history with individuals who were physically or verbally aggressive. Sometimes a safety word is helpful for both sides, when feelings of panic begin to overwhelm.

It is also true that those with AS can be unintentionally offensive. An example of this would be a situation in which Robert was upset by a person who had tattoos on his face and neck. Due to his sensitivity to stimuli, these tattoos were upsetting for him at a purely visual level, as there was just "too much going on," making him unable to process what this person was saying. In addition, the facial tattoos just did not make sense to Robert from a purely logical perspective. This could have become a socially awkward experience. However, Jeanene was able to explain it in a manner Robert could understand. She simply explained to him that everyone has their own way of expressing themselves. She said that some people who have experienced a great deal of pain will sometimes make themselves look more intimidating to keep others away in an effort to protect themselves from additional emotional pain. This was something they both understood and to which they could both relate.

Some additional coping skills which Robert has incorporated include: looking just above someone's shoulder to mimic eye contact, learning to get feedback regarding his attempts to communicate, learning to imitate others in social situations, learning to laugh at himself and gain a sense of humor, learning specific social learns (social skills training), asking for what he needs, learning to identify feeling words, asking for clarification, and listening to the Spirit to help guide him in any type of challenging social situation. It can be helpful for people with AS to actually practice conversational skills or role play social situations in advance. Again, the social skills which just seem to come naturally to most people need to be objectively learned by the person with AS.

One of Robert's greatest gifts was in the family he was born into on this earth. As is so often the case, it seems that where there are great challenges, there are also great blessings.

Robert's mother has been a particular strength to him throughout his life. When he was growing up, there was no diagnosis for what he had, yet she knew he needed special help. She advocated for him with his teachers and with those in their Church ward. She supported him without enabling him. When others told her to just punish him for his meltdowns, she knew that wasn't the answer. She sensed there was something else going on. Both of his parents believed in him and loved him unconditionally.

His sister was a great support as well. She took care of the bullies and protected him when necessary. She, probably more than anyone, knew so much of what he went through each day at school and in other social settings. She encouraged him to become the best person he could be and she too, believed in him, even when she did not understand the nature of his disability due to the lack of information at that time. His parents have passed to the other side now, but they continue to be a support for Robert in many ways. His sister continues as a strong and constant support as well. She (like her mother before her) has learned great patience and has been able to calm him down when he became upset, repetitive, or agitated.

Elder Jeffrey R. Holland stated: "I bear witness of that day when loved ones whom we knew to have disabilities in mortality will stand before us glorified and grand, breathtakingly perfect in body and mind. I do not know whether we will be happier for ourselves that we have witnessed such a miracle, or happier for them that they are fully perfect and finally free at last!" (Jeffrey R. Holland, "Like a Broken Vessel" General Conference, October 2013)

Jeanene has also been able to see the person Robert truly is and will be, in an eternal perspective from the very beginning. She, too, has always believed in him. In the day to day, it has not been easy. She, who has struggled with so many years of abuse herself, has had to set that aside at times to help him work through his own fears. As mentioned previously, there are times when his outbursts of fear or frustration triggered her own fears from past abuse. Jeanene knows with absolute surety that Robert would never do anything to hurt her in any way. However, in the moment, there are times when her past trauma took over and she moved into that fight or flight stance. That is her self-protection and was her survival for many years. Yet, due to their love of one another and to their faith in their Heavenly Father, they have been able to weather many unique and difficult challenges.

Still, as mentioned in my introduction, it has certainly not always been easy. Robert tends to be an introvert while she is more an extrovert. Her adventurous nature struggles with his resistance to change. She has learned to use more direct communication patterns, as he typically is not able to understand the more subtle hints. Jeanene has had to work on not taking things personally after so many prior experiences with emotional abuse and to not be afraid of his physical outbursts, despite her history of physical abuse. This has not been easy. One of the areas that has been especially challenging for Jeanene is Robert's difficulty with empathy. The lack of empathy does not mean he does not care; in fact he cares very much. It simply means he has difficulty putting himself in someone else's shoes. He feels sad when someone else is hurt or sad, but does not necessarily understand what their kind of sad feels like. This has been particularly difficult recently, as she has experienced several major health issues. He has felt upset about her being sick and in the hospital, but struggles to understand how it must feel to be the one who is sick. This difficulty with empathy does not, however, diminish his deep love for her in any way.

As far as my recommendations for family and friends of an individual with AS, I would suggest the following:

1) Education. This is the most important thing you can do for yourself and for your loved one with AS. There is so much information out there now and it can help so much. Sometimes family members are concerned that the label will lead to a stigma, but in most cases I have found the diagnosis just helps them to understand things better. Once you know he has AS, you can begin to understand what he is going through and how you can help. The more you come to understand about this disorder, the better the relationship can become as communication improves and misunderstandings decrease. An excellent resource is the Church disability website at disabilities.ChurchofJesusChrist.org which provides information,

guidance, and teachings for members with disabilities, families, teachers, and leaders.

2) Take Care of Yourself. It is not easy living with someone with Autism Spectrum. It can be challenging and discouraging. It can trigger feelings of frustration, resentment, and your own feelings of inadequacy. You need your own support system. There are great support groups online which can be helpful as well. Reach out to friends and family. This does not need to be a secret, nor is it anything of which to be ashamed. It is what it is, and Heavenly Father loves both of you as you are. Elder Holland has said to caregivers: "In our devoted effort to assist with another's health, do not destroy your own. In all these things be wise. Do not run faster than you have strength." (Jeffrey R. Holland, "Like a Broken Vessel" General Conference, October 2013)

3) Keep Realistic Expectations of your loved one with AS and of yourself. There's a saying in 12 Step Recovery that advises "Accept, not Expect." One thing I have learned as a therapist for about 25 years is that there truly is no such thing as "normal." There is no such thing as the perfect family or the perfect relationship. Living with a person with AS is challenging, but also rewarding. In a talk from the February 1989 *Ensign*, we are reminded, "Tragedy and difficulty are part of mortal life. When we understand this we will be more willing to share our struggles with others. This sharing can lessen the isolation and shame we feel when we encounter serious problems."

4) As far as how those outside of the immediate family can help when someone is struggling with any type of mental health challenge or disability, the following three

suggestions were spelled out quite succinctly in the *Ensign* in 1989: "Express love and interest to both the individual and the family. Withhold judgment and increase acceptance. Give needed help." (Jan Underwood Pinborough, "Mental Illness: In Search of Understanding and Hope." *Ensign*, February 1989)

SPIRITUAL CHALLENGES AND REWARDS

It can be very difficult for people with AS to go to Church, have certain Church callings, attend Church social functions, or speak in front of any type of Church group. Sometimes, just being asked to say a prayer in Sunday School can be terrifying. Sometimes individuals, like Robert, are able to serve full-time missions and sometimes they are just not able to do so. Since many people with AS do not marry, it can be difficult to be part of a family ward, yet even more challenging in some cases, to be part of a singles ward. While they may have strong testimonies of the gospel, they often struggle a great deal with the social part of Church activity.

As ward members and leaders, it is very important that we are loving and non-judgmental. In the article, "Living with Autism," Elder Rex Pinegar stated: "If Church activity plans do not include disabled members, then we are not reaching out to everyone. We have got to be willing to reach out and include everyone in our lives."

In another article at ChurchofJesusChrist.org entitled, "General Information: Disabilities," it states: "Sometimes, in the case of disabilities, individuals may react unintentionally with fear, rejection, or discomfort. Often these reactions are due to inadequate information and inexperience. Learning about a person increases understanding and acceptance for a person with a disability. As we worship together, all can experience, as Paul taught, the 'peace of God which passeth all understanding.'" (Philippians 4:7)

In 1989, the First Presidency issued a statement urging increased awareness, understanding, acceptance, and appreciation of those with disabilities, asking members to "help them feel respected, loved, and understood," and stating, "it is the members' opportunity and responsibility to follow the example of Jesus in loving our neighbors."

Christopher Phillips, manager of Disability Services for the Church, said that beyond providing resources: "...the greatest need the Church strives to meet is to help members demonstrate love, respect, and understanding toward individuals with disabilities. Our goal is to help leaders and members as they try to understand and meet the individual needs of those with disabilities and recognize their gifts." (Church Provides a Wide Array of Disability Resource, Newsroom. ChurchofJesusChrist.org)

There is not a doubt in my mind that the area in which I have learned the most from Robert and Jeanene is in their spiritual approach to their world. Many of us know we "should" pray, read our scriptures, attend our meetings, pay our tithing, go to the temple, do family history work, and keep the commandments. However, for both Jeanene and Robert, all of these things are not just a list of "shoulds" but a daily way of being. Without their spiritual beliefs, I do not believe either of them would be where they are today.

Robert has not always felt loved and accepted at Church by others, but he has always felt loved and accepted by his Heavenly Father. His faith is just absolute. When those in charge doubted his ability to serve a mission, he knew he was supposed to serve, regardless. His dear father advocated for him and he was eventually able to serve a successful two-year mission in South America. When he struggled with other people at times in his various callings, he was able to ask for help from above to do what he needed to do, and he did it. In some ways, his AS has provided a type of protection from many of the temptations of this world. Those things simply held no appeal for him as he sought always to simply stay by the light. Right versus wrong was just always very clear.

In addition, Robert has a unique talent in genealogy. His combination of strengths makes this a perfect endeavor for him. His only frustration is that he does not have more work within his ward, as he is so eager to help. He lives close to the Spirit and therefore the veil is often thin, as he spends so much time trying to help those who have gone before.

In the words of President Joseph F. Smith: "Our fathers and mothers, brothers, sisters, and friends who have passed away from this earth, having been faithful and worthy to enjoy these rights and privileges, may have a mission given them to visit their friends and relatives upon the earth again, bringing from the divine presence messages of love, warning, reproof, or instruction...Their presence may or may not be seen or known. Loved ones who have died may also serve in the capacity of angels to comfort or warn." (Joseph F. Smith, "Gospel Doctrine," Salt Lake City: Deseret Book Coll., 1959, p.

436)

This eternal perspective leads naturally to Robert's other Church calling, which is that of temple worker. When he and Jeanene were first called to be workers at the new temple in their area, he was somewhat apprehensive about how much he would be able to do, given his limitations. To my knowledge, he has been able to fulfill all the roles for which he has been asked to fulfill, and has even been able to go beyond his earthly capabilities. Jeanene has shared on several occasions that it has been amazing to watch his growth in that area and to see him become closer to the person she knows he will be one day. They have shared spiritual experiences which they have been a part of in that special setting. Again, it has become obvious to me on several occasions that the veil is indeed very thin, particularly when it comes to love from the other side.

Finally, I believe it is important to remember that whatever challenges we face in this life, those challenges do not define who we are. Robert's diagnosis also does not define who he is.

As Elder Holland has stated: "Also, let us remember that through any illness or difficult challenge, there is still much in life to be hopeful about and grateful for. We are infinitely more than our limitations or our afflictions. Know that one day the dawn will break brightly and all shadows of mortality will flee...Broken minds can be healed just the way broken bones and broken hearts are healed. While God is at work making those repairs, the rest of us can help by being merciful, nonjudgmental, and kind." (Jeffrey R. Holland, "Like a Broken Vessel" General Conference, October 2013)

It is our priority as followers of Christ to reach out in love and acceptance to all of our brothers and sisters. As we get to know those with various disabilities, mental health challenges, addictions, and those from backgrounds much different than our own, we are blessed and enriched in many ways in our own lives.

our continuing journey

CHAPTER TEN
LIFE IN PASSING

"Ethan, I know these past few chapters written by my family and friends have been very helpful to you and your family. They have been very informative and emotionally impressive, during this part of our journey, as you have really tender emotions. You now have a wealth of information presented to you which I know is helping to lift your burdens and lessen your struggles in a magnificent way. It is also greatly helping your family, and it will be of great assistance to others involved in your life. I, Robert, now have some more very important information to present to you, as well as to your family and friends, along with all of you who are sharing this journey with us.

"I know that after having come this far in your reading, on this journey with me, and having applied this life-changing information to your daily living, that you have already noticed improvement in your life to some degree.

You should feel more confident now, and be able to positively interact more with others. You should also notice that your Asperger's characteristics have decreased. This is part of your progression, as our Savior has planned for you. You will continue to progress and improve during your life's journey as you live the gospel and continue to apply the principles in this book to your life."

We are all progressing in a positive direction as we continue living the teachings of the Lord through His gospel.

"Ethan, as your mother and sister have also received very valuable help here, you may have noticed how they have improved as well. This is how we all want our life's journey to continue, as we become older and more mature as our lives continue passing forward, and as we have more of the good teaching experiences in order to help us to keep growing in positive ways, no matter what disabilities we may have."

LIFE'S TRIALS

Even as we continue to positively progress, our Savior will allow us to have challenges and trials, as these will actually help us more in our progression in life. We just have to overcome them and deal with them, by using the principles and suggestions mentioned earlier, by utilizing the advice of your "safe" person, and through sincere prayer. As we stay close to the Lord and have more faith, He will help us, and our trials will be easier to live with each day. Our family and friends can also help us, so our lives can be more enjoyable. We should be very grateful for their love and assistance they have given us.

"As you know, Ethan, you and your family members have experienced a more major challenge and trial: your sister's illness and death. Our Lord is fully aware of this, and He will help you, along with help given by other people in the Church. There are many good, caring members of the Church who will also give the needed help to those who have real needs. You can make friends with them. They will have great concern for you and will really care about helping with your needs as well as comforting you, as they would for anyone who has a major life challenge. You may experience deep depression and grieving, and feel very much alone. Something may have recently occurred which would have triggered this. Just know that there are people who want to help you feel happier and provide caring assistance, and will help as you invite them to do so. Look to parents and family for this help first, and then look to other friends. They want you to feel happier, not depressed. This is what our Savior would want for you too. They want the best for you, and they want you to have great, positive experiences and a joyful life as they see your progression.

"You have lost a close family member. This is always a very difficult trial for anyone to experience, accompanied by much grieving, but this trial also produces an added emotional level to the person who has Asperger's Syndrome/ASD. This is due to the fact that Asperger's people are more sensitive and tender, just as little children are. They need extra comfort and emotional support, to help with their increased grieving and depression. They may need help from a good counselor as well, who understands about the Autism Spectrum Disorders.

Spiritual help, such as a priesthood blessing, would also be appropriate."

I mentioned earlier that my wife, Jeanene, really helped me at the passing of each of my parents. This was a very new experience for me each time, with a tremendous emotional effect, as I was very close to them. They were also my "safe" people. It is extremely emotionally difficult for an Asperger's person to be alone, without a "safe" person to give needed help in many areas of his life and help him in his progression. Jeanene was able to give me great emotional comfort, especially after having experienced this herself when both of her adoptive parents passed, along with her oldest son. She, indeed, has been my much needed "safe" person, and I thank her so very, very much. I would think of my parents often, which is normal, and she would remind me of what I know, which is that they are enjoying being together again in a very joyful situation, free from any physical and emotional pain, or any kind of anguish. They know much more where they are now, but they also know that we have an advantage, having our bodies. We would both talk about how they are participating in the Lord's work, teaching and helping others in the spirit world, which is right here on the earth, and how they are watching over us, helping us in our lives. They want us to be happy during our earthly life. I know that this is true. Talking about this makes me feel happier.

"For you, Ethan, having experienced the death of a loved one, this chapter in our journey will be of great comfort."

For others with Asperger's, if this hasn't yet occurred in your life, you will be much better prepared with this information I will give, in addition to the help I have already given concerning the passing of my parents.

As I have mentioned, my Church ward is excellent, where there are many wonderful, caring people who think very well of us, and we show our love and kindness toward them.

Jeanene would greet many of the sisters with a hug, in our Church meetings and in the Temple. She has always been a very understanding and caring, loving person. She wants to spread around happiness and help everyone have a happier day. As a result, many people have been greatly uplifted and thanked her. Many of them have said that Jeanene's hugs really made their day.

I, having Asperger's, have been learning how to be more socially positive with people, and I have shared much of this information with you. Other people have seen more of who I really am. My unusual characteristics related to Asperger's Syndrome have decreased, and more people are respectful around me. Of course, I have had to put forth much effort, doing things I have discussed here in this book every day.

To illustrate, I have been able to naturally have more social interaction in my Church meetings. Greeting people, shaking hands with them, and looking at their faces and asking how they are doing has become much more natural for me. I may engage in a short conversation with them. This is due in part to watching Jeanene and what she has taught me about the proper ways of being sociable with people and showing interest in them.

As I enjoy music, I have also participated in stake choirs during stake conferences, and even at the dedication of a new stake center. Doing this has brought me great joy, and I felt much more normal, participating in this way with other people. This has also brought more spirituality in my life, singing many spiritual, uplifting hymns and Church music.

By staying close to our Savior and following His teachings, along with doing the items I have taught during our journey, I have been able to participate more in our class discussions at Church, like many other members would normally do. The Lord helps me to give some enlightening responses, which are beneficial to others. People have noticed that as I do this, I don't exhibit any characteristics of a developmental disorder, and there are no associated odd behaviors. They see that I am very normal, even more so than some of the other members there. I'm not saying this to brag, but rather to illustrate what can realistically be accomplished in the life of an Asperger's person by working on the simple steps which have been presented during this journey.

"Ethan, you can easily achieve the same results."

By becoming more socially aware, I have also been able to help Jeanene easily understand certain areas in her life better, such as when people would try to manipulate her, for whatever reason. She has learned the appropriate response. I have also given Jeanene many priesthood blessings, to help her know what the Lord wanted her to know as she was especially progressing more during this time in her life. These blessings also gave her needed comfort when she experienced trials.

HELPING JEANENE IN HER LIFE

During our marriage, Jeanene needed to have opera-tions on her joints (knees, shoulders, etc.). However, a few years ago, she noticed that she was becoming more tired, which is normal when a person enters his or her later years in life. Jeanene is a few years older than I am. However, she seemed to be increasingly more tired at a faster rate. Medical evaluations indicated that she had a liver problem, but hepatitis was ruled out. We had to stop doing our bakery and pizza home business at that time. Her doctor was teaching her ways to be healthier, which could help her liver to improve. We were doing these, such as eating better and going on walks together.

We were continuing working on our temple shifts as workers there. We were doing two shifts, with Jeanene having a snack in between. However, a couple years later, that was becoming too much, so she changed to just working in the first shift, and rested while I was finishing the later shift. She was becoming even more tired very quickly. This was due to her liver problem. We were con-cerned about this, and she was having increasing balance issues. We moved to a one-level house in our same Church ward, so that she would not have to deal with stairs in the two-level house.

Jeanene was starting to have some new medical symptoms occur, so I had her checked at the medical cen-ter. It was found that some of her blood levels had changed significantly, due to her liver problem, and she was given medications to control this. I was thinking of her even more at this time, and I was doing everything I could to help her feel better and to continue enjoying life.

I was feeling more concerned about her health, comfort, and wellbeing. She was starting to have more pains and discomfort, and had to be in the hospital a few times to control her medical situation.

Later that year, in late summer, we were at our morning shift in the temple, when Jeanene started feeling extremely tired and had to lie down and sleep. We had to leave our shifts and take a medical leave of absence, as her condition had become worse. It was determined that she would need a liver transplant, and we were in the process of completing the requirements so that the transplant could take place. I had to stay around her to help take care of her needs. She had to be in the hospital more often now, as she needed care to help keep her stable, and she needed a couple of blood transfusions, among other things. She was about to be on the transplant list, so I understood that her condition would be taken care of soon. I knew that the Lord was aware of all she was experiencing, including all her discomfort, as she was having more stomach cramps. I also knew that the Lord has His plan for her and would help her. She was staying close to Him through prayer and through our scripture reading.

Jeanene had numerous medications to take in order to keep her medically in balance, as well as to help her feel more comfortable. As she was not able to think as clearly now, I was giving her the medications throughout each day. It was quite a process, but I really cared for her and wanted to help her with all her needs. I stayed with her in the hospital as well.

A few days before Christmas, Jeanene was home and was ready to be on the transplant list. She had been sleeping much more. That evening, she was in bed and was saying that she wasn't feeling very good. She had become quite weak. She had gone to Church the previous Sunday using the assistance of a walker, and had kindly greeted all her friends in our ward. They were happy to see her, and they enjoyed seeing her smile at each of the meetings. During this particular evening, I felt prompted that she needed to stay at the medical center that night, where they would then have her in a care center. The staff there would be able to assist her with mobility, as I was physically not able to get her up for a bathroom break or for anything else. She had become extremely weak and had more balance issues. A couple days later, Susan and I, along with her husband, went to the care center to visit Jeanene. Our grandson, whom Jeanene loved very much, along with his mother, were also there with us. We shared Christmas gifts and had a very enjoyable time together.

The next morning, I received a phone call from the care center, saying that Jeanene was coughing up some blood, and had developed pneumonia. They had taken her back to the medical center for more care. Susan and I went to see her, and Susan then stayed overnight with me at the house to spend some Christmas time together. The next day, I went back to the hospital and stayed with Jeanene a couple more days. I then went home to take care of some needs, planning to go back the next day. However, at about four in the morning, I received a phone call from the doctor on duty, who indicated that Jeanene's pneumonia was worsening, and she was experiencing some other difficulties. He said that they needed to transport her to a larger hospital and have her in intensive care. I was very worried about her, but I thought that they could take care of her situation, so that she could be ready for the liver transplant later. I let my sister, Susan, know about this.

Two days later, the hospital notified Susan and me of Jeanene's situation and said we should come up and see her. Susan and her husband took me up to the hospital, where Jeanene's condition had become much worse. I was feeling that this was the Lord's will. A few devices were connected to her in order to keep her going. She was not very aware of her surroundings, but when I came up to her bedside, she looked at me very clearly and smiled, and I told her I love her, and that it would be okay. The doctor there said she would continue to get worse and that there was nothing more they could do. They disconnected the devices and I saw my sweetheart look up with a pleasant, peaceful smile on her face, looking at some important people in the spirit world who we knew were there, and then she peacefully went through the veil and was gone. Heavenly Father had called her home.

I felt numb; it seemed like it was a dream. It seemed like she was in a coma and would wake up later. However, I again felt through the Spirit that this was the Lord's will. Why would the Lord take her right now? I had just lost my wonderful, loving companion, and my "safe" person. I felt like I had lost a part of me, like I had just had an amputation. I had an overwhelming surge of many emotions, and I had to hug my sister, Susan. She and her husband stayed with me at my house that night and went to Church with me the next day. Susan and her husband knew I needed the closeness right then. Susan told me that the shock would be like ocean waves coming in and going out, affecting my grieving intensities. She knew this after losing her son. This subsided over the first few weeks; however, the grieving was still quite intense. I felt an added, more intense level of grieving, associated with my increased emotional sensitivities. I had a lot of help from the good members of my ward, who provided dinners and came to visit me often. A couple of them had also gone through this process, losing a spouse, and were able to help me by sharing how they dealt with their emotions in these very intense situations.

OTHER PEOPLE CARE ABOUT YOU

This intense loss continued to add a whole new level to my grieving emotions during the following months, having Asperger's Syndrome, as I also have more tender spiritual sensitivities. Having progressed this far in my life, being able to incorporate the items I have discussed in this book, gave me a tremendous advantage in managing this trial. I know that the Lord told my mother that I would not be alone when my parents passed on. This was before I met Jeanene. My father had also told me through priesthood blessings at that time that I would soon be meeting Jeanene. With all three gone now, I am utilizing this advantage to deal with being alone, along with the added grieving and the emotion of really missing Jeanene. The Spirit then told me that Jeanene had completed her time on the earth, and that our Savior needs her on the other side now for some very important work. However, my love for her remains even stronger. Love is truly stronger than death.

Our Savior has been very caring for me. I found out later that Susan and another ward member knew that Jeanene was going to pass on, a couple weeks before she did. However, the Lord didn't want me to experience any added intense emotions than I had to, so in His wisdom and love, He didn't let me know until the day of her passing that she was going to experience this. I am very grateful to Him for this love and His grace which He showed me. I also know that our Savior has His wonderful plan still for me in this life, and I trust in Him that He will let me know, little by little, His important will for me. This shows how He helps everyone's faith to grow. This new experience which the Lord has given me has helped me to progress even more. I am learning to have more faith in our Savior, and to be even closer to Him. He knows what I need.

With my parents and my wife on the other side now, I am seeing more of the reality of the continuing progression toward our eternal family. I am learning how to be even stronger, and to develop more Christlike love toward others, like Jeanene did. She really taught me how to do this. I realize even more how helpful she was. I know that I will be with Jeanene again later, along with my parents, and that this occasion will be an extremely joyful, grand reunion with her as well as with my parents and other loved ones, some of whom I have not known in this life, but they have.

To help me during this present trial, I stay close to many of the good friends I have made in my ward, and they have become closer to me and understand me better through this experience. Many of them are very loving and caring about me. I have also learned more about them, socially, and I am very grateful for all they have done to help, with sharing meals, by visiting, and by sharing their friendship. A few in particular have been especially helpful by talking to me when I needed that support, and have even helped me with some projects such as assisting me with putting up some more pictures around the house.

I have felt Jeanene's presence as well, helping me at her funeral as well as other times. Her funeral was very touching. Susan and I planned it together, and we felt that Jeanene was helping, through direct impressions we received. One instance was selecting a hymn to be sung there, "Our Savior's Love." (*Hymns*, #113)

I know that Jeanene is in a very beautiful place, free from any pains, difficulties, and worries. She does not have her diseased body anymore. She understands much more information, has Christlike love, and is greeting and helping people there as she did here. The fact that Jeanene and other family members are on the other side, actually in the spirit world, is truly showing the progression in the reality of the Lord's process of families toward the ultimate realization of living with Heavenly Father again, and it is also showing how they are greatly involved in helping others toward this goal on both sides, in this life and in the spirit world. I have felt the presence of my parents, along with Jeanene, to help me through this difficult time, by feeling their love and their guidance. They know much more about my future, and they want to help me to fulfill it. They know that I will be doing more of the Lord's work, and that Asperger's Syndrome will not be hindering me. This is a tremendous, wondrous fact, along with knowing that the spirit world is right here, which shows the real importance of accomplishing the Lord's work for our families, so that we can all be together forever.

"I know that you, Ethan, have gone through quite an emotional experience too, after what you have been through. I have taken you through quite an emotional, yet wonderful journey, experiencing emotions of joy, and tender, spiritual feelings, as well as those of sadness, grief, and anguish. You have already experienced similar emotions with the loss of your father and the death of your youngest sister, and you know how hard it is to deal with your day-to-day life. I know that all this information concerning Asperger's Syndrome/ASD I have presented in this book to assist people, during this great journey, will be a tremendous help to you and your family and others, now as well as in the future.

"It is very important to cherish the moments you now have together with your family. This will bring you closer together. Communicating and showing love with good family members and relatives in person, or by using many of the means of communication available to us these days, will be of great assistance for you and for other people with Asperger's, especially during times of intense emotional situations. Your family and others involved with you will also know how to better empathize with you and help you at these intense times. You will find that there are other people, many in the Church and local community, some you may not have known very well, who care about you more than you realized. As you make friends with them, while your life continues to improve through applying these principles I have discussed and through the help of others, you can see that there are a greater number of people who care and will be more involved in helping you. They will be able to communicate with you better. As they learn more about you and about the information in this book, they will be able to have much improved lives as well.

"So on we go. Life continues moving forward, with all of us experiencing whatever the Lord sees fit to put in front of us, knowing that He has His plan for each of us, which is what is best as we do our best. Stay true to our Savior, and you will be successful and happier. I leave you now, Ethan, with my hope and prayer that you will have an excellent, even happier life, as I know you will. I will be with you in spirit. I see tears running down your face. I know that some of these are tears of joy. I regard you and your family very deeply. Your mother and sister will also have better lives, along with you, and will feel more loving toward others as you all feel our Savior's love."

"Wow! Robert, I just don't have words to express my feelings right now. This has been a very emotional journey, and I don't want it to end. I'm really thankful to you for showing me how to have a better life!"

"Thank you, Ethan. You are an extremely important person. All three of you have very important work to still accomplish, and you will all be doing much good, which will bring you great joy during your remaining time on the earth. I have seen your tremendous progression as we have gone on this awesome journey together. I have especially seen the true, life-changing exciting changes in your life that you have experienced along the way. You will all remember this journey throughout your lives with fond memories. What a wonderful time we have had together. Let's all have a group hug. It brings me great joy to help other people have much more happiness in their lives. I have truly enjoyed going on this journey with each of you, Ethan, Sarah, and Alexis."

Still very emotional, Ethan responds, "I have never met anyone as helpful as you are, Robert. You're truly amazing! I've really felt your spirit as you were speaking to us. I don't know how you did it, but you explained much of my life and my experiences, including my emotions in great detail, without even knowing me. You've told me what I can do to be more like you. I feel much more hopeful now."

"Thank you very much for your compliment. Ethan, you are an extremely valuable person, and you're worth it. I can see that you would like to visit with me again. Maybe we could sometime."

On hearing this, Sarah commented, "We can plan to come and meet with you soon and share some more experiences we've had. Ethan would enjoy this, along with the rest of us. Thank you for all you have done. I know that what you have shown us during this journey is truly life-changing, especially for Ethan."

"Thank you very much. I know that it will greatly help you. Seeing you all again would be wonderful. It has been a pleasure meeting with you and your wonderful family. I sincerely wish the best for all of you!"

CHAPTER ELEVEN
THE GREATEST CHALLENGE

Before we were born, we participated in the Great Council in Heaven, and we all knew what life in mortality would be like. We knew that we would be experiencing some great difficulties and challenges, and we knew this was necessary to enable us the opportunity to continue to progress toward Eternal Life, for which opportunity we "shouted for joy." We completely understood this "Miracle of Mortality," and we were very excited for the privilege of being able to be born on this earth. I understand that those of us who have disabilities in this life knew, before we were born, that we would be living life with these disabilities, and our Heavenly Father and our Savior told us the reason we would have them. After knowing this, we still shouted for joy, knowing that these disabilities and disorders will allow us to individually progress in the most efficient manner. This progression which our Savior has planned for each of us easily provides us the only way to be able to receive the greatest blessings our Heavenly Father has for us and is planning to give us, which will bring us tremendous joy.

Now we are here in mortality, not remembering what occurred in our pre-earth life, so that we can develop the faith necessary for our progression. We have experienced, and many are now experiencing, some very intense struggles and trials, leaving each one of us wondering, "Did I really sign up for this?" Each one of us knew that we would all experience having "Mortal Imperfection Spectrum Disorder," as these challenges can be physical, emotional, mental, social, spiritual, or any combination of these. A person with a disability may also say, "Life is hard enough already, and also having a disability just makes it much worse. Why do I have to live through such difficulty?"

I would like to share some very important information here. As we know, we need to have struggles, trials, and challenges in our lives to help us positively progress, and to learn to choose what is right and to draw ourselves closer to our Savior. We might think, "We need more miracles in our lives." Our Savior will give us miracles when it is part of His divine plan for us. But then we think, "Our difficulties, troubles, and challenges seem to occur much more often than any miracles we might receive. We do what's right and many times, blessings don't come. What's going on?"

In addition to experiencing trials in this life to help us positively progress toward Christ, have you thought about the fact that since having these experiences will help us to become better people and to ultimately receive greater blessings, as we choose what's right, that these difficult trials and challenges, and even disabilities are part of our Savior's plan for us, and are actually "<u>miracles</u>" in each of our lives? Please spend a moment to ponder this. Our Savior's divine plan for each of us in mortality is, in reality, His greatest miracle, which includes tremendous challenges. As we live our lives each day doing the best we can to follow Christ and be obedient, seeking His Light, even if it's a smaller amount of what others are capable of doing at this moment, He will guide us and make our burdens lighter, and we will feel of His tremendous love for us. He definitely wants us to succeed.

In this book, I have taken Ethan and his mother and sister on an exciting, awesome journey, along with all of you, where you have seen how they are able to reduce and overcome many difficulties and challenges which have arisen in their lives. You have seen how utilizing our Savior's assistance is the most important method to help us solve problems and manage disabilities. This has been proven. Our Savior wants to help us with our difficulties as we put more trust in Him. This is how we positively progress. However, we will continue to have challenges in our lives, and some may be very intense or longer lasting. Here, I will provide some great assistance to help all of you when you experience intense challenges.

As I have noted earlier, our Savior has His great plan for each one of us. We each have a wonderful mission to fulfill during this earth life, regardless of any disability any one of us may have. This includes those of us who are helping people with disabilities. Again, the Lord has placed disabilities and disorders in people's lives to help them fulfill their missions in this life in the most effective manner. No matter what imperfection we may have, our Savior wants us to be closer to Him, through prayer and by living righteously, as He has instructed us. By doing this, we will know through the guidance of His Spirit, the important items and milestones we are to accomplish in order to succeed in each of our individual missions in our lifetimes. Some of these are mentioned in our patriarchal blessings.

Because our Savior gave each of us His greatest gift, through His atonement, death, and resurrection, we have the knowledge that we are capable and are very able to qualify to receive the ultimate gift of our Heavenly Father and Jesus Christ, that of living with them and becoming as they are, receiving all that they have. What a wonderful blessing to look toward, as we experience challenges in our lives which are helping us to achieve that goal.

When we think of the greatest challenge which our Savior faced on this earth, that of His atonement, we may be reminded to think of great challenges each of us have faced or are facing in our lives. As we think about these challenges, we know there are people who cannot see or hear, or are not even able to walk or have use of their hands. There are people in this world who don't have families, and others who are refugees, who rely on concerned people to meet their basic needs. There are those who have experienced the sudden loss of a close family member, such as a parent, sibling, spouse, or child, with its associated intense grieving. There are those who have serious diseases, such as cancer or heart disease, and the list goes on. When we think of the greatest challenges we have ever faced in our lives so far, we realize that we have lived through them, and have consequently progressed, and then we may wonder if we will be given even greater challenges. This is where we need to rely on our Savior more, and have faith that He will help us through these trials. Remember that He has already experienced them, and knows exactly what it feels like and also what we feel when we go through the challenges we are now experiencing. He has also experienced future trials and challenges we will have, and knows how we will feel. Through this, our suffering can be reduced. He will help us through His grace and He will always love us.

Those of us who have disabilities already know what it feels like to live life each day with each of our individual disabilities, as well as to deal with their associated challenges. This book has shown how people with Asperger's and Autism Spectrum Disorders in the Church of Jesus Christ of Latter-day Saints actually experience life, so that those who interact with these people will be more enlightened and educated to help them. However, people with these disorders will still have great challenges to face, and these challenges will continue to be more unique for those who have Asperger's Syndrome/ASD. Our Savior is the best help for dealing with these challenges, as He works through other people such as family members and friends. He also gives guidance through His Spirit.

Our Savior knows what challenges are best for each one of us, in order to fulfill His plan for our progression in the best possible manner. We should be grateful to Him for this. I know that He won't reward us instantly every time when we make a right choice. If He did, then our faith would not develop and we would not progress toward Him very well. Accordingly, if He always instantly allowed us to be punished for making a wrong choice, then we would be conditioned to not choose wrong, and we would not especially be making choices from our own agency. Therefore, results from our choices are quite often delayed, and trying times from our challenges may continue for a much longer time than what we wish. I know this is the Lord's plan for us, that we will have our agency and we'll progress, through making right choices and staying close to Him through our challenges. This is all made possible through His atoning sacrifice.

I, Robert, have personally progressed through my experiences and through the challenges I have been given by earnestly praying, enduring, being strong and solid within myself, and utilizing the simple principles I have presented in this book. I have become more normal socially, and have progressed even farther away from Asperger's by staying close to our Savior. I feel more of my true self when I interact with other people. I care about them. I greet many of them and ask how they are doing. I converse normally with them. However, I am now facing my greatest challenge.

When my wife, Jeanene, passed on, I not only lost my sweetheart and my loving companion, but also my "safe" person. Here I am living alone again, after a relatively shorter amount of time. I was living on my own for about 13 years before I met Jeanene. That was when my parents were alive. Now I am back in that position, but with more good experience and knowledge. I've had the good experience of being married, while having Asperger's. Jeanene has taught me much about how to properly socially interact with people and how to be more loving. I have now become aware of previous unknown involuntary movements, so that my behavior is more appropriate in public. Thinking back through my married life, I realize how much concern Jeanene had for me, and how much she taught me in a loving way. I know even more now that Jeanene was the perfect companion for me, brought to me by our Savior's hand. We were brought together so that we could both learn more of what the Lord would want us to know, especially of His teachings. Jeanene has exemplified those to me, including charity. Being married to her has been the greatest part of my life so far. I have learned to not take anything for granted, but to cherish each moment and learn from it. I know to enjoy my journey through life. Jeanene reminded me to smile and compliment others. This also helps them understand me better. Through being married, the Lord has taught me through His Spirit about effective communication and how to be more positive around people and with myself. But yet, I now sometimes experience a little more anxiety.

On Sunday, after being with the good members of my ward at Church, I come home to an empty house with no one around, a condition I thought would never happen to me anymore. I sleep alone at night in an empty house. I prepare my meals alone every day. Many times I feel like I'm traveling alone in the middle of a hot, barren desert where an occasional oasis is far away. At times, your challenges may feel like this also. However, I do feel the strength from Heaven to help keep me going. Having Asperger's, I am still somewhat limited from doing certain normal things that other people do. I don't travel very much on my own, although I am driving more now.

There is no public transportation here. With Asperger's, and my wife's passing, my emotions are at a much higher level, and I do not want to be a higher risk on the road while driving. I am now starting to go to other members' houses more often and do other traveling locally. I am not working right now, so I'm in my house more than most people. Some members of my Church ward have plans for me to meet with more people and families in my ward concerning ministering, and temple and family history work, along with what I have already been doing in my ward calling. This benefits me, as being around more people and helping them helps me feel much better during this time. I am fulfilling temple shifts as a temple worker each week, which is very helpful to me, emotionally and spiritually. I feel very spiritually uplifted afterward. At times, I also invite friends to my house for company and socializing.

Being around more people and feeling a connection with good people is one of the great emotional needs we have, along with feeling loved and feeling secure. I, along with other people with ASD, have increased intense needs in these areas. This is why it is more difficult for Asperger's people to be alone for a longer amount of time. There are members in my Church ward who are aware of this, as they know how people feel who live alone. They help me by being friendly and talking to me when they can. However, living alone naturally causes emotions to increase more often.

Depressive anxiety disorder has crept up on me more during this time, but I am able to subdue this even greater challenge. I stay busy with my interests. I keep up with weather measurements, temperature, and rain and snow amounts, etc., as well as watching the weather information on TV and online. I also watch good educational games on TV where I learn and verify answers to many quiz questions. This keeps my mind active while I increase my knowledge through doing this. Also, I enjoy preparing some delicious meals. I listen to some good music on the radio, so that there will not be so much silence in the house. Uplifting music keeps me happier each day. I will be talking more about all the tremendous benefits that good music has in each of our lives.

I spend some time reading in the Book of Mormon every day, as well as praying to my Heavenly Father. I ask Him for His Spirit to help me through each day, as well as asking for His guidance. I fervently talk to Him, as He is literally my Father. I thank Him for all the wonderful blessings He has given me throughout my life, as well as for all the many gifts and blessings He is now giving me, including our Savior and my family and friends. I thank Him for each "oasis" I am able to reach, and the happiness I feel there. I thank Him for His love and our Savior's love for me. I tell Him about all my concerns and anxieties, and I ask Him for further guidance and comfort through His Spirit, knowing of His love for me and His grace, the help and strength He has given me. There are times when I feel comfort through the still, small voice, like Jeanene is here saying to me, "Things will be all right." Many times I also feel the comforting presence of my parents, which helps me feel better.

My sister, Susan, comes at times for a few hours to visit. I really look forward to those visits. It is one of the highlights of the week. I'm very appreciative of her concern for me, and for her wanting to help me. She has helped with some organizing in the house. To be busier, my stake leader is also helping me within their current program to teach more Church members about their family history and temple work. I have been doing more of this. I am meeting more people and I am of service to them, teaching them about our Savior's plan for them and for their ancestors.

I am working on managing Asperger's and being more normal all the time, especially in this present situation. I know that I have become much more normal now. I feel that my Savior wants me to experience this challenge of being alone for my growth. I will show you what I mean.

Soon before Jeanene passed on, she asked me, "Robert, what if I don't get healed? What if I die?" I didn't have an answer because I couldn't think about being alone, not being with her. I started feeling very emotional, wondering, "How would I live without her?" I couldn't bear the thought of experiencing a challenge like that. She then responded with, "Well, if I do go, I'll say 'Hi' to your parents for you."

I felt very sad at the thought, but I still would accept the Lord's will. I did feel that she would be staying. The Lord needed me to feel this at the time. Soon after her passing, I had an emotional talk with my Heavenly Father. I asked Him, "Why did Jeanene have to go? Thou knowest that I need a companion and a 'safe' person in my life. Thou knowest that it is very hard for me to live without her and that I really miss her. I have faith and I trust in Thee, and I accept Thy will, but why, why, why ... did she have to go?"

I felt His response, telling me, "You know that she is

a very special person. You are beginning to understand more of who she really is, as I know her, and you need to know that she is now needed in the spirit world. I know that you miss her and that you intently desire that she be with you. I know that you have Asperger's Syndrome and that it will be very difficult for you, but your Savior and I will bless you and help to ease your burden as you stay faithful and build your faith. This challenge I have given you will help you to grow and develop in ways you have never known, to prepare you for plans We have for you later."

I truly needed to have these words. They were very comforting to me. I now understand more about our Savior and His plans for us. I know the Lord is preparing all of us through our trials and challenges for greater plans and tremendous blessings He has for us. I also know that He has experienced all that I'm experiencing, including my tender emotions. He knows what it's like to have Asperger's, lose a spouse, and be alone with depression and anxiety at various times without a more constant "safe" person around. He completely feels my periods of intense grieving. He knows what it feels like when my face is covered with tears. I know that He is feeling these emotions during the very same moments when I am experiencing these struggles. His face is also covered with tears. He and my Heavenly Father are truly my loving "safe" people. What a comfort to know this!

Some of these emotions I am describing might not seem to be quite so intense to some people without disorders, but for Asperger's, it can be extremely intense. It is more difficult, having Asperger's, to manage certain more aggressive stimuli being alone, along with periods of grieving. Feelings of extreme loneliness can easily occur, which causes a much greater difficulty in dealing with some sensory stimuli. Handling depressive anxiety attacks can be more difficult. With no actual "safe" person in my house to comfort me, when an extremely loud sound occurs, I have to turn my good music on louder until the loud sounds stop, along with praying and doing the exercises, along with deep breathing I mentioned earlier. This comforts me and prevents me from having any reaction to the loud sounds, just as if Jeanene were here with me, comforting me. Many times she is. If, however, I am out with other good people, these stimuli don't affect me nearly as they did previously. The Lord is truly helping me as I do my part.

I have progressed through this time, through the help of the Holy Ghost after fervently praying, which has given me even more experience from this challenge, being alone, to deal with life and Asperger's. I know that some very important progression is occurring in my life as I am placed in this situation of being alone more of the time. My faith is growing much faster during this time. Our Savior knows what is best for me, and I know He will continue to help me and guide me in the best possible way during my present situation. I am truly not completely alone even though I am physically by myself much of the time, as I feel the presence of the Spirit of the Lord in my life, along with the presence of departed family members at various times, especially the presence of Jeanene and my parents.

I know that focusing on our Savior during this challenge is the most beneficial thing I can do. I focus on keeping a positive attitude, and I work on having positive thoughts by remembering how our Savior views me as a person of great worth. This is how He views all of us, along with tremendous love. I am reminded of our great potential and what we are able to accomplish later, becoming as He is, experiencing true joy and tremendous love, through our Savior's atonement and grace. My struggles through this challenge are greatly reduced as I focus on enjoying each day, being truly grateful for the many blessings the Lord is giving me. I have felt through His Spirit that this challenge I have to experience is only temporary, and I truly know that things will get better. This brings me great joy each day as I live "One day at a time." I also look for good humor in every situation, and I keep my countenance positive, which helps other people have better days as well. I know these thoughts will be very beneficial for all of you, no matter what disorders you may have.

Some years ago, I was told about a book called *The Greatest Salesman in the World*, which I read. Its ten important action items have helped me to succeed. Now, it is especially more relevant, helping me to remember to increase my love for people, to manage my sensitive emotions, and to be cheerful. I know that by doing this, our Savior will help me to progress even more, and I will be able to make each day a very worthwhile day in my life. This is good information for all of you involved with Asperger's/ASD and other disabilities, along with your families. I am learning to increase my faith and to trust in the Lord during this time, as I pray for guidance.

Another thing that has greatly helped me in my life is the power of good music. It has a great uplifting effect on my emotions, and has helped me to better deal with my

Asperger's Syndrome during all my life. There are a great number of benefits of good music, as it has very positive transformative effects. Having Asperger's, it has helped me to feel calmer, as I recognize its artistic patterns. It has also helped me to learn new things throughout my life, as it does with children in school. My brain feels clearer and more settled with good music, and I recognize that I am learning more efficiently and effectively. Listening to, and even studying and producing quality music releases good hormones in the brain, positively affecting emotions, and allowing the listener to improve his life and be able to handle his challenges in life more effectively. All this has helped me tremendously during my entire life, even now during my present challenge. Along with listening to good music, I enjoy singing, leading other people in their singing as a director, organizing music programs, and I enjoy playing the piano a little. This has also helped to keep me busier and to not feel so alone.

I know that this time alone without a companion in mortality is part of my Savior's plan for me right now. I know that He will not let me fail as I continue to increase my faith in Him and persist in good works, including increasing my Christlike love for others. I have been taught about how to be more like our Savior around other people, which helps me feel better. This includes living and being as He would, in every situation. This means thinking in a loving manner as He would think, behaving respectfully, being kind, appropriately being of assistance and of service, smiling, showing interest in all other people, and showing compassion and tremendous love as He would. This helps me to know more of how our Savior really is, and how I can actually become more like Him, even now! Think of that. What a tremendous blessing! This is easily achievable for all of you, no matter where you are now in your lives. I know He views me and you as people of great worth, including those of us with disabilities. When we know of His great love for us, our lives will have much more meaning and purpose. We will feel more of the tender emotions of His love. Sensing of His magnificent power in our lives and the wonderful blessings He is giving us can bring tears of joy and increased love for Him. I know He is preparing us for greater blessings and He will never abandon us. Thinking of this brings me much needed hope.

I feel, and this feeling can be true for you too, that I am approaching an unseen border of entering into a realm of great joy and pure love, along with many wonderful blessings and experiencing, to an even greater degree, the powerful love which our Savior has for us. This, of course, will be when He returns to dwell with us. I feel this through faith and through inspiring music that makes me think of our Savior, along with the great love I feel in the temple and through sincere prayer; however, it is not yet as perceivable in present reality, as my challenges are now in reality. Increasing my faith in this, and in the Lord and His promises, gives me more hope about a much happier, blessed life to soon come. Truly, the night will turn into day. Also, thinking about that great reunion I will have later with Jeanene, along with my parents and other special loved ones, brings tears of joy to my eyes. This wonderful thought gives me great encouragement during this period of time, which is now my greatest challenge in my life.

I know that this information I have presented has been a great help to everyone, whether experiencing any type of disability or not, and I know this will give encouragement during times of greatest challenges, whether you have Asperger's or whether you are helping someone with Asperger's. This will also encourage you during times of anxiety, or great loneliness or depression, even when you are living in a household around other people.

We always have choices to make. We can choose to do good things and show Christlike love, which will make us happy. We can choose to follow our Savior. We can choose true happiness instead of misery. We can do this through "enlightened agency," already knowing of tremendous blessings or great misery, consequences resulting from our choices of following our Savior each day, or leaving Him. However, I know that all of you will succeed and positively progress, and receive help with these various challenges and trials in each of your individual journeys throughout life by increasing your faith and trust in the Lord, including the faith to accept trials He gives us. This is done by keeping our Savior in your lives, by following the prophet, by living the gospel, by sincerely praying and accepting His grace for you, and by showing Christlike love and being of service to others. You will then progress more toward the ultimate blessing available to all of us, that of Eternal Life, living with our Heavenly Father again in great love with our families and experiencing true eternal joy, which will be full as we bring great joy to other people's lives forever.

CHAPTER TWELVE
BLESSINGS ALWAYS FOLLOW TRIALS

After having written this book thus far, along with sharing the writing by my family and friends, I, Robert, need to mention a very important piece of information. I have been talking to various members in my Church ward about how I have been writing a book, explaining about Asperger's Syndrome/Autism Spectrum Disorder in a religious setting. In the process of doing this, one of them mentioned to me that she knew of a family in the Church who was presently experiencing some extremely difficult, major problems in each of their lives, and did not know what to do or where to turn. A boy in this family has Asperger's Syndrome, and earlier intervention had not been as helpful as they had hoped. They had been praying for help with faith, but nothing good had happened yet to really help them. She told them of what I was writing, as I had discussed some of my writing with her. She did this as a very caring, family friend. They immediately knew that this book was the answer to their prayers.

Before this book was published, with my permission she shared my manuscript with them, to help them at this extremely low point in their lives. The family I am referring to is Sarah, Ethan, and Alexis. As you remember, Ethan has Asperger's Syndrome. This book was totally life changing for all of them, bringing them out of the deepest depths of despair, to a completely new, very enjoyable life. To illustrate the life-changing information I have presented here, I have included Ethan and his family in this book.

As a report on their progress, after reading this book, Ethan and his sister, Alexis, did receive their patriarchal blessings. Ethan's blessing mentioned that by being faithful to our Savior, he would be called upon to participate in some very important work within the Church, and that he would also be teaching many people about our Savior with a voice that they will hear. It said that he would be married in the temple, and that the Lord will continue to bless him with great blessings as he does his part. Ethan has since returned to Church, and has been able to socialize better with other members in his new ward, where he and his family have recently moved. His Asperger's characteristics have greatly decreased, he socializes well, he is understood much better, and he is more welcomed and loved. He now has a very strong testimony of our Savior and His gospel, which he shares often. He knows about the power of prayer. He and Alexis go do baptisms at the temple for their ancestors, which they extremely enjoy doing together.

THE POWER OF FAMILY

Ethan has been called to share his life-changing experiences in various talks at Church and at a fireside. He relates his intense experiences concerning the losses in his family, as well as the impact that Asperger's has had in his life, how all this has affected him, and how he was able to turn his life around. He relates how he has felt that our Savior, through His atonement, has completely experienced all the trials and bitter emotions which he has experienced. He expresses our Lord's love for him and how extremely grateful he is, that through our Savior's mercy and grace, he was able to accomplish this great achievement in his life, and become a completely new, better person. He explains how he feels that our Savior is frequently close to him, as well as the presence of the Holy Ghost in his life, to assist him each day, which he describes is an extreme benefit. He is able to handle many of life's trials very easily and in a mature manner. He shows how he is able to help his mother feel better, from his positive attitude and through showing love, and especially how he has assisted Alexis to have a much happier life as well, through his spirituality. She really looks up to him now for guidance. When she is having a hard day and having struggles, she goes to Ethan and says, "Ethan, I need your help." He responds, "Lexi, how can I help you?" She then tells him about the difficulty she is experiencing in one of her school classes. He is happy to help her resolve the problem she is having with one of the students in her class. She now knows what to say to this student to resolve the problem. She then says, "Thank you, Ethan. That was very helpful. I sure feel the

Spirit with you!" He responds by saying, "Thank you. I love you, Lexi." Ethan is also very grateful for the special love various people have shown him, and he tells them often, "Thank you. I love and appreciate you!"

Ethan has graduated high school and is now planning and starting the process to serve a full-time mission. He has been ordained an Elder by his grandfather, which was an extremely spiritual experience for him. He relates, "I felt this overwhelming warm, comfortable feeling travel from my head through my whole body. I felt the presence of departed loved ones there, especially Trisha. I know that our Savior is very pleased with me; I feel His many blessings He has given me, and I especially feel His love for me. This was such a wonderful experience, that I feel that I should do all that I can to serve the Lord and to serve others. I love other people, and I want to do everything possible to help them have happier lives. I am very grateful."

Sarah and Alexis have also benefitted from reading this book, learning about how to better help Ethan when he was experiencing the characteristics of Asperger's. They also were able to really help him as he was changing his life, and they learned how to improve their lives in the process. All three of them now know much more about themselves. They are trusting in our Savior. He lets them know about their important missions here on earth, as they are willing to do whatever they are asked to do to further the Lord's work. They all presently have great callings in their new Church ward, which they are fulfilling extremely well. Sarah is now the Relief Society President, Alexis is in the leadership of her youth class, and Ethan is an assistant clerk in the ward. They know to never give up, and they see that the Lord keeps His promises. Of course, they all still experience difficulties in life, but only those similar to what most other people in the Church and community would normally have. They are much happier. Ethan has given them priesthood blessings when they needed this assistance. He has also dedicated their new home to be a spiritual place for them.

Ethan, now at age 20, has received his endowment in the temple, which he relates, "This was such a wonderful, spiritual experience. I now know much more about our Heavenly Father, and His son, Jesus Christ. I'm really excited about being able to teach others the gospel of our Savior, so they can have happier lives. I'm also really excited about doing more ordinance work for my ancestors. I feel such an urgent need to help them all be part of our family, sealed together. I feel great love for them. I also feel great love for my mom and sisters, and I feel their love for me in all that they say and do, especially when I feel Trisha's presence. We have learned to be more selfless, helping each other, being more like how our Savior would like us to be."

Sarah and her two children have felt Trisha's presence in their lives to help them, especially Ethan. They have felt her love and comfort, and they know that she is very much involved in their lives. They know that she wants them to be happy and to be successful. She wants to help them to be an eternal family.

Ethan and one of the ward leaders gave Sarah a blessing, where she was told that, through her faithfulness, she would later receive a faithful husband, to be married in the temple. She was told that they would all be together, sealed as a family, living together after this life, along with Trisha and future family members. She was blessed with the Spirit to help her through life's trials, so that these blessings will be realized, as they will all soon be doing more important work. This blessing gave Sarah a new hope, after losing a husband and experiencing the death of a precious daughter in this life. This new hope really helped her to have a better outlook on her life and increase her faith, as well as the faith of Ethan and Alexis, through the atonement, mercy, and grace of our Savior. Sarah understood from this blessing that all these trials she and her three children experienced within their family were part of the Lord's plan for them, to help them progress toward our Savior. Ethan's trials with losing two family members, plus having Asperger's Syndrome in his life, were always known to the Lord, and were to help him build his faith and to help him become stronger emotionally, socially, and spiritually, as he did his best. The Lord has a great work for him in his future, helping other people, as he continues on his exciting journey.

Ethan's story shows what a person with Asperger's Syndrome is able to accomplish and what he is able to do for his family. This account also shows the role that each family member has in the process. Sarah and Alexis helped Ethan with his trials through their support and love. Through their prayers and their words of encouragement, utilizing the information presented here, he was able to significantly progress. They also progressed by having this experience with Ethan and Asperger's. This all occurred from the natural strong family connection and the power of love involved among the family members. Even though there are trials, struggles, challenges, and even disabilities involved, by everyone working together with love, the Lord's plans will be accomplished, and everyone involved can, and will progress, as would be the case in any family. People will learn to be more Christlike, and learn to have even more love toward each other as they continue on their journey.

Family members in the spirit world will be helping us by watching over us with great love, by guiding us with thoughts and love we can feel from them as they are very interested in our success and our progression toward our Savior. They will also be helping others understand the gospel. We will be helping them by doing baptisms and other ordinance work for our ancestors, including sealings to connect all of our family members together in love, as part of God's eternal family. We will also be helping them by lovingly remembering them and by doing our best. This is all done because we are showing true Christlike love toward each member of our family on both sides. Remember, this is just the beginning of our grand eternal family filled with everlasting love. This is our Savior's plan for us as families. Doing the things I have outlined in this book, and working on becoming more like Christ, all of our family members will be much closer to becoming a united, loving eternal family in the presence of God. This is the whole purpose of our existence. Blessings really do follow trials. Ethan's experience and that of his family has shown how all this actually happens. This shows the power of family.

As you can see, anyone who is experiencing trials, and especially very intense trials, will receive blessings, now as well as later, as they have faith in our Savior.

They will know that things will get better as they do their part. Be strong in following our Savior and He will help us through our trials and disabilities. They are only temporary and will help us to progress in many positive ways. The Lord has told us that He will not give us a trial that is too intense for us to bear. This includes any disability and its associated trials. Know this when you think about your difficulties having Asperger's, or having a family member with Asperger's. Remember that our Savior knows what is best for each of us. He has His plan for us, which may include disabilities. He wants us to be truly happy now, and He wants us to be able to have true eternal joy along with great blessings as families together, after this life. I, Robert Callaway, know that this is true, and that Asperger's Syndrome/ASD or any other disability is only a great, positive stepping stone toward this extremely important, wonderful goal. This is my Church perspective, seeing "Through the Eyes of Asperger's."

BIBLIOGRAPHY

1. "Four Bs for Boys," *Ensign*, Nov. 1981, p. 41; quoting Edwin Markham, "Outwitted," in *The Best Loved Poems of the American People*, sel. Hazel Felleman (1936), p. 67

2. Boyd K. Packer, "The Spirit of Revelation," *Ensign*, November 1999, (General Conf., October 1999), Salt Lake City: IRI, The Church of Jesus Christ of Latter-day Saints

3. "Home Can Be a Heaven on Earth," *Hymns*, #298, Salt Lake City: IRI, The Church of Jesus Christ of Latter-day Saints, 1985

4. "Honesty and Integrity," *For the Strength of Youth*, Salt Lake City: IRI, The Church of Jesus Christ of Latter-day Saints, 2010

5. "Ether 12:27," The Book of Mormon – Another Testament of Jesus Christ, Salt Lake City: IRI, The Church of Jesus Christ of Latter-day Saints

6. "Did You Think to Pray?" *Hymns*, #140, Salt Lake City: IRI, The Church of Jesus Christ of Latter-day Saints, 1985

7. www.nimh.nih.gov/healthtopics/autism-spectrum-disorders-asd/index.shtml/ Updated 2015

8. Carmen B. Pingree, "So Near and Yet So Far: Living with Autism," *Ensign*, August 1983, (Rex D. Pinegar, *Liahona*, March 1984), Salt Lake City: IRI, The Church of Jesus Christ of Latter-day Saints

9. *Diagnostic and Statistical Manual of Mental Disorders, 5th Edition (DSM-5)*: www.psychiatry.org/psychiatrists/practice/dsm, 2016

10. "Autism Spectrum Disorder," NIMH, December 2015, pp. 2-3 (NIMH National Institute of Mental Health pamphlet)

11. Jeffrey R. Holland, "Like a Broken Vessel," *Ensign*, November 2013, (General Conf., October 2013), Salt Lake City: IRI, The Church of Jesus Christ of Latter-day Saints

12. NAMI: National Alliance on Mental Illness, www.nami.org/#, 2016

13. www.myaspergerschild.com

14. www.medicinenet.com/autism_spectrum_disorder_a sd_faqs/article.htm, 2016

15. www.disabilities.ChurchofJesusChrist.org

16. "Dealing with Disabilities," *Ensign*, June 1993, Salt Lake City: IRI, The Church of Jesus Christ of Latter-day Saints

17. "Serving Those with Disabilities," by Becky Young Fawcett, Church Disability Services, *Ensign*, June 2013, Salt Lake City: IRI, The Church of Jesus Christ of Latter-day Saints

18. "Mental Illness: In Search of Understanding and Hope," Jan Underwood Pinborough, *Ensign*, February 1989, Salt Lake City: IRI, The Church of Jesus Christ of Latter-day Saints

19. www.ChurchofJesusChrist.org/topics/disability/ up-dated March 18, 2014

20. "Reaching Out to Those with Disabilities—and Their Families," Lynn Parsons, PhD, *Ensign*, February 2015, Salt Lake City: IRI, The Church of Jesus Christ of Latter-day Saints

21. www.ChurchofJesusChrist.org/topics/disability/basic s/first-presidency-statement/ (*Church News*, April 29, 1989, p. 7)

22. Christopher Phillips, "Disability Services: Church Provides a Wide Array of Disability Resources," www.newsroom.ChurchofJesusChrist.org

23. Joseph F. Smith, "Gospel Doctrine," Salt Lake City: Deseret Book Coll., 1959, p. 436

24. "Our Savior's Love," *Hymns*, #113, Salt Lake City: IRI, The Church of Jesus Christ of Latter-day Saints, 1985

25. Og Mandino, *The Greatest Salesman in the World*, New York City: Bantam Books, 1985

ABOUT ATMOSPHERE PRESS

Atmosphere Press is an independent, full-service publisher for excellent books in all genres and for all audiences. Learn more about what we do at atmospherepress.com.

We encourage you to check out some of Atmosphere's latest releases, which are available at Amazon.com and via order from your local bookstore:

A Converted Woman's Voice: Being Valiant in the Testimony of Jesus and in His Restored Gospel, nonfiction by Maria Covey Cole

The Bond: How a Mixed Bag of Foster Kids Became a Family for Life, a memoir by A.M. Grotticelli

License to Learn, nonfiction by Anna Switzer

Between Each Step: A Married Couple's Thru Hike on New Zealand's Te Araroa, a memoir by Patrice La Vigne

Ordinary Zenspiration: Find Your Chill, Find Your Fun, Find Yourself, by April Cacciatori

Waking Up Marriage: Finding Truth In Your Partnership, nonfiction by Bill O'Herron

Eat to Lead, nonfiction by Luci Gabel

An Ambiguous Grief, a memoir by Dominique Hunter

My Take On All Fifty States: An Unexpected Quest to See 'Em All, nonfiction by Jim Ford

Geometry of Fire, nonfiction by Paul Warmbier

In the Cloakroom of Proper Musings, a lyric narrative by Kristina Moriconi

Chasing the Dragon's Tail, nonfiction by Craig Fullerton

ABOUT THE AUTHOR

Robert was born in Los Angeles, then moved to Utah when he was six, and grew up in the Provo, Orem area.

He attended BYU for two years, where he enjoyed studying science and mathematics. He also studied medical transcription and office management.

Robert enjoyed serving a two-year mission for his religion in Chile. He has been self-employed in the food industry.

All his life, he has enjoyed learning about and observing the weather.

Robert was diagnosed with Asperger's Syndrome at age 36. He has overcome much of his Syndrome and presently lives in a small town in Utah.

CPSIA information can be obtained
at www.ICGtesting.com
Printed in the USA
JSHW020541230621
16110JS00002B/9